GOVERNING IN POST-DEFICIT TIMES

ALBERTA IN THE KLEIN YEARS

Barry Cooper Mebs Kanji

University of Calgary

To

Ed McNally, LL.D.,
patriotic Albertan,
entrepreneur,
purveyor of the world's finest beer,
and
outstanding fisherman.

TABLE OF CONTENTS

Canadian Cataloguing in Publication Data

Cooper, Barry, 1943-
 Governing in Post-Deficit Times: Alberta in the Klein Years

(Monograph series on public policy and public administration; no. 10)
Includes bibliographical references.
ISBN 0-7727-8612-7

1. Alberta – politics and government – 1971- 2. Finance, Public– Alberta.
3. Surplus (Economics). I. Kanji, Mebs, 1969- II. University of Toronto. Centre for
 Public Management. III. Title. IV. Series

FC3675.2.C66 2000   971.23′03   C00-931075-4
F1078.2.C66 2000

Printed for the University of Toronto Centre for Public Management by
University of Toronto Press.

FOREWORD

In the early-mid nineties, the Alberta government of Ralph Klein blazed the trail – at least for state and provincial jurisdictions in North America – in assaulting and then obliterating its deficit. For this, it received recognition in the international business press, and the story of Klein's success was told in *The Klein Achievement* (1996) by Barry Cooper, the first monograph published by the University of Toronto Centre for Public Management.

But the fact that Alberta pioneered the attack on the deficit meant something else: It would be one of the first jurisdictions in North America to enter the post-deficit era; more particularly, it would be the first conservative political culture to wrestle with the trilemma of post-deficit surpluses: pay down the debt, lower taxes, or raise government spending.

Alberta thus once again provides a leading indicator for North American political economy, raising several important questions. Can a government which successfully slew the deficit dragon equally successfully handle the siren call of surplus? Or is a different kind of leadership called for? Are Albertans, united as they had become in fighting the deficit, now fracturing on the question of the surplus? If so, why? Does a conservative political culture deal with the post-deficit era in a different fashion than a liberal political culture?

These are the questions that Barry Cooper and Mebs Kanji address in *Governing in Post-Deficit Times: Alberta In the Klein Years*, which is fittingly the tenth monograph published in the University of Toronto Centre for Public Management Monograph Series, and funded by a generous grant from the Donner Canadian Foundation. It is not only the definitive academic treatment of the Klein government, but a manual for other governments – as well as citizens and journalists – who seek to navigate the treacherous waters of post-deficit democratic politics.

Andrew Stark
Centre for Public Management
University of Toronto

PREFACE

Andy Stark and the Donner Canadian Foundation originally invited Cooper to undertake a study of the Klein government. As Stark said in the Foreword to the first edition, published in 1996, it was designed to be a "report from the front." Like *The Klein Achievement*, this is a sympathetic report—in several meanings of the term. First, it is sympathetic in the literal sense of being an attempt to "feel with" the major players, to understand them on their own terms. Second, it is sympathetic in the ordinary sense of admiring the skill with which the first Klein government established its priorities, overwhelmed the opposition where it was unable to neutralize it, and achieved its objectives. In part because of the great skill and remarkable accomplishments of the first Klein government, the second seems to be less skilled and less adept. When the environment is less bracing one need not rise to an occasion. Finally, it is a sympathetic report because both in the 1993 election and in a more calculated way again in 1997 Klein appealed to what is best in Albertans, to their virtue. At the time of writing, the winter of 1999-2000, his appeal to virtue is more muted.

Not everyone admires what the Klein governments have achieved (though for the most part we do) so we must examine his critics and weigh their criticism. There is more criticism available now than there was when the first version was published, and it does not all come from the same political direction. Moreover, scholars are involved, not mere intellectuals and pamphleteers, so their words need to be examined with some care.

In the chapters that follow we indicate what the Klein governments have done and how they did it. In addition, this study is also analytic in that it attempts to explain why the Klein government continues to remain popular despite significant reductions in spending in core programs—health care, education, and social services. The Introduction contains an overview of the achievements of the Klein governments. The context for our analysis is found in the political culture of the province and so we provide a brief account of it too. The following chapters contain a narrative analysis of the genesis of the financial crisis faced up to by the Klein government, of how the Klein Conservatives distanced themselves from the Lougheed-Getty Conservatives and won the 1993 election, of the chief sources of the new agenda and the opposition to it, both inside and outside the Legislature, of how the Conservatives won the 1997 election.

Finally, we look at the evidence that the government may have strayed off course during the post-deficit era, how it has surrendered some of its autonomy to the federal government, and to the judiciary, and how it has taken measures to get back on track.

As with any project of this size, a great many thanks are in order. First to Andy Stark, who oversees the production of this monograph series for the University of Toronto Centre for Public Management, thank-you for your patience regarding missed deadlines and for your enthusiasm and encouragement; second to Patrick Luciani, Executive Director of the Donner Canadian Foundation and to Sonia Arrison, formerly with Donner but now at the Pacific Research Institute, thank-you for finding the resources to undertake the third Alberta Advantage Survey; and third to Carolyn Andres, thank-you for all the typing and re-typing. It's hard to get it right the first time.

Calgary
March, 2000

INTRODUCTION
IT'S NOT ROCKET SCIENCE

Political scientists have not ignored the activities of the Government of Alberta under the administration of Ralph Klein. Some of what they have written has appeared in scholarly journals, but much more is indistinguishable from journalism. This is perhaps to be expected for the professional observers would say, that it's too soon to reach a verdict or a disinterested and neutral understanding. And yet, there has been a good deal of highly polemical writing on the actions of the Alberta Government, much of it written from a perspective that, with pardonable simplification, may be called the left. For one reason or another, many academics find it congenial to approach politics on the basis of assumptions conventionally associated with the left. Those who do not are usually called right-wingers, and the term is not meant to be complimentary. Ralph Klein, however, has been called the author of the "Klein Revolution," and revolutionaries are usually found on the left.

It seems to us nearly self-evident that clear terminology might be helpful. Unfortunately, none is available, and we must proceed on the basis of more or less commonsensical clarifications. This is why, in the Preface, we noted our sympathy for the Klein government and invited others to admire its achievements. As will be clear soon enough, this does not mean we uncritically adore every move the Government of Alberta has made over the past few years. There is evidence to present, and the evidence shows that Alberta politicians have both great skill and great virtue, which does not mean they are devoid of vice.

The chief objectives of the first Klein government and, in a more subdued way, of the second one as well is to develop policies that aim at economic prosperity for Albertans (and so for Canadians as well) and to do so by restructuring government. By "restructuring government" we mean, first of all, rethinking the place of government in the economy and society of Alberta as well as in the lives of individual Albertans. In order to achieve these objectives, the government thought it had to reverse the policies of the previous governments. In the immediate short term this meant balancing the provincial budget then running a budgetary surplus to pay down the accumulated debt. Conventionally speaking this is a policy of "fiscal responsibility," and it has attracted considerable attention from critics and admirers alike.

Political activity is chiefly action, initiative, and innovation, not a strategic game of adjusting means to an end. This means that the language of "objectives" or "restructuring" or "goals" is somewhat misleading.1 Ends and means are unavoidably and inextricably blended in political activity. The notion of "fiscal responsibility" in Alberta is a package deal, a basket of policies, including fiscal prudence, privatization, and tax reductions, that seek to achieve a configuration of circumstances, including smaller government and greater individual prosperity. The "goal" in other words is to move society in the direction of increased individual responsibility and increased individual liberty. As we shall see towards the end of this book, it is by no means certain how far the Klein government is willing to go in pursuit of these goals.

The context for this study is wider than Alberta. According to an editorial in *The Wall Street Journal*, "one of the big stories across the industrialized world for the foreseeable future is going to be the scaling down of the twentieth century's welfare states."[2] Governments over the past generation have all more or less followed the same script. It has been described by critics and supporters alike as centering on the desirability or the necessity of the welfare state. The chief assumption of the welfare state *is that governments have the obligation to help citizens who are presumed to be incapable of helping themselves.* By questioning the necessity or by describing the perversity of the welfare state, political analysts of various affiliations (journalists, academics, politicians), have begun to convey their doubts about the truth of this conventional opinion.

The significance of the Klein government's achievement is that, beginning with the 1993 budget, they actually put into practice the heretofore merely verbal criticisms of the welfare state. As Catherine Swift, chief economist for the Canadian Federation of Independent Business, remarked in 1994, "What [Premier Klein] is doing is not rocket science from an economic perspective. What it takes is some political will and guts."[3] Indeed, the first Klein administration acted with great conviction. For example, they understood the phrase "reducing expenditures" in its ordinary sense, namely that they would, actually, reduce expenditures. They did not mean it in its conventionally governmental sense, namely that they would simply spend less than they had been planning to spend. This has meant considerable readjustment on the part of all Albertans with respect to what they can expect from government. Those who have, in the past, expected a great deal from government have also, not surprisingly, proclaimed Ralph Klein a revolutionary, and refer to the Klein revolution.[4] Hence the confusion alluded to above.

But Ralph Klein has said he is not a revolutionary, and his own self-description demands our respect, as it also demands reflection on our part in order to understand what he meant. For example, in his January,

1995 address to the province, the Premier said, "you know, some are calling this 'the Alberta revolution.' But it's not a revolution. We're simply renewing our commitment to the basic values on which we built our province. Alberta stands for commonsense."[5]

Unlike Premier Harris of Ontario, who spoke easily of a "commonsense revolution," Ralph Klein wished to keep the two notions distinct. Perhaps the premier is wrong and there is nothing commonsensical about conservatism in Alberta but that remains to be shown. On the other hand, following upon the damage done by the NDP government of Bob Rae to the economy of Ontario and the widespread acceptance of endless deficits and high taxes among strategically placed Ontario elites, perhaps the commonsense of Mike Harris did look revolutionary because it addressed the fundamentals of economic and political order.

In any event, it is certainly true that the Klein governments, especially the first one have, introduced some new policies and, naturally enough, some people do not like what has been accomplished. Then again, most governments do innovate. Ralph Klein has not sought to overthrow an old regime or constitute a new one, which would be revolutionary. To the extent that the Klein government's agenda aims at reducing the welfare state, most Albertans and many Canadians might consider the goal to be a return to public policies from which it was an error to stray. According to Klein himself: "I am no more radical than the people who elected me premier of this province."[6] There are, of course, those who think the entire province is radical—or, to use the preferred epithet, *redneck*—but that is another issue requiring an extensive analysis of competing Canadian myths.[7] Others are simply rhetorically excessive.[8]

A praiseworthy fiscal performance is an important part of the Klein government's achievement but it is not its essential attribute or purpose. Bill Gold, a veteran columnist for the *Calgary Herald*, which distinguished itself in the early years of the first Klein government by its unremitting criticism, made the following observation: "Ralph Klein's Tories," he said, "actively dislike government, both as a concept capable of effecting changes beneficial to the community, and as an assemblage of people charged with these tasks."[9] Gold was half right because, as many analysts of organizational behaviour have observed, those charged with delivering benefits to the community, namely members of the civil service, often act as if they are really charged with delivering benefits to themselves. One of the groups that greatly admires the achievements of the Klein government is the National Citizens' Coalition (NCC), whose motto or slogan is "more freedom through less government." If they are correct, and an inverse relationship exists between big government and political liberty, then the Klein government is only prudent to distrust the self-serving justifications of senior management in the public service.

Gold also misled his readers by using the verb "dislike." Whether we like or dislike the government, the real question is whether government, as it has come to be experienced in the welfare state, is working. It would be more accurate to say that it is up to public-policy analysts to indicate where the welfare state could be improved, which is to say, to indicate where it is not working well or perhaps not working at all, and up to politicians to do something about it. To use the imagery preferred by David Osborne and Ted Gaebler, whose views have influenced the Klein government, it is questionable whether the government should be "rowing," that is, delivering services, or "steering," that is, setting goals and measuring performance towards them.[10] Gold was correct, however, to emphasize that Klein has sought to reorient government in a fundamental way, to change direction, to introduce new modes and orders.

Outside Quebec, the great innovations in political thinking in post-Confederation Canada were born from prairie experience. Historians and political scientists dispute why this is so and what it signifies, but it is simply a fact that the Progressives, CCF and Social Credit, along with successor parties, were generated west of the Lakehead. The same is true with respect to the current alternatives on both the left and the right. Put boldly, in 1993 the Government of Canada, along with the other eight provincial governments, had either to follow Klein's way or the Saskatchewan route of Premier Roy Romanow. Some comparisons of what Saskatchewan and Alberta have done in response to their respective fiscal crises may clarify the fundamental options, as they appeared to the country in the mid-1990s.

Conflicting Approaches

Premier Romanow has received the better press. His way is said to be balanced and fair, combining judicious reductions in expenditures with measured increases in revenues. Premier Klein's way is said by the media to be much different, as we shall see in detail below. But first, the facts.

In the mid-1990s, Saskatchewan had a GDP around $20 billion with a $15 billion debt; Alberta had about the same size debt but a GDP of $75 billion. To the extent that a large relative debt is a drag on the economy, different orders of magnitude are involved. Second, over a comparable period the Government of Saskatchewan, under the Romanow administration, made no spending cuts; indeed 1996 expenditures were up 4%. Third, taxes are way up: the sales tax went up 2% (to 9%), the provincial fuel tax went up five cents a litre, the top marginal income tax went up 2%, a 10% deficit surtax on net income was imposed on a rate that is 73%

of the federal tax rate (by comparison, Alberta was set at 49% of the federal rate and will soon be entirely decoupled). The bottom line is a per capita tax increase during the 1990s of around $1,200, which works out to close to $4,000 for an average household (in contrast, in Alberta, user fees and health premium increases amount to about $250 per household).

Saskatchewan has also hiked crown utility rates to increase their "profits." These are not really profits so much as rents extracted by government monopolies, owing to the fact that it is inconceivable that SaskTel, SaskPower, or SaskEnergy could ever fail to make a "profit" so long as the province is inhabited. According to the quondam Finance Minister of Saskatchewan, Janice MacKinnon, revenues from increased rates from crown corporations were seen as "an alternative to taxation." Her words summarize generally the Saskatchewan way to achieving a balanced budget. The Alberta alternative is clearly something different.

The chief item on the Klein agenda, conventionally understood, is economic development. It is not simply to reduce the size of government or to cut the costs of government without raising taxes or to privatize government services where privatization makes sense. All those policies are ancillary to individual and provincial prosperity. Although prosperity may not be the most noble aspiration or the highest purpose of human existence, without prosperity, the pursuit of nobility, wisdom or even piety, is much impaired. As we shall see in some detail, Ralph Klein came to his understanding of the importance of prosperity on the basis of direct experience, not by following prolonged study of the texts of the great political philosophers or of the theories of renowned economists.

Premier Klein and his government were of the view that the road to prosperity did not entail increasing the taxes on existing citizens or increasing the public debt and thereby deferring tax increases for future citizens. Preston Manning, the leader of the Reform Party of Canada, has often said that you can't get out of a hole by digging it deeper. Likewise you can't get out of debt by increasing it. This is why the first item on the agenda was deficit reduction and elimination followed by annual budgetary surpluses to reduce the debt.

It is not that Albertans are adverse to paying taxes that are reasonable and fair and that constitute payment for essential services and public goods. It is, however, irrational to pay taxes and receive nothing in return, which is what debt-servicing charges amount to. This logic, combined with the government's appeal to citizens' pride and virtue, has persuaded Albertans to support the Klein initiative to reduce unessential services and to substitute private provision of goods paid for by fees, whenever possible. The contrast with the Saskatchewan strategy is sharp, and judging by results there is a clear "Alberta advantage."[11]

The Klein Achievement

On 12 January, 1995, *The Wall Street Journal* made its now famous announcement that Canada had "become an honorary member of the Third World in the unmanageability of its debt problem." A couple of weeks later, the *Journal* observed, "Canada may well have reached the limit of its ability to tax its citizens."[12] If the debt was approaching the limit of manageability, and taxes were approaching the limit of effectiveness, the appeal of the obvious remaining option, namely expenditure reduction, was clear enough. Because this was the course that the Government of Alberta had chosen, it was on the receiving end of lavish American praise. Saskatchewan and New Brunswick had taken hesitating steps in the right direction, said the *Journal*, but "the most impressive performance is in Alberta." In fact, the "province of Alberta is home to North America's most radical revolution in budget downsizing," which makes it "a great Canadian success story" from which both Prime Minister Chrétien and President Clinton could learn important things.[13] The Alberta economy consistently outperformed the Canadian economy, unemployment had been significantly reduced, and the government's share of Alberta's GDP was falling. All these were good signs.

Moreover, *The Wall Street Journal* was not alone. Another important American paper, *The New York Times*, observed: "Alberta is now the model for other provincial governments and the federal government, which also face budget problems."[14] The last time New York took a serious look at Alberta was half a century earlier, when the Rockefeller Foundation gave a special grant to the Social Science Research Council to commission studies of the Social Credit movement. In 1944, admiration for the achievements of Premier William (Bible Bill) Aberhart was firmly under control, whereas it is clear that admiration for Premier Ralph Klein has been far more generous.

As the American journalists observed, Alberta was not alone in Canada or, indeed, on the continent, in having a debt and deficit problem. The means chosen to deal with this problem, namely to reduce expenditures without raising taxes, to do so directly and quickly, to confront rather than appease the immediate beneficiaries of tax-based expenditures, and to appeal to the civic virtue and pride of citizens in order to gain and retain their support, was so unusual in 1995 as to place the Klein government in a minority of one.

The conventional interpretation of elections assumes that political parties seek to capture the support of a notional "average" voter who is supposed to exist in the middle of a one-dimensional, left-right ideological continuum, whose distribution of opinion is more or less in a bell curve. There is, of course, a trade-off between seeking the support of most voters and taking a position; the conventional conclusion is that parties are indiscriminate vote-grabbers more than principled position-takers. The Klein government is, in this respect, highly unorthodox. Between 1993 and 1997 the Government of Alberta did not simply move in a direction counter to the conventional formulas that describe successful political rule—to temporize, to appease the major interest groups, to proceed by quarter-measures when half-measures look too radical—they have moved successfully against the stream. At a time when many governments were confronting problems similar to those of Alberta, two in particular drew useful lessons from the successful Klein agenda.

In 1995 Mike Harris led the Ontario Conservatives back into office. They were a rather different organization than the Big Blue Machine of an earlier day and the difference lay in the emphasis on fiscal restraint that the Klein government pioneered. During the campaign, Ontario Tories sought and received advice from Klein's closest advisors and shortly after his victory received even more advice—some of it public—on how to enact his "commonsense revolution."[15] The Ontario Tories repeated their victory in June, 1999.

Alberta also set an example for Ottawa. On federal budget day, 1994, Finance Minister Paul Martin remarked: "For years, governments have been promising more than they can deliver, and delivering more than they can afford. That has to end. We are ending it." Jean Chrétien said practically the same thing a decade and a half earlier, so Martin's words were quite properly received with a certain scepticism. The federal finance minister was apparently surprised at the response to his budget and was determined to earn the respect he thought his words alone ought to command. Borrowing again from the Alberta government's restructuring initiative, the vehicle was "Program Review," which subjected each department to six tests devoted to determining the necessity of specific programs and, if deemed necessary, measuring their efficiency. This review led to reductions in the size of line departments and of business subsidies, some privatization, and expenditure reductions.[16] It is true, as several observers have mentioned, that if the 1994 federal budget had been reduced in the same proportion as the Alberta one, the cuts would have been on the order of $70 billion, not $15 billion. However, it is also true that, without the Alberta example before them, it would have taken a major international crisis to persuade the Liberals in Ottawa to reduce expenditures at all.

The Klein government received several accolades. In 1994, for example, Klein received the Colin M. Brown Freedom Medal, awarded annually by the National Citizens' Coalition (NCC) to individuals considered to have advanced significantly NCC views on the size of government.

Likewise, The Fraser Institute has twice awarded the Alberta Government a certificate of achievement for coming first in North America in the area of fiscal performance, based on a 12-variable index that even Premier Klein's most committed opponents would have to analyze before criticizing.[17]

The achievements of the Klein government raise a larger issue as well. Nearly everyone would agree that economics is connected to politics so that the economic performance of the province under the Klein government has a bearing on what those achievements were. Many fewer people, however, go on to specify what that connection is. In our view, it is morality or, more precisely, virtue. Economics is not a quantitative science like nuclear physics. It is not even an applied quantitative science like civil engineering. Rather, it is, at least in its origins, a moral science, even if most economists may be scandalized to discover this. It may be prudent, therefore, for economists to take a cue from the moral insights of pre-economic thought: namely, that the succession of good and bad times really is irremediable and that therefore they do not possess the remedy. There is no remedy. But if governments act as if they have a remedy, they can for two related reasons only make matters worse. First, by attempting the impossible, they are doomed to fail. But second, because the governments involved have willfully blinded themselves to the reasons for their own failures, they become morally culpable.

To put the matter more directly, it is clear to nearly everyone that the consequences of "tending" the economy, whether in the form of full-blown Keynesian or even socialist experiments, or in more modest efforts in "economic diversification," job-training, and similar attempts at managing social welfare, have fallen far short of the promises held out by the advocates of such policies. It may be true that among the blind the one-eyed man is king, but must this still be true among the wilfully blind? In fact, the imagery of blindness, whether accidental or deliberately self-inflicted, is misleading. We would be better to talk of those who have merely refused to open their eyes. In this respect, the Klein government was the first to open one eye. Politically speaking, they view the governed as self-reliant citizens, not subject taxpayers. As we shall see, it was not ever thus, even in Alberta.

Much has been accomplished by the Klein governments, but much more could have been done. As a preliminary assessment, it may be useful to recall a controversy that erupted in the op-ed pages of the *Globe and Mail* some five months prior to the first electoral victory of Mike Harris in Ontario. The dispute centred on whether or not the achievements of the first two years of the Klein government could be exported to other places. Mark Dickerson, a political scientist at the University of Calgary (and in 1997 a defeated Liberal candidate), and Greg Flanagan, an economist at Mount Royal College in Calgary, gave five reasons why Klein's achievements could not be duplicated outside Alberta. First, revenues from oil and gas were so high that Alberta had no need for a sales tax and could afford to maintain the lowest provincial income tax. This was unique. Second, per capita spending was so high in the early 1990s that there was plenty of room to cut. This was rare. Third, Alberta suffered from a higher than average ratio of bureaucrats to non-bureaucrats, so pruning the rank growth would be healthy. Fourth, it had a conservative political culture to begin with. Fifth, the cuts to social services had simply exported welfare recipients to B.C. or Ontario.[18]

A Calgary-based freelance journalist, George Koch, disagreed. Alberta has indeed had high revenues from resource royalties, but the budget was not being balanced by increasing them.[19]

Second, Alberta has high per capita spending compared to whom? Not compared to Ontario or Ottawa. It is true that a large government bureaucracy can be cut, but the Government of Alberta, Koch said, was doing much more than that: by 1995 it had privatized liquor stores, consolidated health, education, and licensing bureaucracies, cut public sector salaries and ended pensions for MLAs elected after 1989. Fourth, Alberta's political culture is a boon to the world not a private stock to be hoarded. Fifth, it is misleading to say that all social services were cut when in fact the chief category to have been cut was that of employable single males.[20]

We agree with George Koch so far as his argument goes. But clearly there is a good deal more to be said than can be accommodated in a short newspaper article. In principle every act by any government is unique and incapable of duplication. No one but the Government of Alberta could ever have passed the first Deficit Elimination Act, but nothing is preventing the Government of Canada or of Quebec or indeed of P.E.I. from doing the same thing within their jurisdictions. That is, notwithstanding the unique configuration of circumstances that conditioned the achievements of the Klein government, the principles upon which those achievements were based can clearly be applied elsewhere in the world. In our opinion Diane Francis was right when she suggested that Alberta offered a model for Ontario.[21] Similarly, an Alberta MP, Ian McClelland, observed "what Alberta is doing today, Canada must eventually do as a nation."[22] Considering the number of governments that have followed where the first Klein government led, the words of Francis and McClelland were genuinely prophetic.

At the same time, it is no coincidence that the particular historical experience and political culture of Alberta has made it relatively easy for most Albertans to support the Klein government just as many Albertans have supported the Reform Party of Canada at the last two federal elections and the Conservatives and Socreds before them. But such an observation hardly explains why Albertans are, and have been, ready to support less government and lower taxes. Of course, the usual explanations, from the genteel academic Marxism of a C.B. Macpherson to the hostile appraisal of generic prairie, "redneck" populism, contain a germ of insight that cannot be denied.[23]

In his budget speeches and in interviews, it was easy for Treasurer Jim Dinning to refer to Alberta's pioneer spirit even though he, like us, has had no pioneering experience. "There is," he told Peter Newman, "still a tendency towards a pioneer spirit here that says 'God damn it, we've got a problem. So let's not point fingers and lay blame, let's not spend a lot of time wringing our hands about it, let's get on and solve the bloody thing.'"[24] The virtue to which Dinning alluded, civic pride, is hardly confined to Alberta.

It is not therefore the particular configuration of Alberta's political culture that made the early Klein initiatives an export commodity. Rather, it was what might be called the purity with which political conflict has been understood within the province and between the province and outsiders. By purity we do not refer to any special virtue. Albertans are as honest and as venal as other Canadians. Rather, the pioneer mythology within which political struggles have been understood in this province has kept the real issues in sharp focus. Politics in Alberta is unsullied by ethnic particularism, as in Quebec, or the pretension of speaking for the nation, as in old Loyalist Ontario, or indeed by demands for pensions and other emoluments because of one's much esteemed and valued culture, as in the Maritimes. But it is precisely the purity and conceptual clarity, the common sense and vulgar bluntness, of Premier Klein's rhetoric that suggests that others can find their own, not Albertans', lessons in the achievements of the first Klein government.[25]

CHAPTER ONE
ALBERTA'S POLITICAL CULTURE

Major fiscal difficulties, like major constitutional ones, do not develop quickly. The Government of Alberta did not suddenly find itself in a fiscal crisis, nor did Albertans wake up one morning and find themselves disappointed in the fiscal irresponsibility of their government. In fact, the seeds of their disappointment were sown during the triumphal years of Premier Lougheed. Peter Lougheed was a very popular premier and yet his undoubted achievements led to consequences that Albertans found disappointing. To understand this apparent paradox we need to look briefly at Alberta's political culture. After all, just because Albertans were disappointed does not mean that Canadians living in the midst of other traditions when faced with similar irresponsibilities will feel the same way. They may, instead, simply ask their governments to take more money from them in taxes, or they may ask foreigners to extend or increase their loans.

Political culture is a term that is used in both a wide and a narrow sense. In many respects Albertans share the experience and the understanding of their fellow citizens in other provinces. If there is a Canadian political culture, Albertans share it. At the same time, there are important differences between Albertans and Saskatchewanians (just as there are commonalities) or between citizens of the prairie west and the inhabitants of British Columbia or New Brunswick. These differences are expressed as much in the work of painters and poets as in public policies. The point about making all such distinctions is not to insist that they are absolute but that they provide more insight than obscurity. As Plato said in a similar context, we should strive to be good butchers and carve at the joints.

The Early Days
The foundations of Alberta's distinctiveness were laid during the nineteenth century, with the settlement that began when the North West Territories included most of the prairie provinces. Alberta was at the end of the road. If you wanted to get farther west, you booked passage 'round the Horn. Then came the big ranches and the railroad, along with settlers, barbed-wire, and homesteaders from the south as well as from the east. The memories of the pioneers are still alive in Alberta and their legacy is recalled with pride among their descendants.[1]

To say that self-sufficiency for the individual and cooperation in the community were the twin principles of the pioneer experience simplifies but does not distort reality. Of course Albertans were dependent on the banks for seed money and on the railroad to market their products, but they took no pride in that. Their interests were served—but for a price. The same can be said of the Dominion Government. It was remote and it made deals that chiefly helped its friends, most of whom seemed to live in Montreal, headquarters of the railroad and the country's largest bank, or Toronto, headquarters of many other banks.

One such deal was struck in 1897, the Crow's Nest Pass freight rates. In exchange for an $11,000 per mile subsidy to push a line west from Lethbridge through the coal-rich Pass into the mineral-rich Kootenays, the Canadian Pacific Railway (CPR) agreed to reduce rates for eastbound grain and for westbound settlers' effects. The prairie settlers gained from the 20% reduction and the CPR built its first industrial subsidiary, the Consolidated Mining and Smelting Company, Cominco. The Crow rates stayed in effect until 1983. The Cominco smelter still dominates the *rive droit* of the Columbia River at Trail.

Following the extended struggle for nominal provincial status in 1905 and then for real provincial status, which included control over natural resources, in 1930, the first major political conflict between the Government of Alberta and the Government of Canada took place during the extended bad times of severe deflation during the Great Depression. In 1934 the Social Credit League was established under the leadership of radio evangelist William Aberhart because the United Farmers of Alberta (UFA) Government had refused to incorporate Social Credit doctrine into their political platform. In the 1935 general election Aberhart triumphed and identified the application of Social Credit with the actions of the provincial government.

The chief problem the new government faced was the size of the public debt. During the first twenty-five years of provincial existence, the rate of public investment in Alberta considerably exceeded the relative rate of settlement. Grants, loans and loan guarantees to build railway branch lines and to encourage livestock and grain production were intended to assist economic development, but far exceeded the basic needs of the province. Alberta was, for example, the first province to begin the development of a comprehensive telephone infrastructure. By 1922 Alberta's debt was twice that of Saskatchewan, a province with a third more people. The problem became much worse a decade later. It was exacerbated by differences between the provincial and federal governments over the proper economic policy to be pursued during the depression and by the inevitable complications that politics brings to a federal regime.

Low commodity prices and high interest rates made the public debt both large and a burden to carry. As the Rowell-Sirois Report of 1940 put it, "it is consequently evident that the provincial debt at its original coupon rates was in a technically rigid and vulnerable position, and only small reductions in carrying charges would have been possible through orderly refunding."[2] If "orderly" restructuring of the provincial debt would have achieved little by way of effective relief, and if relief were nevertheless needed, it could only be achieved by "disorderly," which is to say, unconventional, means.

The new Social Credit government was decidedly unconventional. Shortly after taking office, Premier Aberhart asked Ottawa for $18.4 million to meet the urgent needs of the province but received $2.25 million. Late in 1935 E.C. Manning, then Acting Premier, wrote the provincial bondholders and requested a reduction in interest rates. No positive responses were forthcoming from the banks and investment houses. Meanwhile, the newly elected Liberal government in Ottawa under Mackenzie King had made public finance a high priority. A sub-committee of the Dominion-Provincial Conference in December, 1935 recommended, among other things, the creation of a National Loan Council, which would convert existing provincial debt into bonds guaranteed by Ottawa. Each province would establish a Loan Council comprised of the federal finance minister, the provincial treasurer, and an advisor from the Bank of Canada. The job of the Council would be to approve "orderly" restructuring of existing debt and proposals for new borrowing. The necessary amendment to the British North America Act (now the Constitution Act, 1867) was sought and received from London by the Canadian government, but Alberta was, in fact, far from pleased with the scheme.

Worse, the province was under the gun: a $3.2 million debenture was due to be paid out on 2 April, 1936 and the Alberta government could cover less than 20% of the amount owed. This was the chief reason for Manning's request to debtholders in December, 1935. In consequence, Treasurer Charles Cockroft requested a $2.7 million loan from the federal exchequer. At the same time, the Alberta Government unilaterally reduced interest rates on the existing debt, which provided the federal finance minister, C.A. Dunning, with a reason to refuse Cockroft's request.

In the exchanges that followed it was clear that Alberta would not consent to the National Loan Council because it would entail supervision by Ottawa of provincial finance activities – such as the unilateral reduction in interest payments – and Ottawa would not cover the impending debenture maturity without Alberta's adherence to the Loan Council, including the provision for financial oversight. Two days after the last exchange of telegrams between Edmonton and Ottawa, the impasse led to Alberta's default on the April debenture payments.[3]

In retrospect, the National Loan Council looked like a kind of prelude to so many post-war shared-cost schemes. As Mackenzie King's biographer observed, "provincial approval of a Loan Council would thus be completely voluntary—except that there would be no federal loans unless it was approved."[4] Later in the century this unilateral exercise of the federal "spending power," that is, the ability of the federal government (more formally, the crown in right of Canada) to make gifts to individuals or other governments with or without conditions, would become an ongoing source of contention between Ottawa and all the provinces, not just Alberta. The constitutionality of the spending power, derived from the Royal Prerogative and the common law, has been most forcefully argued by Frank Scott,[5] though it remains politically contentious.

The default and the reduction in interest payments brought an immediate response from bondholders who had counted on the Loan Council to protect their interests: they took a train to Edmonton and sought to negotiate an acceptable compromise. The bondholders made the case that unilateral action by Alberta would harm widows, orphans, poor clergymen, and hard-pressed educators. It would also severely hamper any future attempts by the Government of Alberta to borrow money. The indifference of the government to such appeals was palpable: those worthies who allegedly were harmed by the default were not Albertans. More important, as good Social Creditors, they knew that government debt was the problem, which is to say that the threat of impairing the ability of the province to borrow was empty. The provincial government refused to restore interest payments, and temporized in a time-honoured way by agreeing to join a committee established to study the ability of Alberta to meet its financial commitments. When the committee recommended that the solution lay in increasing revenue, not decreasing expenditure, the government thanked them for their efforts and continued to pay at a reduced rate. Eventually the legislation was declared ultra vires, which also made no difference. On the eve of World War Two, defaults amounted to some $12 million.[6]

The debenture problem, the default on payments, and recourse to litigation began what became a pattern in the relations between Edmonton and Ottawa. During the summer of 1936, the Alberta government issued "prosperity certificates" which it declared to be a kind of tax that could be used as money. The Supreme Court of Canada declared it to be illegal tender and Albertans dubbed the scrip "funny money." The harm caused by the depression continued without let, however, and the ability of the federal government to prevent Social Credit remedies from becoming effective merely confirmed the validity of provincial measures in the eyes of many Albertans.

In August, 1937, the province passed three acts designed to extend credit, to reduce the influence of the banks, and to prevent recourse to the courts if anyone objected. All three acts were promptly disallowed by Ottawa. Premier Aberhart replied that the power of disallowance was obsolete, called the Legislature again into session, passed three more acts, and, on 6 October, 1937, they were "reserved" by the Lieutenant Governor for the approval of the Governor General, which is to say, for the approval of the Liberal Cabinet of Mackenzie King. Cabinet did not approve. In the spring of 1938 Alberta passed another batch of acts that were assented to by the Lieutenant Governor but two of them were subsequently disallowed on 15 June, 1938.

The reasons given for disallowance were of more than passing interest inasmuch as those reasons and the objections to them subsequently were incorporated into the lore, the mythology, and the self-understanding of Albertans. It became clear in retrospect that Albertans' attempts to defend their own interests would be treated differently than similar attempts by other provincial governments, especially by Quebec Governments.

According to the Attorney General of Canada, Ernest Lapointe, the Alberta acts were vaguely worded. But more important, they interfered with certain fundamental rights of Canadian corporate persons, such as banks, who wished, in this case, to do business in Alberta, and by so interfering, imposed a burden on the rest of the country. In other words, while the power of disallowance remained practically unlimited, so that no reasons needed to be given beyond the residual "conflict with Dominion policy," the actual reason seemed to be that, by convention, the provinces could not interfere with fundamental civil rights. If, nevertheless, the provinces did interfere with these fundamental civil rights, notwithstanding the provisions of section 92 of the BNA Act, which gave the provinces the power exclusively to make laws in the area of property and civil rights, their actions would be disallowed by Ottawa.[7]

Three weeks later, it became clear, at least to Albertans, that the Dominion Government was not in truth as interested in the civil rights of all Canadians as it had claimed to be in its defence of the disallowance of the Alberta legislation. In July the same Minister of Justice refused to disallow what became known as the Quebec Padlock Law. Instead, this law was eventually declared illegal following lengthy and costly litigation. The Quebec law was easily as vague and arbitrary as the Alberta legislation and was clearly a provincial invasion of the field of criminal law, which was under the exclusive jurisdiction of the Dominion and bound to be *ultra vires* on those grounds alone.[8]

Consider the provisions of the Quebec law. It prohibited the use of any building for the propagation of "communism and bolshevism," terms undefined in the Act. It gave the Attorney General of Quebec, Mr. Duplessis, who was also the Premier, the power to close premises for up to a year without proving anything about the undefined Bolshevik activities. It denied appeal to the courts. It permitted the Attorney General to seize and destroy undefined Bolshevik literature. In short, the Padlock Law was clearly as great an interference with civil liberties as anything envisaged by the Alberta legislation. So why, Albertans wondered, did the Government of Canada do nothing?

Mr. Lapointe did allow that the Quebec law was "not free from difficulty" but considered it "preferable" to proceed through the courts. He never provided a reason for this preference so observers such as Eugene Forsey looked to the context for a clue to the reasoning of the Dominion Government. With the Alberta legislation, opposition came from the banks, the insurance companies, and mortgage organizations; opposed to the Padlock Law were not the rich and powerful but the poor and weak, and in its favour were the Roman Catholic Church, the editorialists of the major Montreal papers, and many of the same business organizations that opposed Alberta.

For Forsey and for the Social Credit Government of Alberta, it was all a question of politics. Ottawa was on the side of the big battalions and all the talk of civil liberties was dismissed in the province as so much hot air. Premier Aberhart drew the practical conclusion that so long as the banks were opposed and were backed by the federal government it would be impossible to introduce Social Credit in Alberta. In response he turned his attention to providing "good government," which is to say frugal government. Following his death in 1943, Aberhart's policies were continued by Ernest Manning. But the popular lore remained: Ottawa would do nothing to help the economically destitute in Alberta and would act to prevent Albertans from helping themselves with a lot of legalistic double-talk. To make matters worse, they didn't even apply the legalistic double-talk consistently. The notion that Quebec was the spoiled child of Confederation was current in Alberta long before the demands for special and distinct constitutional status emerged during the 1980s.

At the end of World War Two, Alberta's prospects did not look rosy. Twenty-five million tons of mineable coal sat in the ground; 171,000 square miles of forests remained practically untouched. Several million hydro horsepower went to waste as Alberta's wild rivers flowed to the sea and billions of barrels of oil remained trapped in the tar sands around Fort McMurray. Worst of all, young Albertans, many of whom were returned veterans, were moving out. Then, on a cold Thursday in February, 1947, thirty years of fruitless petroleum exploration came to an end when a well drilled by an Imperial Oil crew headed by Vernon "Dry Hole" Hunter blew in at Leduc. One of Canada's greatest resource booms had begun and the energy economy of the country was transformed. The resource base of Alberta underwent a phase shift from agriculture to energy. In comparison to the vicissitudes of agriculture, the energy industry looked relatively stable. It was also much more profitable.[9]

Economic Diversification During the Lougheed Era
The old lore was not forgotten under these new circumstances. Albertans still distrusted eastern bankers and big-shots, and showed it by persistently electing an unreformed group of Social Creditors to the House of Commons. So far as oil and gas resources were concerned, the memories of perfidy at the hands of remote rulers in Ottawa extended back beyond Social Credit to the preceding UFA government. One of the reasons the UFA pressed so strenuously for control over natural resources during the 1920s was that Ottawa had left unregulated the Turner Valley oil field and the result was an astonishing waste of natural gas. Premier Manning increased the regulatory strength of the Oil and Gas Conservation Board (later the Energy Resources Conservation Board, the ERCB) after the Second World War, during the 1950s, he created Alberta Gas Trunk Lines (AGTL), a new kind of corporate and legal instrument that combined private capital from producers and exporters with investment from Alberta utilities. AGTL was intended to forestall the penetration across the Saskatchewan-Alberta border by the American- and eastern-owned Trans-Canada Pipe Lines (TCPL), which had been chartered by Ottawa to transport gas interprovincially.

A final factor that set the stage for the conflicts of the 1970s and 1980s also developed during Premier Manning's day. Prior to Leduc, the future of the province seemed tied to grain farming, chiefly wheat, and to cattle ranching. Increased mechanization promised a decline both in the rural and in the total population. Only the development of oil and gas resources held the potential for economic growth and the possibility of diversification away from agriculture. At the same time, oil and gas exploration was both expensive and risky. "Dry Hole" Hunter had earned his sobriquet the hard way. Between the discovery at Norman Wells during the 1920s and Leduc, Imperial Oil had drilled a string of 133 non-commercial wells. In consequence, venture capital was growing scarce. Premier Manning was not about to risk the taxpayer's funds, and the eastern or "national" banks and financial institutions were not eager to invest either. They had neither forgotten nor forgiven Premier Aberhart's Social Credit initiatives. So far as the Government of Alberta was concerned, they had been refused, rebutted, and insulted by their fellow citizens. Accordingly they turned to the Americans and the major international oil companies.[10] The majors were eager to explore the western sedimentary basin, they were welcomed, and they found a great deal of oil and gas.

By 1971, when Peter Lougheed led a revived Conservative Party to victory over a by now worn-out Social Credit government, he also became the leader of an increasingly well articulated and self-conscious political community. Many newcomers had settled in the province, including oilmen from Texas and Oklahoma, but also many more ambitious Maritimers and Europeans, anxious to prosper in a region that rewarded brains, hard work, and the courage to take risks. Wherever they came from, new Albertans arrived in order to pursue economic opportunities. They had no difficulty adapting to the myths and folkways of earlier generations of Albertans. They favoured self-reliance, smaller government, and soon enough adopted the perception that most threats are external. The memories of the federal assault on the Social Credit legislation of the 1930s had faded, and in place of Social Credit measures, "province-building" institutions such as AGTL, the ERCB, and a stable royalty structure—all of which were made-in-Alberta devices—would ensure that financial resources would be in place to diversify the economy and modernize the province.

By any account, the Lougheed victory was a critical electoral realignment that reflected the economic, demographic and social changes that had taken place in the generation after Leduc. The political meaning of the 1971 election was simply that the center of gravity in the province had shifted from the pious countryside to the secular city, though the 1967 election provided a preview of what lay ahead. One of the major criticisms made by the Lougheed Conservatives against the Socreds was that Alberta had remained too dependent on the production of raw, unfinished staples—oil, grains, and cattle. What the Tories called a "third phase" was necessary. In economic terms this meant establishing forward and backward linkages with respect, for example, to oil extraction. Forward linkages refer to ways of generating additional income in industries that use oil and gas as an input or feed-stock and transform it further. Refineries and petrochemical industries are obvious examples. Backward linkages refer to adding value by way of industries that provide inputs to the oil industry—engineering, seismic and technology companies, research and development firms, and so on.

The sum total of Social Credit economic strategy was criticized as being little more than ensuring cordial relations with suppliers of investment capital. Under the more energetic and ambitious Lougheed Tories, the direction switched to support for Alberta capitalists. For 25 years, indigenous Alberta capital had had to settle for a marginal and dependent role. The reason: the combined weight of the major oil companies, Socred preferential policies towards external capital, and the facilitation of takeovers of Canadian enterprises by the majors using the traditional mechanisms of central Canadian finance operating through Calgary branch plants. All this changed after the 1971 election.[11]

For the next 20 years the Government of Alberta took on the role of entrepreneur in regional capitalist development. The great rumble in the background was caused by the increased demand at higher prices for Alberta energy and the increased demand by the Alberta government for higher royalties. During the early 1970s, there was an inevitable shift of power towards the oil producers. The response of the Lougheed Government was to mobilize its own talent, power, and energy to strengthen its control over the Alberta economy, to foster regional capital accumulation, to reduce Alberta's dependence on external political and economic forces, and to diversify the economy away from primary resource production in order to decrease its long- and short-term vulnerability. In short, the Lougheed government would be a more hands-on administration, and what they put their hands on was the oil and gas industry. Increased prices meant increased profits for the oil companies, but it also provided an opportunity for an aggressive government to divert some of those profits to its own use by converting them into economic rents. During the 1970s the oil boom was never seen by the government as an oil boom: it was a path of economic expansion that was a novel, entirely satisfactory, and, they confidently expected, a permanent feature of the economy.[12]

One of the measures proposed was to alter the royalty structure that had been in place since 1948 and had resulted, by 1970, in a situation where 30 companies produced 95% of the oil on 50% of the acreage while drilling only 28% of the wells. This was considered by the Lougheed government and by the junior oil companies to be highly improper. It meant that a small number of relatively large companies produced nearly all Alberta's oil but were not equally active in exploring for more. In short, the major oil companies seemed to be operating on the assumption that the western sedimentary basin in general and Alberta in particular had reached the point of maturity, so that returns measured by barrels of oil found for each dollar spent on exploration had begun to decline. There was still plenty of oil to be discovered, but because it was located in smaller reservoirs, it would be relatively expensive to find, at least compared to the early "elephant" pools that had been discovered during the years immediately after Leduc.

Accordingly, the majors had little incentive to look for new oil when they could make sizeable profits from pumping "old" oil. If exploration was to be undertaken, therefore, the junior companies would be the preferred vehicle, not least of all because their interests more clearly harmonized with the new priorities of the Lougheed government. The 1972 Natural Resources Revenue Plan effectively increased the old royalty rates from just under 17% of gross production to 23%. Premier Lougheed then announced that royalties would rise along with oil prices. The main objections to this new regime, couched in terms of the sanctity of contract, were voiced by the majors. The juniors, in contrast, were more willing to go along with the Alberta Government in exchange for greater prominence in the industry and with the expectation that royalty rates for "new" oil might be the subject of future negotiation. One of the purposes of the 1972 Plan was, therefore, to bring the juniors on side.

Compared to Premier Manning, Peter Lougheed was a committed interventionist. The difference between the two men was dramatically expressed in Lougheed's creation of the Alberta Heritage Trust Fund, a revenue-producing "rainy day" public account into which "surplus" royalty revenues were diverted.[13] On the other hand, as Robert Mansell observed, the Heritage Fund may well have been created "because it would have been impossible for the provincial government to increase spending further without creating excessive inflationary pressures."[14] Whatever the government's reason for establishing the Heritage Fund, it soon came to symbolize a major change in Canadian politics that was very much not to Ottawa's liking. Politically speaking it was equivalent to the Social Credit legislation a generation earlier insofar as it gave contemporary expression to a long-standing conflict with Ottawa.

The response of Ottawa was swift and brutal. If there was any intervening to be done, the federal government had long been of the opinion that they, not their counterparts in Edmonton, ought to do it. In 1973, the federal government imposed an export tax on crude destined for Chicago, the major pipeline hub, and in 1974 they removed the provision that allowed oil companies to deduct provincial royalties when calculating income taxable by the federal government. No such analogous export tax on energy produced by Hydro Quebec was ever considered—probably because Hydro Quebec seems to be capable only of absorbing revenue, not generating it. But Albertans neither knew nor cared about the burden Quebeckers placed on themselves. What they noticed was that Hydro Quebec was in the energy business, as were Ontario Hydro and B.C. Hydro for that matter, and those companies remained untouched.

As Mansell and Percy observed, there is a major inconsistency in the way the oil and gas industry has been treated compared to other sectors of the energy business. For example, hydroelectricity production in Canada is heavily subsidized, and substantial economic rents remain uncollected and untaxed.

> The oil and gas industry, on the other hand, pays considerable taxes, does not have its debt guaranteed by governments, and has the rents associated with its production collected and distributed by governments.
>
> This also results in an inconsistency in the federal government's treatment of regional fiscal capacities. For example, Alberta is a highly successful collector of energy rents, and this has allowed the province to build up the Alberta Heritage Savings Trust Fund. But the existence of this fund has often been used as justification for subjecting the province to special taxes or giving it a less-than-proportionate share of federal expenditures, or both. By comparison, Ontario and Quebec distribute energy rents through artificially low electricity prices. Since the benefits do not show up in a highly visible fund, they escape notice – and measurement as part of regional fiscal capacity. It is interesting to note that, as of the end of 1986, the combined retained equity of Ontario Hydro and Quebec Hydro alone was $11.7 billion, an amount roughly equal to the financial assets of the Alberta Heritage Savings Trust Fund.[15]

The details may have remained vague, but Albertans did know and they did care that they were being singled out for involuntary contributions to the federal treasury. They didn't like it one bit and looked to Premier Lougheed to champion their cause.

Ottawa's move was a textbook example of federal encroachment on a major provincial source of revenue; but it was also an opportunity for Premier Lougheed to change the 1948 rules and get rid of the old and inflexible royalty arrangements. In the conflict between Edmonton and Ottawa, the oil companies, chiefly the majors, were caught in the middle and pulled their rigs out of the province. Eventually a compromise was reached, and exploration resumed. In this conflict, Alberta proved more successful than it had been during the 1930s. The Alberta government also backed AGTL in its negotiations with TCPL in order to introduce competitive, which is to say, higher, prices into the Canadian gas market, most of which lay in Ontario.

The strategy guiding the Alberta government was laid out in the 1972

"Natural Resources Revenue Plan." Additional royalty revenue was to be used to stimulate economic diversification and bring an end to the familiar boom-and-bust cycle. A massive acquisition of resource revenue was of little significance in itself unless it was used to ensure the cycle was ended.[16] The fact that the image of a wasting asset was never far from the consciousness of Alberta politicians added a sense of urgency to their strategic plans.

The National Energy Program

To say that Albertans' view of the provincial energy policy was misunderstood by easterners is a grievous understatement. It was simply incomprehensible to easterners that what they saw as the nation's richest province was aggrieved that it was not getting richer quicker. Albertans, however, thought they were doing no more than following the example of Ontario, which earlier in the century used legislation and taxation policy to ensure secondary processing of mineral and forest resources, to say nothing of Ontario Hydro. Easterners did not see imitation as flattery and redoubled their criticism.

One reason for this regrettable truculence was the fact that, at the same time as westerners were enjoying increased prosperity, the economy of Ontario was not performing well. Indeed, for much of the 1970s, Ontario's growth rate in per capita GDP, income, public investment, residential construction, and other key indicators of economic performance, ranked last. Not surprisingly, Ontario's poor showing was seen as a consequence of the west's buoyancy—especially Alberta's. It was easy for residents of Ontario to reject the notion that a rising tide lifts all boats when their splendid and ornate yacht was still on the beach. In its place was the view that economics is a zero-sum game. In fact, however, for Alberta's prosperity to account for Ontario's misery, Alberta would have had to be able to exercise sufficient market influence to have brought about the oil price increase in the first place—which is patently absurd. It was brought about by OPEC, the Organization of Petroleum Exporting Countries, without the advice or assistance of Peter Lougheed. Moreover, western oil was marketed in the east at prices substantially below world prices even though the price of manufactured products shipped from the east embodied the world, not the domestic, price of oil.

Higher oil and gas prices and attendant increased royalty revenues led to a series of budgetary surpluses, which enabled the government to invest public funds in expanding Alberta's infrastructure in the hopes of diversifying the petroleum and agricultural industrial base. Equally significant, the Lougheed government invested in sufficient bureaucratic and political expertise to be able to meet on more or less equal terms with federal officials. It was as if Premier Lougheed had revived the prewar political legacy along with symbolic opposition to Ottawa, only now from a position of greater economic strength and not merely out of a strong desire to safeguard and maintain what might be called a distinct Albertan society. During the 1970s the eastern banks came to Alberta to invest, not to take the government to court or have the Dominion Government selectively exercise its powers of disallowance and reservation. In policy terms, Premier Lougheed and economic and political leaders across the province had abandoned the strategy of working from within the central government for national economic development, in favour of greater regional or provincial economic autonomy, a strategy sometimes called "province-building."[17]

One might also note a subtle but significant shift in political strategy. During the Manning years the provincial government minded its own store and made minimal intrusions into the federal domain. Premier Manning did express reservations about some policies of the Pearson Liberals, but he certainly never attacked them. During the 1970s, however, relations between Ottawa and Edmonton went from reserved and formal to adversarial and downright hostile. Albertans had noticed that Prime Minister Trudeau was very concerned with policies that had little or no interest for or appeal to them, such as official bilingualism. Other policies, such as massive social spending, they found worthy of suspicion and distrust. A new era had begun.

Alberta advocated and undertook regional development policies by way of the provincial government. Ottawa advocated and enacted "national" policies that neither served Alberta's interests nor respected the pioneering elements so important to Alberta's political myth or political culture, which soon enough came to be disparaged as being redneck. Even more astonishing, at least to Albertans, their objections to being prevented from leading the country in a new direction were categorically dismissed as being sentiments of "western alienation."

For their part, Albertans were of the view that during the early years of the century they had contributed a great deal to Canada's industrial heartland. The wheat boom was almost universally acknowledged as being crucial to Canadian economic expansion, but the legitimacy of contemporary resentments stemming from the administrative restrictions of the Dominion Lands Policy, the appropriation of land and mineral revenues "for the purposes of the Dominion," and the CPR monopoly, were unacknowledged outside the prairie west. In any case, Albertans widely shared the view that it was time to move on to another chapter. They could see what had happened in the U.S. with the decline of the rustbelt and the ascent of the sunbelt. They saw similar causes at work in both countries: rising energy costs, obsolescent smokestack manufacturing industries, and labour and capital mobility. Moreover, in Peter Lougheed and Pierre Trudeau the two governments found strong leaders to personify their respective sides in the conflict. At the close of their 1979 book, *Prairie Capitalism* Richards and Pratt warned of a "counter-assault on the west," when Ottawa and the two larger provinces in the St. Lawrence valley would respond to what had taken place. In 1980 old Canada attacked, and the counter-assault was ferocious.

The National Energy Program (NEP) was presented to Canadians as part of the October, 1980 budget. In coming to terms with the NEP, there are many contexts to consider. Probably the most significant thing about the National Energy Program for the themes we are concerned with in this book is that federal policy-makers, both elected and bureaucratic, did not see it as a temporary or emergency measure. As a report from the C.D. Howe Institute observed early-on, it was intended to be "the cornerstone of a strategy that would shape the nation's economic destiny for years to come."[18] As we shall see, the NEP was based on assumptions but remotely connected to reality, and was sufficiently rigid and inflexible to ensure conflict so long as it endured. Apart from a few interventionist guardians of the Trudeau legacy, the consensus is that the NEP was misbegotten and ill-conceived. At the same time, its genesis, content, and justification also expressed a vision of Alberta that had great appeal to the "national" government. Perhaps it still does. Much of the continuing assertiveness of Alberta business and of the first Klein government has been a direct and creative response to the imposition of that Ottawa-based vision upon Canadians who did not share it one bit.

Trudeau had returned to lead the Liberals to victory in 1980 after Joe Clark's inexperienced Tories had shown their ineptness at Parliamentary procedure. In Trudeau's mind there were four issues: Quebec, the energy question, the economy, and the constitution. It turned out that Quebec and the constitution were two sides of the same issue, as were energy and the economy. The logic was clear but never could be admitted: if Alberta's energy revenues could be appropriated and redirected by Ottawa, the economy would hum; if the constitution could be changed, Quebec would feel at home in Canada.[19]

There were three elements to the Liberals' 1980 energy platform: (1) they would ensure lower petroleum prices than the Conservatives; (2) they would "Canadianize" the oil industry; (3) they would ensure energy-security through self-sufficiency. At the end of the day what the NEP actually achieved was: (1) the highest energy price increases in Canadian history; (2) a drastic reduction in the importance of the Canadian sector of the oil industry (the fate of Dome and Turbo provide the chief examples); (3) an increase in supply uncertainty similar to that of the first OPEC crisis because of massive disincentives to conventional exploration in favour of the much more risky frontier that remained wholly under the control of Ottawa. These were the so-called "Canada lands" in the far north, and they have produced comparatively miniscule amounts, notwithstanding their great potential.

Peter Foster has provided a detailed and accessible account of the origins and significance of the NEP.[20] Two of his observations were particularly astute. First, the major initiative came from the bureaucrats in the Ministry of Energy, Mines and Resources (EMR). The fact that the oil was produced in Alberta but consumed in central Canada was for them a *problem*. Higher oil prices redistributed wealth through the market to Alberta and to a lesser extent to B.C. and Saskatchewan. This, they decided, was clearly an "imbalance." A few years earlier Premier Davis of Ontario had called upon Ottawa to undo the "excessive and imprudent" claims of the oil-producing provinces by taxing western resource revenues, recycling the money through Ontario, and ensuring thereby that "the management and future of our country" would remain in good hands.

As Trudeau himself acknowledged in his *Memoirs*, if the imbalance were left uncorrected, the equalization program would have to be scrapped because "even Ontario would have become a have-not province," which was, of course, totally unthinkable. In short, it was not "fair" that Alberta should collect so much revenue. The ultimate cause of this unfairness was the irrationality of nature in putting oil in Alberta in the first place. Surely it was now up to the rationality of the "super-bureaucrats" in EMR to set things right. More to the point, it was politically self-evident that Alberta could not be expected to use its new financial power in the interests of Canada. What made it self-evident was the undisputable fact that Albertans had shown their complete irresponsibility, not to say irrationality, by refusing to elect a single Liberal to the House of Commons.

Trudeau and his energy minister, Marc Lalonde, had failed to realize it was impossible to base any long-term economic strategy on an industry characterized by a volatile market and unstable political conditions. Not even so mighty a cartel as OPEC could eclipse the influence of the market for long. Even though economic science is not rocket science, the fundamentals of the market and how it works were forgotten, neglected, overlooked, and ignored by panic-stricken bureaucrats in the Departments of Finance and EMR, the latter having mutated during the previous decade from a dull, technical line department to an aggressive and powerful central policy-making agency. In short, the assumption upon which the whole massive NEP edifice rested—constantly rising oil prices—was demonstrably wrong. There were to be no shortages of supply and prices were soon to fall.

During the late 1970s high prices for oil led to lower demand, as conservation measures and product-substitution had their inevitable and predictable effects. Lowered demand led to lower prices as companies and producers bid for customers. That is how markets worked, including commodity markets for finite natural resources. The Ottawa bureaucrats and Liberal politicians had forgotten or never learned about the old textbook standby, the corn-hog cycle. Instead, they invoked the terrifying image of a last barrel of oil sold for an astronomical price. But here we are reaching the outer limits of credibility; such images belong in movies like "Road Warrior," not in the rhetoric of political leaders. Yet political leaders used such fantasies regularly.

The economic thinking of Trudeau and his Cabinet and advisors revealed a great deal about their parochialism, their pseudo-communitarian commitments, their allegiance to what Michael Lusztig has called "command liberalism," and the imprudence of developing an industrial strategy that aimed at something so artificial and abstract as "fairness."[21] To begin with, Trudeau was of the view that the price of oil was politically determined, pure and simple, by OPEC, and was hardly influenced by the market. If OPEC could operate that way, he reasoned, so could Canada: hence the NEP. But Trudeau was wrong. Second, to the federal Liberals generally, and not just to the Prime Minister, foreign oil companies were bad. If they reinvested their profits in Canada, they were bad because they got bigger; if they didn't, they were bad because profits went abroad. Presumably the only good foreign oil companies would not make a profit. But even then they would be bad because they would leave. Such logic, at least to non-Liberals, of whom there were many in Alberta, was perverse.

Peter Foster reported a revealing conversation between Trudeau and Jack Gallagher, former president of now bankrupt Dome Petroleum, but at that time president of one of the major short-term beneficiaries of the NEP. Dome had obtained what were called "super-depletion tax allowances," the result of which was that Canadian taxpayers spent a lot of money in Dome's Beaufort Sea exploration play. "Well," said Pierre, "that means they really drilled the hole for free."

"But Pierre," said Jack, "that's not the point. The point is, there is a hole there now and there wasn't before. And at the bottom of that hole is a lot of oil. Besides, the taxes are only deferred, not lost forever."

"Well, Jack," said Pierre, "I heard they got it for nothing. That's all." As the oilmen say, Pierre saw the hole, not the doughnut.

The drive towards "Canadianization," which induced outfits like Dome to the Beaufort, had tremendous and perverse unintended consequences. To begin with, there has never been an economic rationale for Canadianizing the oil industry. Taxes and regulations are more effective ways to ensure that "windfall profits" are not exported. They are also much cheaper. Consider the following: once the incentives were in place for Canadian companies to acquire foreign ones, the Canadians had to go to the banks for financing because foreign equity markets were, by definition, closed. But Canadian bank loans increased the leverage and thus the vulnerability of the new and larger Canadian company. Direct foreign investment in Canada, the "bad" foreign ownership of Canadian oil and gas operations, was replaced by an almost equal amount of (presumably "good") foreign-held debt because, while Canadian oil companies were induced to go to Canadian banks, the banks were free to go to New York and London. This shell game created a significant inflow of debt capital in exchange for an even more significant outflow of interest obligations that were hostage to interest rates and to the exchange rate between Canadian and U.S. dollars. With the kind of exquisite timing that only governments seem able to achieve, the NEP-inspired acquisitions spree took place at the peak of the oil boom: in mid-1981, the Toronto Stock Exchange index for major integrated oil companies hovered around 3,400; a year later it stood at 1720.

Moreover, by discriminating against foreign-owned companies and retroactively changing the rules for resource ownership, the NEP immediately stimulated the flight of foreign capital. This put additional downward pressure on the Canadian dollar, raised interest rates further, and added to Canada's already significant balance-of-payments problems. By encouraging smaller Canadian firms to expand rapidly using debt financing rather than the more usual and more prudent equity financing, and by basing incentives on the number of holes drilled rather than on the size of the reserves discovered, the NEP contributed directly to the subsequent failure of many of these firms by making them an offer they couldn't refuse, which is also an offer that never should have been made.

In addition to the junior companies, several medium sized companies also got into major financial trouble and even the banks saw that they had become overexposed with their massive policy-driven loans to the oil companies. There were occasional whispers of a general financial meltdown. In the end, Canadian taxpayers were called upon to foot the bill for what had begun as a series of private-sector acquisitions of foreign assets. Finally, since most of the foreign companies were American owned, U.S. retaliation against Canadian exploration companies was swift and sure.

Looking back on the disaster of the NEP, it seems perfectly obvious that its sole purpose had been telegraphed by Premier Davis even before the bright lights at EMR turned their attention towards Alberta. It was essentially a policy aimed at generating revenue by transferring money from the productive private sector in the three westernmost provinces to Ottawa, and thence to Ontario. The assumption was that state control was preferable to private sector control where the state meant Ottawa, not Edmonton, and control by government was assumed, wrongly, to be interchangeable with, and indistinguishable from, control by private interests.

What made the NEP so acceptable to the voters of central Canada was precisely the appeal made by Ottawa to the public good and the "national" interest. It is true that the market and the oil companies are not focally concerned with the public good. They are primarily concerned with creating wealth and finding oil. The federal government claimed to have higher purposes, namely spending wealth for the public good. The credulous will always harken to their siren song, and they did on this occasion. Productive Canadians, particularly in Alberta, are still paying for the gullibility of their fellow citizens, most of whom live elsewhere.

The Heavy Price of Fiscal Federalism

The volatility of oil prices means that revenues based on oil royalties cannot provide a sound basis for any long-term economic policy. Even within Alberta, good faith projections of royalty revenue have varied enormously. As we shall see, when Jim Dinning used a five-year moving average to calculate the basis of oil prices, and thus provincial revenues, a great deal of volatility and especially of over-estimation of revenue was removed from royalty estimates.

In the 1980s, however, matters were made even worse, and estimates and revenues even more unstable, when two governments with competing agendas, existing in relative isolation from the industry, were involved. When prices and costs of production changed, as inevitably they did, though not in the direction everyone thought, then the solemn agreements that governments signed to divvy up the royalty revenues had to be rethought, scrapped, or imposed on the industry whatever the circumstances. But excessive royalties imposed on a reluctant industry may make production uneconomic, in which case both oil deliveries and revenue are reduced; on the other hand, if royalties are adjusted because of unforeseen circumstances, then the case for stable projections for government revenue is thrown out the window. Neither option seems to have occurred to the bureaucrats in EMR and Finance, nor to the federal Liberal or provincial Conservative politicians.

The most important legacy of the NEP was political not economic. Shortly after the NEP legislation was introduced Premier Lougheed delivered the same message to the Alberta Legislature and to audiences in Calgary and Edmonton: the NEP, he said, was part of a plan to centralize economic power in Ottawa and thereby to change the very nature of Canadian federalism. In 1978, Alberta had produced its own vision of Canada's future, *Harmony in Diversity: A New Federalism for Canada*. It was a much more decentralized version than could ever win the approval of the Trudeaucrats. For Albertans the NEP was also a political move on the part of Ottawa to enhance its power over the industry and over the producing provinces. *Harmony in Diversity* was a prelude to the series of reports—Bélanger-Campeau, Allaire, and all the rest—that were produced in Quebec a decade later in response to an analogous problem with decentralization.

It is, of course, true that large changes in oil and gas prices were a problem, but they also provided an opportunity to demonstrate the flexibility and resiliency of Confederation. Looked at in terms of a business arrangement or as "fiscal federalism" pure and simple, Confederation can be considered as a means to promote regional stabilization. Each region can specialize in areas of comparative advantage without suffering the instability that comes along with specialization because the federal government could make compensating fiscal transfers when one region is hit by an economic downturn and other regions are prospering. A more or less equitable fiscal federalism would mean that the overall fiscal balance that the federal government runs with any particular province or region would vary with that area's economic performance. For example—and assuming for the sake of simplicity that the federal government is running a balanced budget—Ottawa would run a surplus with the "have" regions and a deficit with the "have-not" regions. That is, the federal government would extract more revenue from the have regions than it returned in goods and services and provide the have-not regions with their goods and services at relatively cheaper prices. In fact, something like this arrangement actually exists with social welfare payments to, and income taxes from, individuals. Things become more complex in reality when transfers are between regions, insofar as poorer individuals in richer regions may end up subsidizing indirectly richer individuals in poorer regions.

Leaving that question aside, the net fiscal transfers between regions are pretty much what one would expect if the country were run along more or less equitable lines. Thus per-capita deficits with low-income provinces such as Newfoundland have been larger than they have been with higher-income provinces. Provinces suffering a temporary or cyclical downturn have likewise run higher deficits with Ottawa than have more stable provinces.

Unfortunately, things do not always work out the way they are "supposed" to do. In 1986, two economists at the University of Western Ontario, John Whalley and Irene Trela, published a study for the Macdonald Commission, which had been asked to examine the "Economic Union and Development Prospects for Canada." The Whalley/Trela study examined the "price" of being Canadian in different parts of the country. Whatever the technical difficulties of the approach they adopted, *Regional Aspects of Confederation* did indicate as clearly as possible that the four western provinces *all* paid more to be Canadian than they received in benefits. The highest price for being Canadian was paid by Alberta, and the biggest payments went to Quebec and Atlantic Canada. When they examined the question of costs and benefits of opting out of Confederation using this same bookkeeping approach, it turned out that all the western provinces would be better off, including the "have-not" ones, Saskatchewan and Manitoba; none of the eastern ones, including Ontario, would benefit by opting out. The conclusions reached by these two respected academic economists writing a technical report for a major Royal Commission came as a shock to many easterners and especially to Quebec sovereigntists.[22]

Another study, by University of Calgary economists Robert Mansell and Ronald Schlenker, developed a way of asking the same question as the Macdonald Commission study, but avoided some of the technical problems with using the Whalley/Trela approach. They sought to determine the actual difference between federal government revenues and expenditures when all taxation, transfer, and expenditure policies are taken into account. It was written in the wake of the constitutional agitation surrounding the Meech Lake Accord and sought to examine the probable effects of Quebec independence, of Alberta independence, and of a looser federation. Like the pre-Meech conclusion of Whalley and Trela, Mansell and Schlenker showed that, for the 1961-1990 period, only B.C. and Alberta, of all the provinces, experienced a net financial outflow. In the example of Alberta it amounted to $2,500 a year for every individual in the province (1990 dollars) or about 12% of GDP for the 1970s and 1980s. These payments can be best understood as federal surtaxes, which means that Albertans paid the highest, not the lowest taxes in Canada.[23]

As a result, the overall macroeconomic effect of federal-provincial relations during this quarter century was to reduce the size of the Alberta (and the B.C.) economy. Gross Domestic Product (GDP), population, and employment were all lower than they otherwise would have been. By the same token, the economies of the Yukon and NWT have been greatly enhanced, as has the economy of Atlantic Canada.[24] Saskatchewan, Manitoba and Quebec have significantly larger economies than they otherwise would have had. There is, of course, considerable redistribution away from Ontario, but a good deal of it is offset by indirect effects of trade linkages to the rest of the country that result in large amounts of the Ontario-based transfer payments leaking back to their province of origin, just as Bill Davis advocated in the 1970s. That is not true for Alberta. The NEP, by the Mansell and Schlenker account, cost the province $40 billion. Between 1970 and 1991 Alberta contributed $165 billion more to Ottawa than it received in benefits—an amount, incidentally, that is close to the excess that Quebec received over revenues collected. In a bookkeeping sense, Alberta has paid for federal transfers to Quebec.

The general or macroeconomic effects of Ottawa's policies, therefore, are clear. What would have happened without these transfers out of the west is not clear—Heritage Fund investments lead to different consequences than tax reductions, and both would have been options. Nor is it easy to predict the detailed effects on per capita income had Ottawa not taken so much revenue—except, of course, that Albertans were left with a lot less jingle in their jeans. What is clear, however, is that the decisions would have been made by Albertans.[25]

The short-term effects were entirely predictable. The recession that began in 1982 lasted longer and was more severe in Alberta than in the rest of the country. Even after 1983, when in eastern Canada the economy was in recovery and in the west it was still depressed, the heavy outflow from Alberta served to delay recovery further and to stimulate the Ontario economy, which was already expanding quite well. As a result, measures were then taken by the Bank of Canada to slow down the Ontario economy, which then also provided additional drag to the Alberta economy. In 1986, with the collapse of energy and agricultural commodity prices, recovery in Alberta was again slowed down. Moreover, a general imbalance between eastern and western regional economies made matters worse for Albertans. Because Alberta relies on international markets for most of its exports but on eastern Canadian markets for most of its imports, expansion of the Alberta economy provides direct benefits to the east whereas a prosperous St. Lawrence valley by itself generates few benefits in Alberta.

In short, the economic downturn of the 1980s was accentuated and prolonged by the NEP and only provincial reduction of royalty payments and agricultural support policies prevented things from being even worse. The response of the federal government was not to increase its discretionary spending in the west to a degree that it would have any discernible inter-regional stabilizing effect. On the contrary, as we saw, the heavy extraction of revenue by Ottawa at a time of economic distress simply made matters worse.

The most immediate and obvious result of the NEP for Canadians liv-ing in Alberta was found in the considerable (and avoidable) dislocations affecting families, businesses, and other social institutions that are inevitable when large parts of the economy and society of an area are compelled to make major adjustments in a short period of time. The availability of these disruptions and adjustments has remained an ongo-ing source of irritation in the years after the NEP came to an end. Considering how large a price Alberta paid for the NEP alone, it is sur-prising that something like the Klein agenda was not advanced earlier than it was. Even more surprising is that the fight between the outsized personalities of Peter Lougheed and Pierre Trudeau was not continued by their respective successors.

CHAPTER TWO
THE PRELUDE TO ELECTION '93

In the fall of 1984 the Liberals were temporarily removed from control of Ottawa. By June of the following year the Mulroney government had reached the "Western Accord," which over the next four years phased out the perverse tax and incentive provisions of the NEP. The "Halloween Agreement" later in the year deregulated natural gas pricing and markets. Together they stimulated reinvestment in exploration, even with relatively low oil prices. Moreover, the end of government incentives led to the collapse of a number of companies and the consolidation of their assets in larger and more financially stable firms. It amounted to a Darwinian cull following the predatory mutations created by the NEP.

However ill-advised many of the policies of the Mulroney administration seemed to Albertans, the dismantling of the NEP was not among them. Had it been continued or revised to take account of lower oil prices, bad times would have been much worse. Despite the NEP, the Alberta economy had matured during the 1980s with the growth of manufacturing, high tech industries, food processing, and petrochemicals—the latter, for example, directly employed over 6,000 people and generates over $1 billion in export earnings (1990 dollars). The responses of business people thrown out of work by downsizing as a result of federal policies has been creative rather than passive. Instead of returning to Ontario or Nova Scotia and collecting pogey, many of these highly skilled entrepreneurs struck out on their own and developed new businesses or diversified and specialized within their existing industry.[1]

From Lougheed to Getty

Meanwhile, Peter Lougheed announced he was stepping down from the Premier's office in order to become a business consultant in Calgary; he then assumed the edifying role of national statesman during the Mulroney phase of the constitutional gavotte. For twenty years Lougheed had presided over a successful and innovative political organization, and he had presided alone. As Sheila Pratt, who but slightly admired Lougheed, said, "Lougheed's one-man rule had one major flaw. It didn't prepare the party for life after Lougheed."[2] Because there were no aspiring successors, he encouraged Don Getty, a long-time friend and senior cabinet minister during the 1970s, to allow his name to stand for the leadership.

Getty was popular enough with the Conservative Party faithful and particularly with senior ministers. They correctly assessed his style of leadership as being much looser than Peter Lougheed's and were eager to perform on their own, while Getty served as caretaker. Unfortunately he was not up even to that modest task and the ambitions of his ministers soon outstripped the ability of the government to pay for their expensive initiatives. In short, Premier Getty inherited the on-going costs of the Lougheed expansion in a vastly changed economic and political climate, and unlike Lougheed, he lacked the desire, the initiative, and perhaps the ability to ride herd on a group of ambitious big spenders around the cabinet table.

When the price of oil dropped from $30 US a barrel in the summer of 1985 to $15 by Thanksgiving weekend that same year—when Getty was elected leader—the implications were significant. Over the longer term, between 1981 and 1985, for example, resource revenue had averaged around $4.3 billion a year; starting in 1987, resource revenue averaged $2.3 billion a year. This spelled trouble at a time when over half the province's income was derived either from royalties on oil and gas or from investment income from the Heritage Fund. At the same time, the high per capita expenditures from the Lougheed years had become "deeply entrenched," as Mansell put it.[3] Between 1986 and 1991, for example, per capita debt increased 340% (the next highest, Quebec, was a mere 42%). By fiscal year (FY) 1987-88, revenue from resources had fallen to about 35% of the province's total revenue. Instead of raising taxes or cutting expenditures, the Getty government followed the lead of the Government of Canada: use the credit card and keep up appearances. In the sober light of day, this meant amassing huge debts while hoping for another oil boom to bail you out, which is about as prudent as investing in lottery tickets. On Don Getty's watch, Alberta never knew a balanced budget.

Long-time provincial Tories sensed the party was coming apart at the seams. It lacked vision and direction. It lacked confidence and competence. In simple terms, Don Getty was no Peter Lougheed. Gordon Shrake, an MLA at the time, said Premier Getty "seemed utterly incapable of making any significant decisions." Caucus meetings showed "a complete lack of reality" because the Premier "just wanted to be praised and left alone."[4] Getty was virtually unavailable outside caucus, and caucus was hardly a forum either for debate or for the implementation of a well-considered agenda. No wonder that during the later months of his premiership he and his advisors were said to have had a bunker mentality. The government had lost touch with the electorate and the Premier had lost touch with his own party.

Not until the spring of 1992 did a whiff of economic and fiscal reality finally penetrate the bunker. In April, Premier Getty said he would balance the budget, but everyone around the cabinet table knew it could not be done. Then Ray Speaker, who began his political career as a Social Credit MLA under Premier Manning, quit to run federally for the Reform Party. In Speaker's mind the Getty Conservatives were doomed and deserved their doom: they had not addressed the spending problem and had lied to Albertans that they had done so.[5]

Don Getty did not fumble the ball or miss an Argo bounce, and Peter Lougheed was not just lucky. In many respects their two administrations should be considered as an ensemble. Don Getty's government was the Late Show of the Lougheed years. Like his predecessor, Premier Getty assumed that oil and gas revenues would be enough to keep Alberta prosperous. Even during the early 1980s, there were plenty of indications that world oil prices were softening and yet the Provincial Treasurer, Dick Johnson, projected continuing long-term increases in energy prices. In any event, oil revenues are really just rents, not the results of effort, and so remained inherently vulnerable to price fluctuations over which the province had no control and little influence. The promised rewards of diversification had not (or had not yet) been realized, and meanwhile Alberta taxpayers still had to pay for on-going programs.

The causes of the problem were clear enough, but the relative weight of each of the factors is still controversial. Lower oil and gas prices along with royalty rate reductions and royalty holidays clearly reduced revenue. Public expenditures during an economic downturn meant growing budgetary deficits. With the accumulated deficits came debt servicing costs. Most of the fiscal difficulties encountered by the Getty government resulted from revenue shortfalls. Things were made worse in fact and much worse in perception by the unrealistic expectation that oil prices would improve. The government's refusal to make major program reductions in health, education, and social services or to reduce capital expenditures connected with the Lougheed-era dirigiste diversification program called into question the managerial competence of the Getty administration.

Some analysts went so far as to claim that capital expenditures and associated operating costs, not program spending, were chiefly responsible for the province's economic problems. According to University of Calgary political scientists Mark Dickerson and Stan Drabek, and Mount Royal College economist Greg Flanagan, "if the government had not embarked on all its economic schemes, we would be a debt-free province."[6] Spending on what the Alberta Government classified as "Resource Conservation and Industrial Development" grew from $35 million in 1965 to a high of $3 billion twenty years later—an 85-fold increase. According to Dickerson *et al.* the Alberta rate of spending in this area was between three and five times higher than in other Canadian provinces.

Alberta's budgetary history was not in dispute: prior to 1970 budgets were generally balanced; between 1973 and 1985 budgetary surpluses were banked in the Alberta Heritage Savings Trust Fund; after 1985 the accumulated surplus was wiped out and deficits accumulated into debt. Dickerson *et al.* pointed to a serious policy error, whatever the weight it should be given. "It was an underlying assumption that government expenditures could get the economy moving." This meant that governments were in the business of "picking winners" and betting taxpayers' money on the soundness of their choices. But what they almost invariably picked were losers. That is, the answer to the question "Where did the money go?" seems pretty clearly to be: into ill-conceived grants and loans designed to ensure economic diversification and industrial development as well as into the traditional fiscal sink-holes associated with the ever-supportive welfare state. As left-wing critics have correctly pointed out, government-directed spending on "economic diversification" is little more than corporate welfare.

The list of money-losing enterprises backed by the Government of Alberta has taken on legendary significance in the province. In 1987, the Edmonton-based Principal Group of companies collapsed, and the Court of Queen's Bench appointed Bill Code, a Calgary lawyer, to find out why. Among other reasons cited was the failure of the provincial regulators to do their job. Code indicated that the Minister of Consumer and Corporate Affairs, Connie Osterman, had neglected her duty to administer Alberta's investment law properly. At the end of the day the failure of the Principal Group cost Alberta taxpayers $100 million and ordinary Albertans who had invested in it many millions more.

In 1990 the Government provided the cash for the purchase and expansion of Alberta-Pacific Terminals, a grain-handling facility in Vancouver, just before it went bankrupt. Cost: $10 million. Peter Pocklington, owner of the Edmonton Oilers and, in the 1980s, of Gainer's Meats, failed to make payment on a $12 million dollar government loan secured by an outdated packing plant; the Government foreclosed, acquired a lot of old equipment, and eventually sold it at a loss of $200 million. Probably the most expensive mistake was NovAtel, a joint venture between Nova Corporation, the successor to AGTL, and Alberta Government Telephones, AGT (now Telus). Together they proposed to manufacture cell phones. In 1989 Nova sold AGT its share for $40 million; in the fall of 1990 the Government began to privatize AGT, including NovAtel. In the event, NovAtel was excluded from the AGT sale and the Government was left as the sole owner. NovAtel had never made money; its best year was 1989 when it lost only $3 million. The eventual cost to the taxpayers was close to $600 million, real money by anybody's standard.

The list of other failures, on a smaller scale, includes investments in a steel plant, pulp mills, a computer design company, a canola crushing plant, a magnesium plant, and a company that manufactured machines that cut things with lasers. Perhaps the success rate or failure rate was not out of line with similar activities by private speculators and venture capitalists, but as Mark Lisac reported, "no one ever had a clear account of how the government ended up putting money into these firms."[7] Moreover, private speculators and venture capitalists rely on private funds and can go out of business. Governments don't.

The Getty government's error was to have carried on the original Lougheed policy under conditions when failures could not be overlooked. The Principal Group, for example, was in the forefront of the futile Lougheed initiative to establish Alberta as a North American financial center. During the last spasms of the constitutional melodrama, Premier Getty continued to play his allotted part. By the summer of 1992, pressure on him to step down had increased. He did so early in September, just as the referendum campaign for the Charlottetown Accord began to get underway. Considering he had invested a good deal of time, effort, and reputation in constitutional questions, it seemed strange that he chose to lead the Yes forces on Charlottetown as a very lame duck. At the time, political pundits and ordinary Albertans who could remember life before Lougheed were saying it would be the end of the Conservative "dynasty." Don Getty's successor would be sure to suffer the same fate as Harry Strom, who succeeded Ernest Manning and was swept away when Lougheed obliterated the Social Credit "dynasty." But Ralph Klein, it would turn out, refused to take the place of Harry Strom.

The Klein Story
From high-school dropout to mayor:
Ralph Klein was born in Calgary in 1942. After his parents divorced, he lived there with his grandparents. He dropped out of Crescent Heights High School after grade ten and joined the Royal Canadian Air Force. After his discharge he went back to school, picked up high school courses by correspondence, and enrolled in Calgary Business College. He was asked to stay on and teach, and wound up as principal. In 1963 he became the Alberta public relations director for the Canadian Red Cross; three years later he took a similar position with the United Way for

Calgary. His background and early life was hardly patrician. It was relatively detached from public affairs as well.

In 1969 he began an eleven-year stint as a TV reporter with CFCN, which as a radio station had carried the Social Credit message of William Aberhart to the far corners of the province. He was, by all accounts, a persevering investigative reporter with a special interest in City Hall and in the gritty subculture of the city—bikers, whores, and native drifters. During the 1970s his documentary reports were very much anti-establishment. The mayor, Rod Sykes, did not appreciate the Klein reportorial approach and pretty clearly didn't like him very much either. Klein had little regard for the performance of Sykes' successor, Ross Alger, and produced a documentary highly critical of City Council's plans to create a showcase civic center that would entail the dislocation of a large number of residents from the downtown core.

The next page of the Klein story has the status of an urban legend, like that of the Corvette across town for sale for only $500 because someone died in it. But by all accounts Klein's legend is true. When he told Thompson MacDonald, his boss at CFCN, that he was going to run for mayor, MacDonald didn't believe it. Klein then gave the story to the *Calgary Herald*, took a leave of absence from the TV station and sunk his life's savings, $300, into the campaign. Alger was the first of many political opponents to underestimate Klein. On 27 October, 1980, Klein was sworn in as the city's thirty-second mayor. He went on to two more victories as one of Calgary's most popular mayors and was particularly successful as the official civic host of the 1988 Winter Olympics.

Shortly after Klein resigned as Mayor of Calgary in March, 1989, Rod Sykes was asked about Klein's alleged populism. "Faults that would have destroyed almost every politician I know," said Sykes, "are tolerated with Ralph. He's looked on as a fat little drunk and as a great guy." Worse, so far as former mayor Sykes was concerned, Klein was attracted to politics for all the wrong reasons. "It used to be that you didn't run for political office until you had something to offer—experience or achievement." Sometime during the seventies politics became attractive to "young, inexperienced, and frankly, unsuccessful people." Such individuals, according to Sykes, "were looking for political achievement as some sort of solution to their own problems."[8] This kind of visceral contempt, disguised here as pop psychology, typified much of the early dislike of Ralph Klein. It remains characteristic of a lot of the current anti-Klein sentiment as well, particularly among patricians and intellectuals.

In the early days, suspicion of Klein was not unmixed with resentment that he had succeeded at all, let alone so conspicuously. In 1980, for example, Ross Alger was the clear choice for mayor among the Calgary establishment, a real and a normally effective old boys' network, centered on the Stampede Board, the Petroleum Club and the Ranchman's Club. Alger, in their view, had been a fine mayor. From the start he had been part of the team that bid successfully for the 1988 Winter Olympics. He was a tall, good-looking man, a well spoken gentleman. The other gentlemen who put the successful Olympic bid together and then sat on the Olympic Organizing Committee, (OCO) were not all that enthusiastic about the arriviste TV reporter who took Alger's place. As Frank Dabbs observed, "Klein was not their kind of people; he was an intruder, the kind of man you sent around to the back door."[9] Klein was very much aware that he was distrusted and disliked by many of the Calgary establishment. Indeed, the high profile Olympic backers, including Premier Lougheed, tried to keep the mayor on the sidelines. They were unsuccessful, not least because, according to Olympic protocol, the host city, not the province or the country, is given official representation. That meant the mayor.

One of Klein's first tasks was to mend fences with the establishment; with a few months hard work behind him, delivering speeches to the appropriate clubs, inviting senior businessmen in to chat, they came on side. Klein saw that the Olympics ought to be, and could be, more than an international TV show. He informed OCO and its two senior organizers, Bill Pratt and Frank King (both solid establishment men), that, if they wanted his cooperation, the citizens had to feel that they, not OCO, owned the local side of the Games. This act was the source of Klein' reputation as a "populist" politician. It was also astute politics.

The statutory responsibilities of the office of mayor in Calgary are two-fold: to chair City Council meetings and to represent and report to the people of the city. The politics of being mayor is about 80% ceremonial. Such power or influence as a mayor has stems from being elected at large, and from the ceremonial responsibilities of the office. This means that the Mayor has much greater media exposure than the aldermen and so has a much greater opportunity to influence public opinion than they. The power of the aldermen, in contrast, is collective, not individual, and is exercised in Council. Mayor Klein used his position not to lobby aldermen to line up votes before meetings but allowed Council to work out its own solutions under his chairmanship. He was, in this respect, a natural student of Heraclitus, a believer in the principle that strife is the law of all things—and it's fun, and good for you as well. Not everyone enjoys or can handle a procedure stressing confrontation and bringing opposed points of view into public. Ralph Klein mastered the style. As mayor he was a skillful chairman, and Council was able to negotiate solutions more or less on its own, under his guidance.

The third source of power at City Hall is the professional administration charged with actually running the day-to-day operations of the city. In Calgary the senior officials are called Commissioners. Mayor Klein had a close and mutually respectful working relationship with the Chief Commissioner, George Cornish. Klein was both a salesman for the city and a conduit for public opinion back to the Chief Commissioner, as well as to Council. A good deal of Council's agenda was, in fact, a reflection of the thinking and planning of the administration, not of the Mayor or Aldermen. And much of that agenda was premised on the plans of bright and highly trained urbanologists who saw the boom years of the 1970s and 1980s extending into the indefinite future. City planners were in favour of arterial roads, extensions of the Light Rail Transit System into the northwest quadrant of the city, and sewer and water main construction to service endless suburbs. Council, persuaded by the mayor, agreed.

Looking only to his leadership style, it has sometimes been said that Klein was a "big spending mayor" while in office. This is misleading for several reasons. First, a good deal of the debt incurred on behalf of the city was tax-supported debt for utilities: water and sewer services in Calgary have always been user-paid. Second, the most spectacular of the civic-related building was connected to the 1988 Winter Olympics, and the federal and provincial governments helped finance these installations. Finally, in 1985 Mayor Klein presided over the establishment of a debt-control policy designed to reduce the City debt by $500 million by 1999. The Klein-initiated plan succeeded in reducing the percentage of debt servicing costs from 24% of the operating budget in 1985 to 15% in 1994.[10] This is particularly remarkable because, at the same time as the provincial government began racking up large debts, Klein (and Cornish) put in place a mechanism that would reduce the city debt.

Klein's reputation as a big-spending mayor is therefore unwarranted, but that does not explain his enthusiasm for the Olympics or for spending substantially on infrastructure even while doing as much as possible to reduce tax-supported debt servicing costs. The explanation does not lie in economic theory or even in bookkeeping. It is found in the combination of Klein's personality, his own experience, and the historical experience of his city and province. Calgary has always been the entrepreneurial center of an entrepreneurial province. Obstacles to prosperity have from the beginning been perceived as being external to the will of Albertans and especially foreign to what Calgarians have sought. Distance, the CPR, the Dominion Lands Policy, the disallowance of Social Credit legislation, the National Energy Program: all were seen as unfortunate or unnecessary brakes on economic development—for the region, the province, and the city.

Among the prominent constituents of Ralph Klein's character are toughness, demotic exuberance, and a great imaginative capacity to understand the misfortunes of others. He was a new mayor when Trudeau's National Energy Program devastated the Calgary-based oil patch. Indeed, Klein's inauguration took place the day before Marc Lalonde rose in the House of Commons to introduce the NEP. He was mayor when the price of oil fell by half. He was mayor in 1986 when 6,500 jobs in the energy industry were lost in his city. And, like most Albertans, he was heir to the popular perceptions and the political culture of the province regarding the Ottawa government and its embrace of the welfare state. There were real external constraints on the ability of Calgary and of Alberta to prosper, some natural, but most political. This fact was reflected in the rapid and extensive downsizing of the oil industry during the mid-1980s. It was reflected as well in Calgary City Hall and in the anger and distress the mayor experienced in cutting staff.

The city was vulnerable to outside influences, but it was not helpless. One of Klein's initiatives, undertaken to mitigate the unfortunate effects of that vulnerability, was the Calgary Economic Development Authority, conceived by an early ally at City Hall, Arthur R. Smith. Smith had been active in all three levels of government, had been an outstandingly successful international businessman and President of the Calgary Chamber of Commerce. Together with Smith, who was the veritable incarnation of the Calgary establishment, they brought together City Hall officials, such as the Chief Commissioner, local politicians, and senior business executives to attempt (once again!) to deal with the structural problems of economic development in the city. The basic argument that Smith made was that the best long-term incentive for capital investment, and thereby for diversification away from dependence upon a single industry, was to provide an economic environment friendly to potential investors. If you get the economic context right, that is, if you allow the market to work, investors will come. Other things, from making the city a nuclear free zone as in Vancouver, to purchasing a hockey arena as in Winnipeg, are best ignored.

The chief lesson Ralph Klein learned as mayor, a lesson he was to act on when he became premier, was that a long-term solution to Calgary's and then to Alberta's economic difficulties required *indirect* action. Klein saw that long-term prosperity could not be assured by government intervention; only the private sector had much of a chance to do that. Trudeau and the NEP had shown, however, that government intervention in the economy could certainly do a lot of harm. The role for government, he concluded, was to make it easier for others—investors, entrepreneurs, business people—to act. In that way the jobs of the secretary and of the dump truck driver would be more secure.

Ralph Klein has probably never had a strategy for economic development, at least not in the sense of a doctrine or blueprint that could be communicated as a position paper suitable for discussion at Davos or a G-7 summit. There is however a coherent logic to his action. Economic development for Klein means chiefly that working people keep their jobs. The best contribution any politician can make is to encourage those with investments to make them here, in his or her bailiwick. One way of doing so is to keep the degree of government involvement in the economy as low as possible. Fiscal responsibility or, if one prefers, fiscal conservatism, is not an end in itself or an ideological principle to which Klein is devoted. It is, however, a policy that is useful in promoting economic development. In order to act on it more effectively, Klein would have to move on to a larger political arena.

The path to the Premier's office:
After the spectacular success of the Olympics, it was almost inevitable that Klein would seek higher office. Brian Mulroney offered Klein a seat in the House of Commons, but he declined to accept. Ottawa was too remote, he said, and his wife, Coleen, refused to move. The Alberta Liberals were interested in recruiting him—and he had on previous occasions assisted Liberals.[11] Klein canvassed his friends for their advice and it was unanimous: Liberals in Alberta are perpetual losers. When at last the provincial Tories made their offer, he accepted the nomination in Calgary Elbow, defeated Gib Clark in the March 1989 by-election, and became Environment Minister in Don Getty's cabinet. He then began to travel the province, speaking extensively, making friends, building support. As Environment Minister, he introduced the first broad and public environmental impact procedures. He saw himself as a referee, much as he had been as mayor. The environmentalists, however, wanted an advocate and, when Klein did not agree with them on all things all the time, he became an enemy.

Premier Getty had been elected at a traditional convention filled with the usual hoopla and backroom deals. Many members of the Conservative Party were pleased neither with the process nor, especially after Getty's poor performance in the 1989 election, with the result. Getty was a weak leader. He had tarried too long in office, and his refusal to leave had simply accentuated the divisions among those who sought to replace him. Klein was one, and he became the chief beneficiary of a general dissatisfaction with the old method of choosing a party leader.

The usual way of selecting delegates is by constituency association and within each association provision is made for specific categories of delegate—women, youth delegates, ethnic delegates and so on. Under

such a structure, long time party members and spokespersons for speci-
fied and designated groups have an inside track. Ralph Klein was not an
old-time Tory insider. His appeal to ordinary citizens with rough-and-
ready views of the political process was stronger than it was to traditional party activists. Many of the old-time Tories were supporters of chrono-
logically younger leadership candidates, such as Health Minister Nancy
Betkowski or Energy Minister Rick Orman. The Tory veterans, as
Betkowski and Orman, had been active in the party since the early days
of glory with Peter Lougheed. Moreover, many of them would have quietly agreed with Rod Sykes' appraisal of Klein, and others were more
openly contemptuous of him. Other older MLAs, however, especially
those from rural and northern ridings, such as Ken Kowalski, Ernie Isley,
Peter Trynchy and Peter Elzinga, were concerned about their own and the
party's survival. They saw themselves marginalized by Orman or
Betkowski but not by Klein, and, to a man, they believed a Betkowski victory at the convention would mean a Tory defeat at the polls.

A traditional Tory convention would have been dominated by old
friends from previous constituency-level campaigns keen to recall past
triumphs and eager to elect someone to carry on in the old style. But the
new rules—one party membership, one vote—had changed the entire
process. First, it removed the decision from the convention delegates.
Klein supported this change early on. He knew from experience that he
appealed strongly to the ordinary members and he knew they were
unlikely to pay their own travel costs, hotel rooms, restaurant meals and
registration fees to attend a traditional convention. The consequence was
to turn the province into one big constituency, making it easier for traditional convention-goers to forget about past, face-to-face loyalties to
other candidates.

A second rule change also worked in Klein's favour, though he did
not know it at the time. Now it was possible to sell PC memberships, and
therefore the right to vote, between the first all-candidate ballot and the
run-off second ballot.

It was in this context that Klein decided to run using the same up-
beat, happy, good-time campaign that had worked so well to get him
elected mayor. He did not emphasize policy and even appeared to take a
positive view of fiscal problems. "We are," he said, "dwelling too much
on these things. You can't sell investors on coming here by saying 'hey,
why don't you come to Alberta? You know what? Here's a good reason to
come, because we have a big debt and a terrible deficit.'"[12] The thinking
in the Klein camp was clear enough: there was no point in appealing for
blood, sweat, toil and tears if it meant that Nancy Betkowski would be the
premier that led the Tories to defeat. At under 20% in the polls during the

fall of 1992, defeat seemed likely no matter who replaced Getty. Certainly the provincial Liberals knew from polling data that they could demolish Betkowski and were quite prepared to purchase PC memberships and vote for her to become the new Tory leader. In Klein's view this was one more reason to ensure that it was she and not he who became the Harry Strom of the Lougheed-Getty party.

The first-round results amounted to a dead heat between Klein and Betkowski, who led by a single vote. The other candidates dropped out, announced their support for Betkowski, and Klein seemed about to lose his first election ever. But in fact, Klein was well positioned. He had won outside Edmonton, although Betkowski had run up large pluralities in the capital. If the votes had been tallied by ridings, Klein would have won with 45 out of 83 constituencies voting for him.[13] When the other candidates backed Betkowski—almost all of them were long-time Getty cabinet ministers, and many, such as Betkowski herself, came from upscale urban ridings—it looked as if once again the establishment was closing ranks against Klein. As former Labour Minister Elaine McCoy said later, Klein's victory was a "revolt of the caucus against the cabinet."[14]

What looked like establishment solidarity worked against Betkowski among rural Members and rural Tory supporters as well. She was a career politician; she was well educated, having obtained an M.A. in French literature at Laval; she was seen as being in favour of lavish social programs but also was said to be in favour of closing rural hospitals. But for many Tories the fact that she was an attractive forty-something woman made her less not more appealing as a potential premier. In the nature of things, many of these sentiments could not be voiced or acknowledged, which had the result of making Klein, not Betkowski, look like the underdog, especially in the media. As had happened nationally a few weeks earlier with the popular vote against the Charlottetown Accord, the elites were all on one side, but the people seemed to want to go the other way. Doug Main, Minister of Culture under Premier Getty, and a strong supporter of Nancy Betkowski, could not have been more mistaken when he declared that Klein had "zero growth potential."[15] Klein benefitted from a mood that was already there, but he also used the week between votes to help deflect it in his direction.

A rural MLA, and Minister of Agriculture, Ernie Isley, had been instrumental in persuading Klein to run. He immediately began phoning other rural and northern Members who had supported Klein and told them to get out the vote because, he said, if Betkowski won the nomination, they would all be out of work after the next election. Ken Kowalski, another rural MLA and minister in charge of lotteries (among other things) mobilized his office to remind his friends around the province who had benefitted from allocations of lottery money how important it was that Klein win.[16] In short, the Klein team woke up and used the phone-tree, and Betkowski's went, if not to sleep, then into a mode of comfortable confidence. Two very experienced organizers and pillars of the Tory establishment, Jock Osler and Ron Ghitter, were working on the smooth transition from a Getty to a Betkowski administration; Betkowski refused to debate Klein on TV and asked him to withdraw. He politely declined, and by the Thursday between the weekend votes his trackers were telling him he would win.

According to David Stewart's survey of delegates, 55% of those voting joined the Party only in order to elect a new leader and many of them had not voted Tory in the 1989 election. This gave credence (after the fact) to Klein's claim that Betkowski's support came from Edmonton Liberals. The charge stuck, and it helped her even less than all the support from the Getty cabinet.

About 53,000 people voted in the first ballot and 78,000 in the second. As Thompson MacDonald, his former boss but now a member of Klein's team, observed, the new voters "weren't on anybody's list. You didn't know who they were. We're talking about the general public."[17] According to Stewart, Klein won 80% of the votes of those who registered between the two ballots. He also gained 80% of the support of ranchers, farmers, those with lower educational achievements and those paid an hourly wage. It is probably fair to say that individuals so described were not in regular attendance at PC conventions though they were likely to be PC voters. While it was well defined socio-economically, Klein's support, said Stewart, came from all across the demographic and geographic map: north and south, young or old, male or female, all found a reason to vote for Ralph.

On the second ballot Klein effectively crushed Betkowski, 60% to 40%, and as Frank Dabbs observed, it looked as if Klein had modernized the old Aberhart-Manning coalition of agrarian Alberta, small town business, and blue-collar workers. To these traditional bases of support he added "the immensely powerful and influential leadership of the petroleum and financial industries."[18] It proved to be a stable and effective coalition.

There was little enough on the public record to indicate what kind of premier Klein would be. He had many Liberal friends; before joining the Tories, the Liberals had cultivated him. As was indicated above, during the leadership campaign he had played down the importance of the provincial deficit and debt, and as Mayor of Calgary he had gained the reputation of a big spender; everyone knew the 1988 Winter Olympics were not cheap. Not surprisingly, therefore, he was expected to continue the big-spending ways of Premier Getty.[19] Indeed, the *Toronto Star*, hardly known west of Mississauga for the reliability of its reporting on events in remote, outlandish Alberta, went so far in the wrong direction as to declare "it looks like business as usual in the conservative province of Alberta."[20]

Among the early commentators on the Klein phenomenon, Ted Byfield of *Alberta Report* was the most astute. According to him, Klein "realizes that political parties no longer represent anything permanent or even definite.... Hence all attention focuses upon the leader, or at least on the media's image of the leader, and Klein's image is about as far removed from Peter Lougheed's and Don Getty's as it's possible to get."[21] There was, in fact, no real need for continuity or for business as usual; quite the contrary: Klein had every reason to change the image of the Conservative Party. His first task, therefore, would be to distance himself from the burden of the Lougheed-Getty legacy. Nancy Betkowski presented him with the first opportunity to do so.

Cleaning house:
Betkowski sulked in her tent for a week. Unlike the great words of Achilles, however, her first post-leadership announcement was timid: she doubted whether a Klein-led party could win the next election and wasn't sure if she wanted to be part of it anyhow. Then she asked for a senior cabinet position and control over Edmonton patronage. "She doesn't get it. The media don't get it," said one unnamed insider. "He won. She lost. Her finish doesn't mean she owns 40% of the party. He won't allow her to have 40% of anything he's involved with. The party she knew between 1967 and 1992 is gone. It no longer exists. Welcome to the Ralph Party."[22] Klein himself said of Betkowski's requirement that she be allowed to set policy, "how could I accept that?"[23] As the chief advisor to the crown in right of Alberta, the new premier was constitutionally as well as politically correct.

Moreover, behind the public exchanges there was a history lesson that Klein had learned from the federal Conservatives. One of the conditions extracted by Joe Clark for graciously turning over the leadership of the federal Party to Brian Mulroney was that he would strongly influence, not to say control, patronage in the West.[24] One of the consequences for the federal Tories was that Mulroney's western supporters were not on the inside when patronage decisions were being made. This added to the internal animosity between Clark Conservatives and Mulroney Conservatives. Ralph Klein and his advisors were not about to repeat the mistake.

Klein knew from first-hand experience that the Lougheed loyalists had been a source of dissent in the Getty cabinet; they and their successors, the Getty loyalists, would soon be gone from the Klein administration. One of his first major acts, reducing the size of cabinet from 26 to 17 provided the occasion for a purge.[25] At a stroke, 16 Getty-era ministers were gone and only two survived from Peter Lougheed's day.

At the same time, the Premier replaced the existing array of legislative committees with five Standing Policy Committees (SPCs), each of which is chaired by a backbencher, not a minister. Each SPC has responsibility for scrutinizing the legislation and budgets of four line departments. Their chief means of changing ministerial proposals is through public discussion rather than direction, but considered only as a change in administrative style, the significance of the new system was clear: for the first time, politicians and not just bureaucrats scrutinized a minister's proposals.[26] The *Calgary Herald* was moved to declare the old Lougheed-Getty establishment dead and buried. The Conservative Party of Alberta was under new management.[27]

But how would they manage? We said that Klein's record as mayor and even as Minister of Environment left few public clues about what his personal agenda was, or even if he had one. There were, nevertheless, clear indications of what the agenda would have to be for the next Premier of Alberta, whoever it was. For example, when a seasoned and nimble politician such as Ray Speaker left the Getty cabinet to seek the nomination of the Reform Party for the House of Commons, one did not have to be particularly prescient to conclude that Speaker thought he had a brighter political future with an essentially untried federal party than with a provincial party that had been in power for nearly a generation. But more to the point, the Reform Party, like other political parties in Canada, is a coalition of several different interests and visions,[28] and one of them is undoubtedly fiscal conservatism. As David Taras and Allan Tupper remarked, by 1992 Reform had succeeded in "reshaping and focussing the public mood."[29] Alberta, in other words, was already prepared or "primed" by the Reformers for the message that Premier Klein was about to deliver. In addition, the provincial Liberals, under Laurence Decore, were promising fiscal rectitude in place of Tory profligacy. The only strategy that might succeed lay in outflanking the Liberals on the fiscal issue. In order to do that, some real distance had to be put between the Klein Conservatives and their predecessors.

Defeating Nancy Betkowski and the old guard won Klein control of the party, a necessary first step. His next one was to prove to the Alberta electorate that it really was the Ralph Party. The changes began shortly after the Klein victory at the December convention. Planning a strategy to win the next election began in January, 1993 and continued throughout the spring. The late spring election campaign was essentially the execution of a strategy that was initiated in December.

In his March, 1995 speech to The Fraser Institute, Premier Klein recalled how, after years of distrust, the Alberta electorate would not believe *any* of the figures produced by the Treasurer's office. After all, Treasurer Johnston had long been promising a balanced budget and yet never achieved one. The new Premier had every reason to think Albertans distrusted their government. "So," he said, "we started by appointing a financial review commission, an independent objective group of respected private sector Albertans chaired by the former President and CEO of TransAlta Utilities, Marshall Williams."[30] The Alberta Financial Review Commission (FRC) was appointed by the new Treasurer, Jim Dinning, on 21 January, 1993 and reported "to all Albertans" on 31 March. The Commission was given authority and responsibility to examine the appropriateness of the accounting principles currently used by the Government of Alberta and to provide an accurate picture of the financial position of the province.

Accurate and timely financial reporting is obviously essential for prudent fiscal management. Since a majority of commission members worked for accountancy firms, it is perhaps to be expected that many of their recommendations were concerned with reporting, accountability, and management control. These are doubtless important matters, but the importance of using Generally Accepted Accounting Principles (GAAP) was probably clearer to members of the accounting profession than to ordinary mortals.

Two major items, however, had a wider significance and a greater immediate implication for public policy. The first was that government "loans, guarantees and investments create risk." Four reasons were advanced to explain why such intervention in the marketplace increased, not lowered, risk. First, the commodity industries to which loans had chiefly been made, namely energy, forestry and agriculture, were much more strongly influenced by economic activity outside the province than within. Hence, whatever stability government support appeared to give was fragile at best, and more likely, illusory. Nothing the province did would influence the price of wheat, of wood products or of oil and gas. Second, and as a result, a large number of loans had to be written off. Third, there was hardly any debate in the Legislature regarding loan guarantees, so that, fourth, concessionary terms and conditions were granted that either were not accounted for at all or were accounted wrongly, that is as receivable loans, when clearly they were not.[31]

The Commission said, in effect, that the normal and irremedial uncertainties of the economy were made worse by government actions that were intended to provide remedies. Moreover, because the government accounting regime deviated so far from GAAP, those actions were taken in such a way that even the government could never know what, in fact, it had done. One implication of the Commission's recommendation was that loan guarantees and direct government investment may well have a particular and short-term political benefit, but they invariably impose a general and long-term economic cost that good government, by any definition, would avoid.

The second major finding with important policy implications was "that the province has a *structural deficit*, a condition in which expenditures will continue to exceed revenues, even in an improving economy." That is, there existed "an inherent imbalance between revenues and expenditures" that would doubtless get worse as payments from Ottawa decreased and the compounding effect of interest costs became ever more apparent.[32] The main conclusion, stated on page one, was therefore obvious: "the need for Albertans to support change is urgent."

The actual dollar figures involved are so large as to be meaningful only to accountants and economists, but the logic used by the FRC to calculate them is generally intelligible. First, the revenues and expenditures of the largest government account, the General Revenue Fund, were combined with those of the Heritage Fund, the Alberta Capital Fund and 22 other funds, agencies or commercial enterprises with deficits or surpluses of $5 million or more over the previous five years. The objective was to get a GAAP-compatible bottom line figure, and to compare it with the numbers computed according to the idiosyncratic public accounting principles then followed by the province. Employing the method of calculation then in use, the reported net debt at the end of FY 1991 was $2.2 billion; the projection for FY 1992 was $5.3 billion. Using GAAP, the projection for FY 1992 was $11 billion, over twice the amount previously reported. The report of the FRC had the sought-for political impact and the Klein government achieved its first success: the news was bad enough to be credible to Alberta citizens.[33]

Even before the Commission issued its *Report*, the government sponsored a Budget Roundtable at Red Deer College. The Roundtable, which had recently been used in a somewhat different form by the federal government during the constitutional discussions, served many purposes, from manipulating public opinion to determining what it was. In this instance, the Red Deer exercise generated two symbols that evoked clearly what the Klein government saw as the chief problem and the most effective solution. The problem was "hitting the wall" and the solution was "cutting the stupid way." The first referred to the fiscal crisis, the second to across-the-board, rather than refined surgically precise, cuts.

"Cutting the stupid way" was something of a misnomer. On the one hand, it did mean across-the-board horizontal reductions. They were "stupid" in the sense that the revenue source (and eventually the Treasury) simply declared: "next year you get less money; you figure out how to spend what you get." This did not mean the same percentage would be cut from all the line departments but that cuts would reflect the government's strategic priorities. Moreover, cutting this way was anything but politically stupid. In the first place, the cuts were dramatic and sudden, which meant opponents would have no time to organize. In this context the government would either cut the stupid way or not at all, which they thought would be truly stupid. Second, the government could say, with justification, that those who would be affected were in the best position to know how to make the cuts in detail. They had the real expertise in such matters, not the government.

Treasurer Jim Dinning provided a few details regarding the strategy the government would follow in an interview with the *Calgary Herald* on 25 April, 1993. He was asked:

> *Herald*: Is there a feeling in Cabinet that government should be out of business altogether?
> *Dinning*: The answer is yes. It took an industrial policy of 1984 to get us involved in loans and loan guarantees to the extent that we have. It's almost ten years ago.... The taxpayers should not be in the business of supporting business.

At best, the Lougheed strategy had a place in the Alberta of 1984, but no longer. The deficits of the Getty years proved it. The repudiation was clear.

So too was a new sense of realism. Both the Wall Street bond rating agencies and ordinary Albertans, said Dinning, expect the government to bring expenditures in line with revenues. "The rating agencies are looking for a plan. Albertans are looking for a plan. The rating agencies don't expect a quick overnight fix, nor do Albertans."

> *Herald*: Can you seriously tackle the deficit in an election year? Do you feel the public will accept either tax increases or service cutbacks and still vote the Conservatives back into office?
> *Dinning*: We have no choice. Albertans are going to judge us by our actions to begin to get our house in order.

Dinning's response was a variation on the theme, "hitting the wall." It operationalized the conclusion of the Financial Review Commission, that "the need for Albertans to support change is urgent." The time had come to act.

The First Budget and the New Tory Platform

By the time Jim Dinning tabled his first budget, on 6 May, 1993, three things were clear. First, it would respond to the new political agenda crystallizing, thanks both to the Reform Party and to the Alberta Liberals, around fiscal responsibility; second, it would be the budget that differentiated the Klein government from its predecessors; and third, it would constitute a major part of the Tory election platform. That said, however, most pre-election budgets are attempts by governments try to bribe voters with taxpayers' money. This one clearly did not.

The goal, Dinning said, was "a prosperous Alberta with open, accountable government that lives within the taxpayers' means and delivers quality services at low cost."[34] In order to reach that goal, Dinning promised to do four things.

First, the government would legislate an enforceable plan to balance the budget by 1996-97. The Deficit Elimination Act was in fact proclaimed law a week later.[35] It contained target deficit ceilings and provisions for either making up any slippage in subsequent years or directly applying any surplus to the deficit and debt. There were additional provisions covering the use of warrants, audits, supply votes and quarterly reporting. The objective was to reduce program spending by 20% by 1996-97. Health, education and social services account for some 70% of all program expenditures. Necessarily these policy areas would be prime targets. Revenue projections—especially royalty revenue from petroleum resources—were conservative, which was also in accord with the recommendations of the FRC. No new taxes would be introduced. "Other provinces," said Dinning, "have tried to solve their deficit problems with high taxes. But they have not succeeded. They have continued to spend what they take in, and more."

Second, the government would set and stick to a clear set of priorities, the first of which was to ensure job opportunities. Accordingly, education or "life-long learning" would be maintained and encouraged, along with an affordable and more efficient system of health care. So that government priorities and performance could be independently appraised, "benchmarks" were to be developed through a system of business plans for all ministries and agencies.

Third, an economic strategy would be implemented based on the principle of creating wealth by providing an economic environment attractive to private enterprise. "The government will not try to pick 'winners' or increase spending to create short-term jobs."[36] Rules and regulations would be more efficient, deregulation plans would be drawn up, negotiations with Ottawa over corporate taxes would begin, direct business subsidies would be phased out, and so on.

Fourth, Dinning promised to change the way government did business, chiefly by increasing the two-way communication between the government and citizens, eliminating duplication and waste, improving cost-effectiveness through audits based on business plans, privatization, and introducing incentives for improvements in civil service productivity.

Many of these policy proposals were statements of intent rather than detailed action plans. By the spring of 1995, for example, most ministries had published "business plans."[37] These documents indicated spending and capital investment targets; all ministries calculated the gross targets and eleven of seventeen calculated net targets as well. The latter take into account the contribution of licences, user fees, agreements with other governments or the private sector, and so on, to the net revenue of the department. Utilizing business plans became a high priority for the first Klein government, even though they encountered considerable difficulty in recasting the modes of existing bureaucratic procedures.

The general direction of the plans was to emphasize that the highest priority was to reduce the size of government. Klein began, as noted above, by reducing the size of cabinet and by replacing 26 permanent cabinet and caucus committees with five policy committees. This triggered a program of amalgamating, restructuring and eliminating government departments, boards, crown corporations, committees and councils. In response to recommendations of the FRC and the Auditor General that new and more accurate accounting practices be adopted, Dinning introduced a number of other changes. For the first time unfunded pension liabilities were considered as part of the consolidated debt of the province. The Lloydminster heavy oil upgrader was written down, and program guarantees, crop insurance, loans, vacation pay, long-term disability, and crown corporations liabilities were included on more conservative accounting principles than before. The eventual result, as had been estimated by the FRC, was to double the book value of the debt.[38]

The First Election Issue

During the spring 1993 budget debate in the Legislature, an even more intense debate was going on within the Conservative Party caucus over reform of MLA pensions. Of the 59 members of caucus, nearly half would not seek re-election, including many of Premier Getty's former ministers. In 1989 they had all voted themselves a 30% pay raise, which meant a 30% pension raise as well. In the top category, veterans from the Lougheed days stood to collect over $80,000 a year. With the new understanding of the failure of the Lougheed policies under the Getty administration, support for what turned out to be the richest pension plan in the country was not widespread among voters. Initially, Klein favoured leaving the pensions intact, which greatly pleased the Liberals who proceeded to attack the government on a daily basis—even though they too had supported the pay hike and the pension plan. By budget day it was an obvious election issue: the Liberals could rightly claim it was intolerable to reward the very people who had made such a mess of the economy. "They simply do not deserve it," said the Liberals, "vote for us."

The first attempt at pension reform was in place by April, 1993. It was fine as far as it went, but it would not take effect until after the next election. In the words of Kenneth Whyte, "Getty's crew didn't deserve an estimated $40-million in golden handshakes, shouted critics and the public."[39] The opponents of this modest proposal wanted the reforms to be retroactive. Premier Klein again resisted on the abstract and legalistic grounds that generous pensions had been a condition of initial employment. Caucus members who had been door-knocking in anticipation of the election knew the popular mood.

Then came the real push. A new interest group, the Alberta Taxpayers Association (ATA), publicized the terms of the plan, which almost spoke for itself: for every dollar contributed by an MLA, the taxpayers contributed six. Premier Klein made the mistake of getting angry—in public, with the TV camera rolling—with Jason Kenney, executive director of the ATA, and later an MP for the Reform Party. Instantly, concern over MLAs' pensions was at the top of everyone's list of what was wrong. The Premier's office received calls from fundraisers and donors telling him, not asking him, to find the right solution.

On 27 April, 1993 Premier Klein knew what had to be done. He had listened to the public, he said, and now was willing to consider "all reasonable amendments to the bill." In other words, the tirade on TV had backfired; Klein sensed the public mood and changed course in response. Whether one sees this sequence of events as evidence of political genius or of crass expediency, it is a clear indication that Ralph Klein knew how to act but also to acknowledge a mistake. Coming after the Lougheed years, when mistakes were unheard of and after the memories of the bunker mentality of Premier Getty, the Klein style received general approbation. "He may have made a mistake," critics said, "but at least he admitted it."

The way things turned out, the whole sequence could have been minutely choreographed. The contrite reversal following the heated exchange on TV was undertaken without informing caucus. When the members, particularly the outgoing veterans, discovered what the Premier had said, they objected loudly, intemperately, and at great length. As a result they, not the Premier, became the focus of taxpayers' anger and contempt. The solution was clear: if the Tories were to be re-elected, and half the caucus was vitally interested in re-election, then they would have to persuade or shame the other half, who were quitting, into voting for changes. They did so by agreeing to eliminate pension benefits for all existing first-term MLAs, and for all MLAs after the next election. Having given up all their own benefits, the rookie MLAs prevailed upon the about-to-retire Lougheed-Getty veterans to give up enough for the Premier to be able to say he followed the will of the people. The Liberals cooperated with the Tory strategy by denouncing the government for going too far. The following week the Tories took out large newspaper ads: "Premier Klein on Pensions: You have spoken and we have listened."

It was nearly time to go to the people. The budget, including the Deficit Elimination Act, had been tabled. The government had indicated the seriousness of its intent to streamline and reduce its own operations. With the retroactive reduction of pensions for outgoing MLAs and the elimination of pensions for future MLAs, Premier Klein had found the sought-for and defining symbolic event that would make his party distinct from that of Lougheed and Getty. As Kenneth Whyte said, the pension changes made it look as though Premier Klein had "run up against a bunch of Tory politicians found fattening themselves at taxpayers' expense and he'd made them bleed on their way out the door. He'd made voters forget that he himself was a Tory and a politician."[40] He had also out-flanked the Liberals.

CHAPTER THREE
METHOD BEHIND THE MADNESS

If the 1993 provincial campaign did nothing else, it confirmed the Klein-Dinning fiscal agenda. Fully 85% of the votes cast went to parties favouring a balanced budget with no new taxes, and 100% of the elected Members ran on essentially the same platform of fiscal prudence. Did the voters of Alberta prefer *drastic* cuts (then vote Conservative) or *brutal* cuts (vote Liberal)? Decore's Edmonton-based Liberals, however, were badly outclassed in political skill and experience. For the first time since 1921, Decore had a real chance to restore the Liberals to power. Instead, he confirmed the image that Liberals were bumblers by a series of campaign errors, from self-righteous comments on the divisive issue of abortion,[1] to simply failing to adjust campaign strategy to the obvious: he was no longer running against the party of Don Getty. In fact there was very little that the Liberal leader could say to criticize the Klein platform. When he did, Rod Love, who had joined the Klein team when he first ran for mayor, and who was undoubtedly a shrewd political tactician, would fax to the media earlier statements by Decore that contradicted his campaign criticism of Klein. Once the Liberals denounced the Tory pension reform, they were faced with an uphill struggle.

The New Democratic Party (NDP) was out of the picture from the beginning of the campaign. Ray Martin, whose vote base in Edmonton had already been siphoned away by Decore, campaigned on an ideologically inspired, sure loser's platform: the oil and gas industry, which contributes about a quarter of Alberta's tax revenue, was not paying what the NDP thought its "fair share." Second, according to Martin, Alberta did not have an expenditure, a deficit, or a debt problem—let alone a crisis; it had a revenue problem that could be rectified by raising tax rates. The NDP were extinguished at the election and Mr. Martin claimed another moral victory.

Eight minutes after the polls closed it was clear that Ralph Klein's Tories had won, but by how much? When the dust had cleared, the Tories had elected 51 members, down 5, with 45% of the popular vote. The Official Opposition was no longer the New Democrats, who had 15 sitting Members going into the campaign and who kept their 15% of the vote but lost all but one riding. The Liberals elected 32 members (up from 12) and managed to attract nearly 40% of the popular vote. Eighteen of those MLAs were from Edmonton, which meant that Calgary and rural

Alberta had voted strongly against the capital city. The "Ralph Party" strategy had worked; but it remained very much an open question how long he could maintain his consistently high approval rating.

In the aftermath of the election, Decore, like Rod Sykes before him, thought that Klein would be "eaten alive" when he left the Mayor's office in Calgary for life under the Dome in Edmonton.[2] Even political scientists have, on occasion, voiced the same view: on election night, Allan Tupper of the University of Alberta, in Edmonton, said that the Premier's views on balancing the budget without raising taxes were "almost utopian."[3] Klein, of course, is fully aware of his ability to seem inept, vacillating, and, indeed, stupid: "People," he said, "are going to tell me that it can't be done, that balancing the budget without raising taxes taxes is beyond our reach. I have only one response to the cynics—just watch, I've been underestimated before."[4]

Strategic Influences

Academics are fond of looking for meaning in texts to make sense of politicians' actions. Legends are told of how Stalin kept a copy of Hobbes' *Leviathan* at his bedside table or how JFK was always searching Machiavelli for apt advice. Sometimes this is a useful exercise, but sometimes not. In politics one constantly reinvents the wheel. Besides, by their own accounts, most politicians say that events, not books, provided the inspiration as well as the opportunity for them to go into politics. This was certainly true of Ralph Klein, for whom the National Energy Program had a greater impact on his thinking than all the books in the Calgary Public Library.

Even though books influenced the Klein agenda much less than experience, the arguments of two of them, *Reinventing Government* by Osborne and Gaebler, and Sir Roger Douglas' New Zealand memoir, *Unfinished Business*,[5] did have an impact on the Tory strategy. These two books articulate commonsensical strategies and offered clear guidance on the kinds of changes that needed to be made. They suggest a strategy and a logic, not a policy wish-list. Whether the Premier ever read either one is beside the point, though the similarities between the Klein government's approach and the arguments provided by these two books is uncanny.

In Douglas' opinion, for example, free markets, deregulation, and reduction of government-provided solutions are policies that promote individual liberty and responsibility, and the virtues of individual choice and self-respect. With the growth of larger and more integrated markets or, to use a more popular symbol, with "globalization," the real political division is between the internationalists, who are realists, and the isolationists and protectionists, who are not. Nostalgia for the past, in the view of Sir Roger, is a recipe for disaster. His supporting arguments are straightforward.

Consider, for example, his remarks on welfare policy: "By the late twentieth century, the most disturbing question about social welfare and the poor and disadvantaged was not how much it cost, but what it had bought," namely dependency. He took as his model not Ronald Regan but President Kennedy: the disadvantaged should be given a hand, not a handout, JFK had said.[6] Handouts lock those who are already vulnerable to social and economic pressures into the role of passive recipients. Vulnerability gets transformed into permanent dependency. Arguably good intentions have led the disadvantaged into the traps of welfare and poverty.

In economic terms, the poverty trap is one of marginal utility: if there is an inadequate increase in disposable income when there is a real increase in hours worked, why work more? Likewise the welfare trap: when the level of benefits is so high that one is better off not working, why work at all? These are commonsensical questions raised about real problems, not ideological fantasies or resentment-inspired rants. They are questions that clearly address the incentives and self-interest of individuals.

Why, then, have politicians been unwilling or unable to ask direct questions and find sensible answers? According to Sir Roger, "they close their minds to the obvious need for change because they believe that decisive action will automatically bring political calamity upon them and the government." As we said in the Introduction, most politicians find it easier to be vote-grabbers than position-takers so that, in the short term, it looks more appealing to bribe the electorate or blame others than demand citizens accept responsibilities. Both Douglas and Klein saw matters differently: they recognized the importance of pride.

Pride induces a sense of accomplishment, and inspires the sense that we are all in this together, as citizens and not as private individuals, each with his or her own particular interests. It becomes everyone's best interest, therefore, to push for change and see it succeed. The only ones who need protection are those who truly are vulnerable, and who therefore lack the ability to help themselves. These are the genuinely needy: they are mere subjects who can take no pride in their condition because they have only interests to be protected and must call upon government to do it.

Osborne and Gaebler's *Reinventing Government* was, on the surface, considerably less controversial a source of ideas than was Sir Roger's *Unfinished Business*. One source suggests that Elaine McCoy, one of the many leadership candidates defeated by Premier Klein, was the first to consult the book.[7] Others have indicated that former University of Calgary President, Norm Wagner, or Calgary oilman, Jim Gray, sent copies to each member of the Tory caucus.[8] But by the time of the second Dinning budget, in February, 1994, the arguments were familiar enough that the Treasurer could cite them simply in passing.[9] There is a strong element of commonsense in the Osborne-Gaebler analysis, as well as in their recommendations.

Osborne and Gaebler make a point of distinguishing government from governance. The first refers to doing things, such as delivering services, and the second to leading society, which is to say, managing policy by persuading interest groups and citizens to embrace common goals and strategies. When the Hudson Bay Company transported furs across the thousands of miles of rivers in the northwest, the *great canots du nord* divided effort between the voyageurs at the paddles and the *gouvernail* in the stern; in the same way, Osborne and Gaebler distinguish between rowing and steering. Traditional, industrial and bureaucratic government thinks of itself as being in the business of rowing. The very word government, however, comes from the Greek verb *kubernan*, to steer, and Osborne and Gaebler argue at great length that governance should be the chief mission of government, not delivery of services.

The logic of *Reinventing Government* indicates that the goal of public policy is not simply to balance budgets but to restructure government using the budgetary process as leverage. Likewise, Premier Klein and Treasurer Dinning have stated time and again that they were not simply concerned with balancing the budget. If that were all they wanted to do, it could be done in a flash by raising taxes. "The way you don't create prosperity," said the Premier, "is through taxes. That's the stupid way. That's the simple way."[10] The overall strategy is to determine what government can do better than the private sector, what the private sector can do better than the government, and then making the necessary regulatory, administrative, legal, or budgetary adjustments. The budget, therefore, has been and remains a means to that goal.[11]

The Klein-Dinning Budgets: 1993-1996

During the summer of 1993, the long-term plans for debt reduction were put into place. Klein and Love and Dinning were assisted by Vance MacNichol, Steve West, Ken Kowalski and Peter Elzinga. All but MacNichol were politicians; he had been Klein's Deputy Minister at Environment. He was an outstanding administrator and was strongly recommended by George Cornish, who had been so effective as Chief Commissioner during Klein's term as mayor. MacNichol was elevated by Klein to the position of Deputy Minister to Executive Council, which made him the provincial version of the Clerk of the Privy Council. He became a strong advocate of cuts, as did Dinning. West was one already.

Elzinga agreed and Kowalski went along, though he had large reservations, which he kept to himself.

The first public indication of Government policy following the June election came on September 8, 1993, with the Lieutenant Governor's Speech from the Throne. The speech echoed what Dinning had already said in his pre-election budget. The basic "philosophy of government" announced by his Honour was "that government should get out of rather than into the lives of Albertans. People in this province know that more government and more laws mean more expense, red tape, and confusion and less freedom."[12] In order to achieve that objective the Government announced four "commitments."

> My government's first commitment is to balance our provincial budget within four years and to take the steps necessary to ensure that my government will live within its means. The second commitment is to create an environment that will allow the private sector to create 110,000 new jobs for Albertans over the next four years. The third commitment is to reorganize, deregulate, and streamline government to reflect Albertans' desire for a government as frugal and creative as they have to be in these times of fiscal challenge. And this government's fourth commitment is to listen to the people it is privileged to serve, to consult with them, and to be as open, compassionate, and fair as possible in reflecting their wishes, their hopes, and their dreams.[13]

The main difference between the pre-election budget and the September "update," the Lieutenant Governor said, was to change the relationship between government and economy particularly with respect to economic development policy. "The core of this strategy is tax and regulatory reform" and the purpose served by that strategy was contained in the second "commitment," namely the creation of "a climate conducive to investment and job creation." Implementation would be two-phased. The first phase called for each government department to develop a "deregulation action plan;" the second phase involved public review and actual implementation.

Other parts of the throne speech emphasized the government's continued commitment to remove as many business subsidies as possible, and to simplify accounting techniques even further. Finally the government promised, once again, to focus on reducing the costs of health care, education and welfare, the big three, along with debt servicing. "We all know," said the Lieutenant Governor, "that more money is not the answer. Albertans pay enough for these programs already." To maintain high quality services without debt, "the government has to be imaginative. It has to look at everything. It has to take risks and try new things."[14] In short, it had to reinvent itself.

The size of the government's cuts to the so-called MUSH sector (Municipalities, Universities, Schools and Hospitals) left most Albertans both satisfied and astonished. Paul Boothe, at the time Professor of Economics at the University of Alberta, declared it was the boldest budget since the 1930s.[15] On the basis of numbers alone it would be a claim difficult to dispute. The average budget cut among all departments was around 20%. This was chosen, evidently, "because it was the cut in expenditures required to eliminate the deficit without increasing tax rates."[16]

Among the big budget ministries, education and advanced education, which may be considered investments in the future, were cut the least. Indeed, education was hardly touched. In contrast, departments such as Treasury, Municipal Affairs, Economic Development and Tourism, and even the Cabinet Office took cuts far above the average. The largest savings in terms of bureaucratic intervention was in the area of public works, a classic "rowing" ministry and in the Cabinet Office, where the number of positions was cut from over 1,500 to 360. Ministers in the Klein government evidently would have to get by without a phalanx of aides and outriders to clear their way.

The second budget, presented on 24 February, 1994, continued the direction of the first, and provided further analyses of the significance of the entire exercise.[17] In his budget address, Treasurer Dinning again emphasized that balancing the budget was only a means, and tabled two documents along with the Budget Address: the Budget itself and the government's business plan.[18] *Budget '94* "is not just about reducing spending. It is about restructuring government so Albertans can receive essential services at affordable price." An "affordable price" was calculated at $4,000 per person.

The Budget also reiterated the need for speed and decisiveness: gradualist attempts at deficit reduction would not work. The accompanying business plan "is not only a first for Alberta, it is unique in Canada. The standard for effective government operations will be set in Alberta." The business plans themselves were very close to the Osborne and Gaebler model. "By focussing on outcomes," the volume of business plans said, "and keeping track of results, government departments can adjust programs as they learn more about what works and what does not." By the time of *Budget '95: Building a Strong Foundation*, tabled on 21 February, 1995, the four "commitments" of September, 1993, which had been outlined in the pre-election budget, had been routinized into four "pillars" supporting the "strong foundation" of the budget's title.[19]

The Treasurer was now in a position to provide a retrospective analysis and to offer advice.

> For years, governments in Canada have been living beyond their means. Governments have put off paying bills until tomorrow in the mistaken belief that revenue will catch up to spending. Overspending, not lack of revenue, is the problem. And every delay in fixing this problem increases the amount of debt and makes the solution more painful.[20]

Budget '93, he said, was the beginning of the end; by 1995 the goal of living within taxpayer's means without raising taxes was in sight. In his 1996 budget speech, Dinning was understandably exuberant in presenting the first balanced budget in over a decade.[21] In just four years, the Klein government had completed a remarkable record.

Consider the following six areas:

1. *Finance.* Deficit reduction can mean one of two things: to reduce program spending so that costs are covered by tax revenue, or to reduce program spending so that program costs and debt-servicing costs are covered by tax revenue. The Alberta Government tackled the second option, the overall deficit, and developed a four-year reduction plan to put it into effect. By the spring of 1995 the government was ahead of schedule. Accumulated savings were occurring for the same reason that accumulated deficits do: changes in the fiscal regime lead to changes in expectations and alterations in behaviour. Effective control of program spending plus higher than anticipated revenue from oil and gas royalties, and accompanying higher corporate tax revenue, made possible balancing the budget ahead of schedule. The sheer procession of numbers is impressive. In FY 1992-93 the deficit was $3.4 billion; four years later is was gone. Moreover, the savings were drawn primarily from traditional high-cost policies of the welfare state—health, education, and welfare—together with the gradual reduction of debt servicing expenditures.

2. *Health.* Alberta Health (now Health and Wellness) accounts for a quarter of budget expenditures. Between 1983 and 1995 the costs of providing health care increased 178%. In dollar amounts, Alberta's hospitals cost 30% more to operate than do all the hospitals in British Columbia, where the population is 27% larger. There was room for significant restructuring. The major change was to replace 200 hospital boards with seventeen Regional Health Authorities (RHAs), which meant a major reduction in the number of middle and senior managers, and cost savings of nearly a billion dollars.

Alberta Health developed a 3-year business plan (as did other ministries) to reorient health policy so as to encourage individual responsibility, to develop a health care delivery system driven by consumers rather than medical practitioners, and to delist medical services judged non-essential. Additional implementation strategies included raising health-care premiums, reducing wages, closing hospitals, consolidating regional medical boards, and promoting health and fitness.

As we shall see in the following chapter, resistance has come from the federal government, which seeks to defend its own understanding of the Canada Health Act, from physicians who are reluctant to limit their own income and authority, as the province has suggested, and from a militant and highly unionized health care labour force. The new RHAs have also run into difficulties coping with the transition to more home- and community-based care. There have been a number of highly publicized stories of individual suffering and hardship, but no mass public protests.

Health care restructuring continues to be a topic of vigorous debate in Alberta as in the rest of the country, and the Canada Health Act is still strongly defended by a succession of federal health ministers. This is unlikely to change in the near term. RHAs have occasionally run deficit budgets and have had to be bailed out by the provincial treasury. Even so, the overall costs of the health care system appears to be under control. Moreover, the new approach to health spending, as we shall see, is more prudent and selectively targets only the most critical pressure points, such as the need for more front-line services and staff, or the need for more long-term care facilities, in order to free-up acute care beds and the need to expand the current prescription drug program.

3. *Social Policy.* The most important institution of the welfare state in Alberta is called the Department of Family and Social Services (FSS). The objective of the government's reforms in this area has been to ensure that FSS programs do not become "welfare traps" that provide incentives for people to seek the certainty of a welfare cheque over the uncertainty of a job. FSS programs are to do no more than provide temporary assistance in emergencies along with incentives for education and retraining, especially for young singles.

The actual cuts and reductions in the welfare rolls have been much higher than anticipated. Between the spring of 1993 and the spring of 1995 welfare caseloads declined in number from nearly 95,000 to just over 50,000. In Alberta, a "case" works out to about 1.9 individuals, so the actual size of the welfare-dependent population is about double the caseload. The decline in the FSS "client base" has been accompanied by a decline in the number of workers to service them, with a total of 7,138 employees leaving the government payroll.

In FY 1992-93, the Minister in charge, Mike Cardinal, told the Fraser

Institute "over 50% of the people on welfare...were young, healthy Albertans that were employable and trainable."[22] These individuals, he said, "were using dollars that were meant for persons with disabilities, the elderly, and the children that need protection." Accordingly, spending for children, aboriginals, the disabled, and widows—categories that would correspond precisely to the kinds of individuals who are truly unable to help themselves—was increased by over $100 million. The savings to the FSS budget as a result of the two year reduction in the size of the caseload amounted to over $450 million. Plus there was an additional savings of $150 million to the taxpayers of Canada, because of reductions to programs cost-shared with the federal government. At the same time, labour force statistics indicated that nearly 100,000 new jobs were created between December, 1992 and December, 1996.

4. *Education.* Before 1999, education in the general sense was the responsibility of two departments, the Department of Education and the Department of Advanced Education and Career Development (AECD), later amalgamated as the Ministry of Learning. These two ministries took relatively small cuts compared to the rest. This reflects, in part, the view of the Ministers in charge, but more significantly, a kind of rational choice to invest in the future productivity of the young over sustaining the unproductive through lavish welfare and medical expenditures.

At the primary and secondary level, school districts consolidated in much the same way as Regional Health Authorities. One of the objectives of consolidating school boards and centralizing wage negotiations was to make it impossible for the Alberta Teachers Association (ATA) to play boards off one against the other during wage negotiations. The Minister at the time, Halvar Jonson, capped administrative expenditures at 4% of total costs in order to ensure that funds were actually directed towards educating the children of the province and in order to free up an additional $60 million. Local boards can raise additional money for special projects, but the tax increases must be explicitly approved and cannot exceed 3% of the board's budget over any three year period. A new fiscal framework was established to equalize per capita grants, which run about $3,700 a student. The result has been a net transfer of funds from urban to rural students and schools.

Other changes are evident in the overall "philosophy" of education. For example, provision has been made for basic province-wide tests, which have been advertised as a move away from no-fail, "child-centred" learning. In addition, Bill 19, the School Amendment Act, contains provisions for Charter Schools to be established directly under the ministry. At the same time there are a number of conditions, such as the necessity of hiring teachers certified by the ATA, that limit the effectiveness of

Charter Schools as genuine centers of competition for the school boards.

Funding to AECD, which included universities, colleges and technical institutes, was cut by 15.3% over the period 1992 to 1997. Tuition fees were raised by 20% and are scheduled to increase by another 10% in 2000. In other words, consumers—that is, students—are being asked to pay for a larger part of the service received. Moreover, universities have been forced to compete with colleges and technical institutes for the available pool of "adult learner" dollars. The combination of "advanced education" and "career development" indicates the Government's technocratic and practical understanding of education.

Naturally, universities have not welcomed these changes, but they have responded creatively, with curriculum and program changes. In principle, of course, there is no genuine threat to a liberal education by insisting upon a greater contribution from students. Presumably students will be able to see the value of Latin literature, which has not been related to vocational training for several hundred years. Moreover, even if the belletristic side of the quad has difficulty justifying its own short-term utility, humanists are adept in raising Kant's question, "what's the use of use?" By doing so, they make themselves useful after all. And students who pay more for their education may be under greater pressure to be rationally selective about the programs and courses they take.

5. *Regulatory Changes.* State intrusiveness in the daily lives of Albertans has become a fact of life. All Canadians are surrounded by a web of regulations the intentions of which are, no doubt, of the highest probity—such as promoting health and preventing corruption. The costs, in sheer economic terms, no less than in time lost filling out licences, permits and other forms, is often much greater than any possible benefits. Anyone who has ever tried to build a house or even undertake a modest renovation has experienced first hand the frustrations of red tape.

The Klein government seems to be aware of the difficulties for economic activity that are created by regulations that stifle initiative, impose external costs, and serve no public purpose save to employ regulators and inspectors. An indirect measure of the effects of government regulation (and deregulation) can be found in the government share of GDP. In FY 1994-95 it dropped from 17.3% to 15.6%; by FY 1996-97 it reached 12.9%, where it has remained.

As examples of deregulation that have made the interaction of supply and demand more efficient one may point to the following: (1) The Dairy Industry Amendment Act (1994) relieved the Government of Alberta from financial responsibility in the event of bankruptcy of a milk processor; (2) The Brand Amendment Act (1994) simplified brand registration to a once-in-a-lifetime action; (3) The Agricultural Statutes Repeat Act (1994) repealed nine obsolete agricultural acts; (4) The Dairy Board Act (1994) deregulated wholesale milk prices; (5) The Industrial Wages Security Act (1995) was repealed, and over a million dollars held in trust was returned to Alberta businesses; (6) changes to the administration of oil and gas royalties also resulted in major reductions of administrative costs.

The spider's web of regulations within government was also cleaned up. A good example of this were the 1995 amendments to The Municipal Government Act (MGA). Section 147 of the 1980 Act required the minister to approve new town crests or logos in advance. Dr. Steve West, the minister, was astounded with his responsibility in such a trivial area. Likewise section 178 of the old MGA required ministerial approval before local streets could be blocked off to create a pedestrian mall; section 128 required all public housing projects to make 10% of all units available to seniors.

The new MGA abolished these and other similar provisions, the intention being to reverse the paternalism that has been the governing assumption of municipal-provincial relations since 1905. The previous MGA listed what municipalities could do; the new one lists what they may *not* do. It has the effect of making local politicians locally responsible. In general, the new act abolished 23 statutes and 80 regulations and gives local authorities much greater flexibility in terms of taxing, borrowing and spending. Deficits are now permitted for emergencies, but must be corrected within three years. Borrowing for individual projects no longer requires ministerial approval, but borrowing limits for types of projects still exist.

In light of their new responsibilities, municipal politicians are now included under The Freedom of Information and Protection of Privacy Act. This is a significant development for the following reason: although most municipal politicians outside Calgary and Edmonton earn under $20 thousand a year, by serving on regional planning boards, rural power commissions, school boards, and so on, they can easily triple their earnings in honoraria, travel allowances and *per diem* payments, all of which are set by the councillors themselves. These expenditures have now been made public.

6. *Privatization.* Historically, public monopolies have been created by governments in the expectation that these organizations would serve the public interest. Often they have ended up serving the interests of those who staff them. High costs and poor service are typically associated with such organizations. Privatization of government-supplied services aims at creating market alternatives to state monopolies, with the objective of obtaining high quality services at lower costs. The most obvious candidates for privatization in Alberta include Alberta Government Telephones

(now Telus), Treasury Branches (a Social Credit era quasi-bank) and Alberta Intermodal Services. Treasury Branches are still under ministerial control, but Telus, along with animal health labs, highways maintenance, water hauling, licensing, parks and campgrounds, and several other services have been privatized.

The jewel in the privatization crown, however, has been the severe trimming of the Alberta Liquor Control Board (ALCB), in September, 1993. In place of 205 ALCB stores and 1,866 unionized jobs that paid around $17 an hour, over 600 stores now sell liquor at competitive prices over longer hours providing jobs at $7 an hour for over 3,000 Albertans. The conversion costs amounted to about $100 million in private capital spending for new or renovated stores; the sale of about 150 ALCB properties brought in close to $200 million to the provincial treasury by January, 1995. Severance pay for ALCB employees cost $17 million and other wind-down costs were just under $20 million.

There has been a slight decline in tax revenue, from $435 million in the last year of ALCB retail operations to $415 in the first year of private operation. The overall price of alcoholic products is up 5% but competition ensures there will be bargains on individual items. Premium liquors are down 10% in average prices and product selection is up 35%. By 1998 there were 117 new brands of beer, 700 new wines and 300 new kinds of spirits. There has been no noticeable change in public drunkenness, though individual incidents, from public brawls to liquor store robberies, have been associated by opponents of privatization with the end of the ALCB.

There is no doubt that the greater convenience to customers is immensely popular. Who would oppose, now, a policy that allowed people to purchase a bottle of merlot or a six-pack of Big Rock on a Sunday afternoon? Moreover, the slight increase in prices is not so much a result of price gouging as it is of an incomplete privatization. The ALCB still has a monopoly on the wholesale market; if that upstream part of the retail liquor business were also privatized, the resulting wholesale market would, no doubt, result in lower prices and greater selection.

To summarize the achievements of the first Klein government: It was the first government in the country to have shown a genuine and realistic commitment to fiscal prudence and less government. Moreover, it did so not as an ideological end in itself but as a means to ensure economic development: balance the books and investment will come. And as Tom Musgrove, a Tory MLA during the Lougheed and Getty years, has argued, the government has deliberately ignored a socially-conservative agenda, preferring instead to concentrate on fiscal issues. This kind of single-issue politics coupled with the Premier's own political skills has led to a consistently high approval rating. There is bound to be considerable opposition when changes of such magnitude are undertaken with such speed and thoroughness. In the following chapter we consider how the Klein government handled its opponents.

CHAPTER FOUR
OPPOSITION AND CRITICISM

Premier Klein is fond of using the imagery of home renovation as a metaphor for the activities of his government. Renovations always create a mess, increase family tension, and guarantee frustration because things never work out as planned. It may not be completely impossible to have a smooth home renovation, but that does not mean that it has ever happened. Similarly, the process of reinventing the Alberta government had its fair share of disruptions caused chiefly by widespread opposition and criticism, particularly from those whose interests had been served by the expanding policy of high expenditures irrespective of revenues. The Klein government, however, has managed to deal with these difficulties in a variety of ways.

The Opposition

Organized labour announced it was against the May, 1993 budget,[1] but no serious opposition was mounted until after the election. In August, 1993 the President of the Alberta Federation of Labour (AFL), Linda Karpowich, promised "a mobilization and a militancy not seen in Alberta since the Gainers strike" if the Government tried to make any cuts in the civil service.[2] In fact, however, the Alberta Union of Public Employees (AUPE) was rather barren ground upon which to sustain the flowering of union solidarity. The Union had been formed during the 1960s from a staff association and had no history of militancy; it was quite unlike the meatcutters who physically resisted the use of replacement workers during the long and bitter Gainers strike.

Then in October, 1993, hospital administrators and unions rejected the government's invitation to reduce salaries voluntarily by 5% "because it fails to respect the legal framework of the collective bargaining process and threatens to destroy the relationship between employers and employees."[3] A couple of weeks later the Alberta Teachers Association (ATA) said they too would fight any salary reductions and announced a $500,000 advertising campaign.[4] They advanced the opinion, widely reported in the media, that Albertans in fact were eager to pay more taxes to ensure educational funding and that 80% of the population opposed cuts. As we shall see in detail in the following chapter, this statistic was far from accurate.

At the end of that same month there was a protest by some 2,000 students and teachers in Calgary, about which Liberal leader Decore remarked, "I think all the wheels have now fallen off the Klein initiative, particularly with respect to cutting back in education. It's now a situation out of control."[5] The *Calgary Herald* later declared that the protests over cuts to kindergarten funding, a program first introduced in 1975, and known in Alberta as Early Childhood Services (ECS), "could turn into the provincial government's worst nightmare—the birth of a true grassroots movement with thousands of angry parents [acting] as willing midwives." Decore then announced that because of the ECS protests, "we're seeing the chinks in their armour today."[6] The premier, the cabinet, and the whole Tory caucus, he went on, "say they're not going to blink. We're going to make them blink."[7] The issue was resolved by compromise. The taxpayers would pick up the tab for 240 hours of ECS while the remaining 200 hours a year were paid for by parents as a fee for service they received.[8]

As November wore on the verbal assault continued. Ed Hanson, President of the Canadian Union of Public Employees (CUPE), promised to "take up the battle." AUPE President Carol Anne Dean warned that "cuts like Klein is demanding will come out of purchases for groceries, school supplies and clothing." Karpowich of the AFL again went public with her concerns: "They have no sense of how people are feeling. Look at the timing of this, just before Christmas." Bauni MacKay, President of the ATA, added: "They're trying to make it look like if we don't cooperate, we are responsible for any lack of quality of education."[9] And David Inkster, President of the Alberta Colleges Institute Faculty Association complained: "It looks seriously like this government is bent on taking apart a high quality post-secondary system."[10]

Things remained relatively calm over Christmas, but heated up again in the aftermath of Premier Klein's TV address to the province in mid-January, 1994. This time complaints came not only from union leaders and health-care spokespersons, but also from social workers, political scientists, and school trustees. In response to Bill 19, the 1994 School Amendment Act, which reduced the number of school boards from 141 to 57 and thereby reduced by over half the number of school trustees,[11] Rosemary Church, President of the Alberta School Board Association, declared: "I think there will be a fairly violent reaction if they mean equal funding for private schools." Similarly, Patti Grier, a Calgary School Trustee (and defeated Liberal candidate) warned: "I think we're headed for a voucher system. This year is going to be gruesome, and the next two years will sort of pale in comparison with this year."[12] Much of the criticism from the Public School Boards concerned either the increased centralization that they thought was coming or increased parental control.

Either way, the power of the school boards to command and direct funds had been compromised.[13]

Margaret Duncan, Executive Director of the Alberta Association of Social Workers, announced that in the wake of the Premier's speech, 50,000 people were without hope because of "this extremely cruel course of action." Meanwhile, the University of Calgary and the Southern Alberta Institute of Technology (SAIT), announced that for two years they had been planning for cuts in the 16-20% range.[14]

Except for his calling the Klein agenda "hidden," Laurence Decore made an accurate summary of the consequences of the government's action: "His hidden agenda isn't deficit cutting, it is the dismantling of Alberta as we know it."[15] Decore formerly an advocate of "brutal" cuts, had become the spokesman for the pre-Klein status quo, which left all the momentum for innovation and change in the hands of the government. This mistake was to cost him his job.

During February, the criticism continued. The AFL promised "flying pickets" at all events where the Premier was scheduled to appear. Sunera Thobani, President of the National Action Committee on the Status of Women, showed up in Calgary and stated: "we see these policies as being anti-woman."[16] The ATA offered to take a 5% wage rollback in exchange for 300 days to study the effects of educational cuts before they were implemented, which is to say, the better part of a year to drum up opposition to the government's policy. To no one's surprise, the Premier rejected the offer, to which Bauni MacKay replied with the warning: "We figure we made the step. It wasn't accepted. Now we get a little tougher."[17]

Meanwhile, the AFL threatened a general strike, the teachers predicted a two-tiered educational system, the *Edmonton Journal* accused Premier Klein of personally forcing welfare recipients into starvation, and the City of Edmonton's finance department said it was thinking about introducing user fees for fire inspection. Even the federal government got involved. The Prime Minister said that Alberta's policies were "overly ambitious" as well as "heartless and short-sighted."[18]Later the federal Minister of Health at the time, Diane Marleau, threatened to penalize Alberta for alleged violations to the Canada Health Act by reducing funds for health care.[19] Next door, B.C. NDP Premier Mike Harcourt said that Alberta was a bad neighbour, claiming the province was buying one-way bus tickets for welfare recipients and exporting them to B.C. He also objected to Klein luring business to the "socialist free" province and thought about excluding Alberta companies from B.C. government contracts.

Opposition in the Legislative Assembly closely tracked that on the outside. On opening day of the fall, 1993 session Liberal leader Decore asked the Premier "to tell Albertans why he doesn't care for these [88,000] children in poverty."[20] A few weeks later Liberal Grant Mitchell, Decore's eventual successor as Leader, asked the Premier about:

> the human costs of this government's across-the-board, arbitrary, unplanned cuts to health care: cases of surgical dressings left unchanged for a week, bloodied hospital walls left uncleaned for literally days, a patient's repeated requests for help to stop his bleeding answered only by housecleaning staff because nobody else was available. My question is to the Premier. How many more of these experiences have to be related to this Premier before he will understand that they are the direct result of the manner in which his government is cutting: arbitrary, across the board, unplanned?

In response to Mitchell, the Premier skillfully replied:

> This is melodrama at its absolute worst. Mr. Speaker, first of all, the government does not run the hospitals. If the hon. member would be so kind as to give me the specifics, I will have the Minister of Health discuss this particular situation with the hospital officials who are directly responsible for their patients.[21]

Bickering among politicians did not end there. In the spring, 1994 session a Liberal member prefaced a question by invoking the image of "many many people crying in the hallways [of an old folks' home] after receiving notices of the cuts...seniors are now trapped. They're trapped by the Premier in the kind of panic that only can be felt by someone with no one left to trust and nowhere to turn."[22] In June 1994, Opposition Leader Decore brought up another unfortunate example where a welfare worker left a child in a home where the SPCA removed the dog because "the home environment was so terrible." The Premier was asked "how can you justify a system where dogs are treated better than children in this province?"[23]

National television coverage of Alberta also opposed the Klein agenda. The National Media Archive, a division of the Fraser Institute, conducted an analysis and comparison of media coverage of the first twenty months of the Klein government with the first twenty months of the NDP government under Premier Bob Rae in Ontario.[24] Granted, Ontario constitutes 40% of Canada's economy, so we might expect that media coverage of the actions of the Ontario Government to be more prominent. In any case, it is undoubtedly true that the Ontario NDP government's decision to fight the recession with increased expenditures had enormous repercussions for the rest of the country. In fact, TV news paid more attention to Alberta than to Ontario.

Moreover, assessments of Ontario's policies were "slightly more negative than positive" on both major networks. "However, on CBC, assessments of Alberta's actions were twice as often negative as positive, and on CTV three times as often negative as positive." Expenditure cuts were said to be much less desirable than increasing either deficits or taxes. Privatization was attacked and the deficit and debt crises were virtually ignored. No one argued that increased taxes in Ontario caused citizens to dance in the streets for joy; rather, the actions of the Rae government were explained and excused by TV reports. On the other hand, the CBC mentioned that Alberta had not raised taxes in only 1% of its stories. CTV did so in 2%. Instead, both networks focussed on the opposition claims that user fees were "hidden taxes."

Seventy percent of the stories on TV were negative at a time when Klein was setting records for popular support. According to the National Media Archive, the media displayed "gross partisanship" that may well indicate that they "have crossed the boundary from news reporting to news advocacy." The conclusion was obvious: "In their coverage of Alberta and Ontario, television news has seriously misrepresented the public mood."

The CBC used health care cuts as evidence of the deviance of the Klein government from what it considered acceptable in Canada. In July, 1993, nurses' protests, using stark and emotional medical imagery, constituted the feature of choice. On 6 December, 1993, an interview with the Premier began by indicating that the deficit and debt were a problem, but "the cure might kill the patient in Alberta." A month later (10 January, 1994), nurses' fears were central: "patients' lives are at stake" and "caesarean babies could die." One interview featured a nurse who commented:

How do you explain to that mother, "well, you know, she [the nurse] wasn't really trained very long, but the baby didn't make it. And we're really sorry. But the cutbacks, you know. Things are just the way they are. And budgets are budgets. And we just don't have enough money. And I'm very sorry, but your baby's dead."

Cathy Tomlinson: These are not isolated fears.

Perhaps such fears were not "isolated," but were they valid? More balanced coverage would have raised this issue.

The CBC also had something to say about the Premier's January, 1994 TV address to the province: Klein had dished out "tough medicine" that "will hurt" (18 January, 1994). As a result, "Alberta today is a shadow of what it was" (6 December, 1993), a place where "nothing is sacred," not after kindergarten fees, health care fees for old people, mediator fees and health inspection fees have been introduced (9 March, 1994). "Poverty is flourishing" in Ralph Klein's Alberta (13 June, 1994); at the end of August, CBC uncovered a "poverty activist" to contest Treasurer Dinning's view that the government's popularity was up as a result of the cuts. All that meant, she said, was that "obviously Dinning and Ralph are in a state of denial" (24 August, 1994). Clearly, for CBC news, only a psychological explanation could account for such unrepentant deviance.

Then on 8 November, 1994 the nation was given the alarming but misleading information that "the [Alberta] government is removing itself from the obligation to provide health care." The Gimbel Eye Clinic's facility fee was really extra billing, viewers were told, and extra-billing was prohibited by the Canada Health Act. There is in fact considerable debate regarding the effects of facility fees. The Alberta Government's position is that by providing an alternative for those willing and able to pay, the line is shortened for those using the publicly funded facilities. Moreover, even if facility fees are identical with "extra billing," which is also debatable, the use of such fees is widespread across the country. It is routinely applied to procedures ranging from using ultrasonic waves to break up kidney stones to performing abortions.[25]

None of this was discussed. Instead, Albertans were simply visualized as deviant. "Albertans," the CBC national audience was informed, "are big on their rights. Particularly their right to spend their money the way they see fit." There followed the clincher, a terrible story of a man with an eye injury who had to be driven from Banff to Calgary in pain, vomiting in the back seat of his car. His misfortune and suffering were directly attributable to cutbacks in health care. The imagery was strong, but the factual information and the logical links highly questionable.

The CTV national news carried a few stories about health care undergoing "some radical surgery" and the government taking "a scalpel to hospital funding" (14 July 1993; 9 December, 1993). By and large, however, they made fewer appeals to emotions. Most coverage concerned protests by nurses, by students, by social workers, union leaders and "social action" groups. Moreover, privatization, particularly of liquor stores, was criticized at the beginning (2 September, 1993), the middle (12 February, 1994) and the end (10 September, 1994) of the period covered.

In addition, an innovative plan designed to ensure that child-support was paid up before ordinary government services, such as driver's licences, were delivered, was said to be unworkable, notwithstanding the fact that it is both simple and inexpensive to keep data available on child-support payments on-line at driver's licence outlets. In fact the plan was designed to support custodial single parents (who usually are women) and are economically vulnerable. It was never presented that way, not least of all because to do so would be inconsistent with the view that the Klein government's social policy was cruel and heartless and, by the conventions of TV news, that would undermine "credibility." As for the Premier himself, he was "media savvy" and "smooth" (28 April, 1994), so nothing he said could be trusted.

In the spring of 1994, the Premier came under considerable adverse criticism from lawyers for efforts that aimed at ensuring that provincial court judges accept a 5% wage cut along with other Albertans whose salaries were paid from the public purse. One Youth Court judge protested by cancelling his own appearance in court in order to devote time to "studying" the question. The Premier then suggested that persons who don't show up for work should be fired, even if they were judges. This, naturally enough, added fuel to the controversy and allowed the judges to raise the question of judicial independence.

Even the Premier agreed that judicial independence is a matter of fundamental importance in a constitutional democracy. In his opinion however, judicial independence was a red herring, designed to divert attention from the real issue, which concerned the ability of Cabinet to cut salaries of all individuals paid from the public purse. If specific judges were singled out for salary reductions, and if such judges had previously rendered verdicts contrary to government policy, then the charge of attacking judicial independence might have been plausible. After all, no one in the provincial universities ever said that academic freedom was at risk when university grants and salaries were cut. It strains credulity to think that professors were happier with their lower salaries than judges were with theirs, particularly since the average judge makes a good deal more than the average professor. It looked as if a privileged minority was defending its privileges and nothing more.

Tensions in the Ranks
Not all the opposition to the restructuring undertaken by the Klein government came from outside the Tory party. Virtually all political parties are coalitions of some sort and the "Ralph Party" is no different. In Chapter Two we saw how Premier Klein learned quickly a lesson that Don Getty did not even know about, namely that those loyal to the preceding premier could disrupt the agenda and do so with the highest of motives. Klein handled the old guard adeptly. Nancy Betkowski quickly disappeared from Tory politics. When Don Getty announced he would never go near the Legislature again, the Premier's office indicated that Mr. Getty would pay for his own office space in downtown Edmonton.[26] And as

Mark Lisac pointed out, for the former premier there was "no official goodbye. The party newsletter ran one small photograph of Getty in its postleadership issue."[27]

When it came to the new guard with retained old habits, Klein, along with Rod Love, was even more deft. Ken Kowalski, for example, was fired twice in the fall of 1994. Kowalski had been one of those who had persuaded Ralph Klein to seek the leadership; he had been rewarded with three titles, Deputy Premier, Minister of Economic Development and Tourism, and Minister of Lotteries. Whatever the debts owed by the Premier to Kowalski, by October, 1994 his overt as well as his backroom opposition to the direction Klein was taking the province had made him a serious liability.

He refused to consolidate lottery funds into general revenues. He managed to secure an almost invisible loan guarantee of $100 million for the Swan Hills hazardous waste incinerator and another $10 million for hospital construction in his constituency. He also resisted privatization of tourism services and opposed the Alberta Economic Development Authority (AEDA), which the premier strongly supported. Even worse, he did so in on-the-record complaints to the media. It was clear that Kowalski would have to go. The only questions were: when? and how?

The manner of his going reminds connoisseurs of such matters of the story of Remirro de Orco as told by Machiavelli in chapter seven of *The Prince*. In October 1994, the conjunction of circumstances came into proper alignment.[28] Kowalski was away on a lavish but unproductive trade trip to Mexico. He had planned a stopover in Las Vegas on the way back, but the Premier ordered him to return directly to Edmonton. Shortly after, on 20 October, 1994, Kowalski attended a meeting with Art Smith to discuss the AEDA and again opposed the innovative initiative. He was then asked to report to the Premier's office and was given three options: to stay on as a backbencher, to quit politics altogether, or to become Chairman of the Alberta Utilities and Energy Board (AUEB). Whatever he chose he would be out of cabinet. Premier Klein gave him a minute to decide.

The AUEB is a quasi-judicial regulative board formed by a merger of the Public Utilities Board and the venerable Energy Resources Conservation Board (ERCB), both of which operated at arm's length from the government. Kowalski was clearly an inappropriate choice and when his appointment attracted loud opposition, the premier admitted his error and withdrew it, cleverly suggesting his own guilelessness. In a little over a week, Ken Kowalski had been transferred from a very powerful and successful minister, flying about the world at taxpayers' expense doing the public's business, to something quite different, a sullen though not always silent, back-bencher.[29] Kowalski was down but not out. In April 1997, after successfully being re-elected as MLA for Barrhead, Kowalski was elected Speaker of the Legislative Assembly, much to the chagrin and irritation of the Premier.

Mastering the Disruptions

By striking fast and spreading the cuts widely, the Klein government succeeded in diffusing the opposition, not stifling it, neutralizing critics, not extinguishing them. The Official Opposition was there, of course, but so was an extra-parliamentary one. Occasionally they joined forces. So, when protesters appeared on the grounds of the Legislative Assembly he was asked during Question Period whether he would address the protesters, to which he responded:

> Absolutely not, Mr. Speaker. Absolutely not. But I'll tell you what: they can stand out there and they can yell and they can scream and they can have all the placards they want and they can have all the billboards they want and they can call me every rotten, stinking name under the sun. I ain't going to be there but I'm also not going to blink.[30]

When necessary, however, the Government would respond with clear answers or rebuttals. In response to the statement issued by the teachers' union—that Albertans earnestly, if not fervently, wished to pay more taxes to maintain educational funding—the Premier asked "when were they elected to make that decision?"[31] Moreover, it seemed odd to him that the same teachers' union that claimed its members were too underpaid to take a 5% cut in salary could mount a half-million dollar advertising campaign against the Government.[32] In the event, the campaign never began.

To complaints that the cuts in welfare payments were niggardly and mean, the Government responded with evidence showing that Alberta was in the middle range of the provinces with respect to payments for couples with children and, quite properly, near the bottom where payments to able-bodied, employable singles were concerned. With a low rate of unemployment, where else should such welfare payments be?[33]

Furthermore, census data indicated that Alberta bureaucrats were not underpaid. Public sector wages were 10% above private sector counterparts, especially in Edmonton.[34] Even so, there were a few occasions when the Government found good reason to side with lower level civil servants against senior management. For example, after meeting with Labour Minister Stockwell Day and AUPE President Carol Anne Dean,

Klein remarked that the administrators of the major public-sector institutions were not cooperating in the realization of the Government's objective. Instead of ensuring that the cuts were equitably spread across the full range of positions at around 5%, the lower-paid employees were given reductions far above 5% and the better paid ones were cut at a lower rate. Klein declared that such a strategy on the part of senior administrators was wrong. "I'm solidly on side with AUPE," he said.[35]

Other responses were symbolic media events. In October, 1993 for instance, Premier Klein returned a $5,000 clothing allowance that, he said, he didn't even know he was getting. It had been introduced by Peter Lougheed, always a snappy dresser, years earlier.[36] If the federal government increased taxes on Albertans, he vowed the provincial government would return the same amount as a rebate.[37] To "victim-of-the-week" stories of how individuals had suffered so badly as a result of health care expenditure cuts, the Government occasionally responded with additional facts.[38]

The economic health of the province attracted the ever-alert and interested eyes of Ottawa. Demographics as well as the seductions of the welfare state ensured that one of the most expensive policies in the future was going to be health care. Alberta had undertaken a few tentative steps toward introducing rational incentives to reduce costs. Suddenly the Canada Health Act was a sacred foundation of the nation, a veritable pillar of national unity. The Chrétien government sent the otherwise undistinguished Health Minister, Diane Marleau, to do battle with her provincial counterpart, Shirley McClellan. The object was clear: since Alberta had plenty of cash, find a pretext to cut off dollars from Ottawa.

From the federal budget 1995-96, it was evident that Paul Martin would eventually balance the federal books, but would do it by reducing contributions for health, education and welfare, all of which are provincial responsibilities. Alberta then asked Ottawa to establish a national and reduced standard for health care, to which Chrétien and Marleau responded with the mantra: no two-tiered health care system. The Prime Minister then intervened directly in a provincial by-election in Calgary McCall using health care as a pretext, and Grant Mitchell, the Liberal health critic, made "two tiered medicine" the constant focus of question period. Even so, the Tories won the by-election, though the Liberals claimed a moral victory because they hadn't lost as badly as they thought they would.

When Diane Marleau began her threats to penalize Alberta for allegedly violating the Canada Health Act, Klein expressed surprise since he hadn't had so much as a word with the Liberal Health Minister. "The debate on health care is between Klein and Marleau, Klein and Marleau,

Klein and Marleau," said Marcel Chartrand, Marleau's press secretary. "And it's escalating." To which Klein replied: "This is not Marleau-Klein, Marleau-Klein, Marleau-Klein. It's Marleau, Marleau, Marleau."[39] In the event, Alberta changed its position on "user fees." The unilateral exercise of the federal spending power and more important, the refusal to spend, had its intended effect. Equally important was the federal propaganda initiative regarding the symbolic significance of state-delivered health care. This particular conflict, which combines large sums of money and alternative visions of the country, is not likely to disappear anytime soon.

The Klein government did not always come out on top when it dealt with its critics. But when the government could make strategic use of admitting an error it did so, usually with the explanation that they had in fact been wrong and that they had changed direction because they had been "listening to Albertans." For example, as we noted in Chapter Two, the original plans formed at the Red Deer Roundtable in the spring of 1993 called for "cutting the stupid way" at 20% across the board in all ministries. Once the principle of major cuts to the largest spending programs had been adopted by the government and accepted by the electorate, it could be changed to cutting in a more focussed way. Accordingly, a policy of differential cuts was announced and implemented.[40] Thus as we noted above, education was cut by a relatively small amount and the difference was made up by other departments and programs, especially agriculture, government operations, and transfers to municipalities.[41]

In defending the 1994 budget, the new minister in charge of lotteries, Dr. Steve West, freely acknowledged that it had been a terrible mistake to have tried to intervene so directly in the economy as had been done during earlier governments of which he had been a part.[42] Likewise, Bill 57, which would have allowed administrative rather than legislative action to privatize ministerially delivered services, was withdrawn from the government Order Paper in order to tighten up the language and ensure that accountability was not sacrificed to efficiency.

By the spring of 1995 it was clear that Premier Klein had secured control of the agenda. His own astuteness was obviously a major factor in this political achievement: politicians usually help make their own "luck." In addition, however, the sheer ineptness of the Liberals was a big help. They created a void that made the short-term efforts, corrections, and U-turns of the government that much easier. With no one to capitalize on errors in judgement and changes of direction, the Premier and his ministers were seldom called to account.

Laurence Decore was rendered ineffective because he was the first to call for fiscal probity and because he was clearly demoralized. A minor indiscretion, for example, quickly blossomed into a major failure of judgement: after a leisurely Friday lunch with one of his female staffers, Decore was a passenger in her new 4x4 when it tore up the legislative lawn and crashed. Alcohol, as police reports say, may have been a factor. When his brother died suddenly in a motorcycle accident in July, 1995, he abruptly resigned.

Grant Mitchell, Decore's successor, was plagued from the start. He came with his own set of old baggage: he had been a vice-president in The Principal Group, the financial company, the collapse of which during the Getty administration had ruined many elderly Albertans. Second, like Decore, he was from Edmonton, which was a liability everywhere else. Third, his election as leader was clouded with suspicion.

Mitchell's main opponent was Sine Chadi, who was accused of buying ethnic block-votes and who in reply charged his detractors with racism. To make matters even worse, the new high-tech voting system used by the Liberals didn't work. Chadi claimed that the breakdown had cost him enough proxy votes that he otherwise would have won on the first ballot. Mitchell's team said there were (unspecified) irregularities in the Chadi proxies but that they could not be determined because Chadi supporters didn't speak English. The result of all this bickering was that the Liberals looked to be deeply fractious as well as technologically challenged. Even worse for the long term, the Liberal leadership race was almost entirely devoid of policy discussions, so no one knew where Mitchell stood on the issues of the day.

Half-way through the first government mandate, it was clear that Klein would receive no significant criticism from the left. The liberal media and the Liberal Opposition were ineffective, and the academic left could simply be ignored. That did not, however, mean there would be smooth sailing. After the deficit and debt issue had been met, what was to follow? How intense should "reinvestment" be, and where should it be directed? And what of other policies?

That these questions were on the minds of Klein and his advisors was telegraphed indirectly in his post-Christmas television address to Albertans, delivered on January 15, 1995. Close observers of the operation of the Conservative Party could sense a significant change in the premier's style. It was nothing like the enthusiastic and spontaneous broadcast of the year before. Instead it was a pretaped and highly massaged production from the cabinet room, from his office, and from the electronic no-man's land of computer-generated graphics. The message was: stay the course; we are almost done. The significance, however, was that the government seemed unsure of its next moves.[43] The general drift of the government was confirmed a few months later at the April convention, when many Tories expressed anxieties that 70% approval rating was not enough.[44]

The April convention was also the scene of the first significant cracks in what came to be called the neo-con/theo-con alliance.[45] The issue was abortion, and pro-life advocates packaged the issue as one of fiscal restraint, not morality. If the government could save $4 million a year by defunding abortions, why continue to pay for them? After all, pregnancy is not an illness.

Ted Byfield in particular directed his criticism at the premier for attacking social conservatives. "In one resounding declaration," Byfield thundered, Klein "denounced politically active Christians, vowed he would ignore a resolution if his party's rank and file adopted it, declared the legislature no place to debate 'moral' questions, and saw one of his top cabinet ministers defy him and vote against him."[46]

It was, he said, "the dumbest blunder of his political career." What had caused the remarks by Klein was a 20,000 name petition to the Legislature asking to defund abortion the way that circumcision and weight removal were excluded from medicare coverage. This was followed by a resolution at the Tory convention asking for the same thing. Klein's "blunder," Byfield said, was to take sides instead of avoiding the issue by, for example, calling for a referendum.

By July the government had struck a committee to study the issue. There would be a free vote in caucus on defunding abortion.[47] By September, following a heated and divisive debate, the government agreed to pay only for "medically necessary" abortions as part of the general cost-cutting in the medical care system. Health Minister Shirley McClellan announced at the same time that it would be up to the physicians of the province to formulate a clear definition of what "medically necessary" meant.[48] The doctors were, at the time, objecting to the decision of the government to remove $100 million from their salary envelope and were in no mood to cooperate.[49] As a result, no definition was forthcoming and no change to existing funding was made.

At the next provincial Tory convention the pro-life group proposed a province-wide referendum to settle the issue. As in 1995, the defunding proposal was packaged as an economy move, and the referendum was promoted as being populist and democratic.[50] The convention rejected the resolution and Premier Klein indicated the party should think about the next election and forget about policies that divide Conservatives from one another.[51]

Another potentially contentious issue for the premier involved the always dangerous question of conflict of interest. On 13 December, 1993 Colleen Klein, the premier's wife, received 10,000 shares of stock in a soft-

ware company, Multi-Corp. Inc. Earlier in the year a number of prominent Tories had purchased substantial holdings in the Calgary company.
The main product was a translation system, called Ziran, which allows
relatively rapid writing in Asian languages using a special 10-key key-
board instead of a conventional one. What was unusual in the Multi-
Corp. stock deal was that Colleen Klein did not have to pay for her stock,
which she could obtain for a dollar a share, until she sold it—presumably
at a higher price. On 19 November, a few weeks before his wife received
the stock option, the premier opened the Hong Kong office of Multi-
Corp. On 6 December, 1993, Klein delivered a speech to the Hong Kong
Business Association in Edmonton praising, among other companies,
Multi-Corp.[52] Early in February, 1994 Mrs. Klein noted on her disclosure
form that she owned stock in Multi-Corp. In November, 1994, the premier visited China and helped Multi-Corp. gain a $26 million contract
with a state enterprise in Guandong province, called Gaozhou Dongling
Electronics.

According to the Liberals, and especially by Calgary MLA Frank
Bruseker was that there was an obvious conflict of interest because Klein
had promoted a company in which his wife had a financial interest. The
Ethics Commissioner, Rob Clark, found otherwise, noting only that Mrs.
Klein's purchase of the shares on credit was a source of "concern" because
it looked very much like a gift.[53] About a year later, Clark completed a
second investigation, this time centred on a dinner in Hong Kong host-
ed by the province at which the president of Multi-Corp., Michael
Lobsinger, was present, along with Premier Klein; he again found no conflict of interest to be present.[54]

There was, at the time of the investigation, considerable speculation
about the damage done to Ralph Klein's reputation as an ordinary guy,
and the effect the whole business would have on the next election.[55] In
the event, as is indicated below, the "Multi-Corp. affair" had as much of
an impact on the election as Klein's promotion of the company had on
the performance of its shares on the TSE—none.

A final area of criticism, which began as early as November, 1994, was
that Premier Klein was no more a fiscal than a social conservative and
that only the perseverance of the Treasurer, Jim Dinning (himself a late
convert to restraint) kept the province on track.[56] Three months later
Ted Byfield summarized an interview Klein gave after the 1995 Tory convention. According to Byfield, reporters asked him "what was next on the
government agenda, after the deficit?.... Beyond the deficit, there was no
agenda, he said. He'd gone as far as he would go."[57] In June, 1995,
Byfield's *Alberta Report* indicated that the premier was already reconsider-
ing the decision to trim $123 million from the health care budget.[58]

In July, *Alberta Report* expressed the opinion, that Klein was quickly turning into a "business conservative," as Getty and Lougheed had been. That is, he was less concerned with smaller government and lower personal taxes than with assisting large business organizations.[59] According to this interpretation, there was little difference between giving corporations tax breaks and "picking winners" in the old style by providing selective loan guarantees, direct investment, and so on. This may be questionable economic doctrine, but *Alberta Report* had clearly discovered a change in the Premier's attitude and actions.

By January, 1996 the criticism had intensified and the suspicion grew that Klein was more interested in "reinvesting" the budget surpluses than he had let on. What, after all, was a surplus but an artifact of arithmetic? If revenue are more than expenditures there is a surplus; but, as *Alberta Report* pointed out, "there is nothing in the [Balanced Budget and Deficit Retirement] Act to prevent a premier from anticipating a surplus and decreasing revenue or increasing spending to wipe it out."[60]

A few weeks later in the *Financial Post* David Bercuson and David Frum both argued that the Klein achievement had come to an end: the books were in good shape, so now the politicians would revert to their old, bad habits and spend money that had not been earned.[61] Later in February, 1996, the results of a survey of Albertans conducted by the government were made public. The largest number (35%) wanted the budget surplus to be used to pay down the debt faster than originally anticipated.[62] The government, however, favoured a "flexible" combination of debt reduction, lower taxes, and "reinvestment," and had clearly constructed the questions to get that result. In consequence, they were surprised that Albertans were still committed to debt retirement.

In June, 1996, Link Byfield, Ted's son and the publisher of *Alberta Report*, indicated the real limitation to the Klein initiative. It was a neat recapitulation of St. Augustine's account of sin: all humans are tempted; then they take delectation in their temptations, imagining what it would be like to "give in;" and then they assent and act. For Byfield *fils*, taxes are not the real problem. "The main issue is how politicians think," and almost by definition they think they can help. That is the temptation, the original political sin. "To the objection that the measures are too trivial to make much difference, the politician replies that their effect is really incremental and cumulative; and to the objection their effect is incremental, he replies that they are really trivial. To which he now adds the comforting thought, 'Besides, they won't cost taxpayers anything extra.'"[63] Here we see the rationalization that both expresses and obscures the delectation that politicians feel as they contemplate all the "help" they might provide. Moreover, the conditions for assent could not have been better. The whimpering lobby groups were still loitering in place, famished for taxpayers' money. Moreover, with most of the bureaucracy intact and eager to justify itself by catering to the infinite and pressing needs of their clientele, it was only a matter of time until the government gave in. By mid-1996 it was clear to the Byfields, *père et fils*, that Ralph Klein had already assented in his heart.

And yet, in the thirty or so months after becoming premier, Ralph Klein had managed to change the financial profile of the province. When Peter Lougheed turned the government over to Don Getty in 1985, the provincial net worth was nearly $13 billion; when Getty left in 1992 the province was nearly $6 billion in the hole. With Klein, the deficit was gone in a matter of three years and it was conceivable in 1996 that the debt would disappear a few years down the road.

Opposition to this remarkable achievement came initially from those whose short-term interests were harmed—civil servants, doctors, teachers, and municipal politicians—denizens of MUSH. The government dealt with this criticism in a variety of ways: head-on, through consistent application of the argument that they had been elected to govern; by providing answers and rebuttals through the media; by using the usual array of public relations sophistry; and by admitting error and correcting its actions. Both substantively and technically, the Government was successful in meeting the initial opposition to its program. The criticism from *Alberta Report* and from other committed social and fiscal conservatives could, for the moment, be ignored. By and large, it was, but it would reappear after the voters rewarded the Tories at the 1997 election.

CHAPTER FIVE
WHY THE KLEIN GOVERNMENT
IS POPULAR

The previous chapters have shown earlier how governments—both federal and provincial—contributed to Alberta's deficit and debt problems, how the Klein government employed a commonsensical yet hard-hitting approach to deal with those problems, how that approach has helped to achieve results but not stifle opposition, and how the Premier has taken advantage of his mistakes and used his rhetorical skills to deflect critics. In this chapter, we explain why Albertans continue to support the Klein government.

In the Introduction we distinguished rather crudely between politicians who wree vote-grabbers and those who were position-takers. The former, we said trim their policies to satisfy the average voter, while the latter seek to distinguish themselves from their political opponents, even if it also appears to push them away from the presumed position of the average voter. "These opposing imperatives," write Richard Johnson and his colleagues in their study of the 1988 federal election—"to take stands which give voters reasons for supporting the party, on the one hand, and to move towards the center to avoid alienating voters, on the other"— create one of the essential tensions in campaigns."[1]

The "tension" is "essential" in the sense that it never goes away. Thus a party that comes close to taking no position will give potential voters no reason to vote for it, and they are likely to drift away; likewise, a party that takes an unambiguous and intense position on a range of issues that are of little concern to most voters may attract a devoted following, but it will be small. Hence the need to balance the two tendencies.

Having said that, however, the left-right spatial model that is presumed to portray accurately enough the normal or bell-curve distribution of public opinion carries with it the implication that most politicians most of the time will be enthusiastic vote-grabbers but more reluctant position-takers. They will, of course, take positions, but the positions they take will be similar to the ones they took last election, particularly if it was successful. If they do this too many times, even successful parties will become stigmatized as "tired" or being devoid of "fresh ideas." When that happens, parties renovate themselves with new policies and give voters reasons to vote for them while, at the same time, they try to keep in touch with old coalitions. In this context political scientists speak of politicians "priming" the electorate—that is, giving voters a simplified message with which they can identify. In other words, if politicians are skilled in controlling the agenda, they will be able to shape alternatives to their own advantage. In the previous chapters we have seen how Ralph Klein was able to take a position that also grabbed votes. It is a skill he learned as mayor of Calgary, when he was able to manage confrontation to enhance his ability to get things done; it is a skill he perfected as premier.

The previous chapters have provided a narrative analysis of Klein's political achievement. In this chapter we will examine the response of Alberta voters to the leadership Klein offered them. We begin with a discussion of some of the implications of the spatial model of voter support.

Four Explanations

In his *Economic Theory of Democracy* Anthony Downs formalized the view that governments plan and undertake policies that are most likely to maximize voter support, and citizens, in turn, form their political preferences on the basis of government actions. It follows that governments are likely to spend when they calculate the benefits to be greater than the political costs of financing expenditures, which can be done either through taxation, printing money, or borrowing, though only the options of taxing or borrowing are available to Canadian provinces. Stated more formally, a "government increases its spending until the vote gain of the marginal dollar spent equals the vote loss of the marginal dollar of financing."[2] The bottom line, therefore, is that to increase its support a government must either increase its spending or decrease its taxing. By this argument, governments calculate what is in their own interests by estimating what is in the interest of their supporters.

As we saw above, after the 1993 election one of the most important and most immediate challenges facing the new government was to balance the province's budget and to bring into control its rapidly escalating debt. A straightforward Downsian response would have been to proceed cautiously, by implementing a balanced mix of spending and financing, designed to maximize voter support and minimize the number of votes lost. In fact, however, the government appears to have avoided both options provided by Downsian logic. First, they began immediately to slash public spending across a broad range of policy areas, including programs that deliver highly valued benefits—health care, education and social welfare; second, although the government did not implement any new taxes, at the same time it did not compensate citizens for reduced services by also reducing their tax burden. Furthermore, despite its explicitly one-sided policy actions, the government won its second electoral mandate in 1997 with even greater voter support than in 1993.[3] The electoral victories and the high approval rating were interpreted by the government as evidence of support for both deficit elimination and spending cuts without tax reductions.[4] Other observers drew the conventional Downsian conclusion that the government's popularity would quickly decline.[5] And yet, despite its underspending and overfinancing, the government grew more popular.[6] Why?

Our analysis considers four possible explanations. The first examines the impact of various long-term influences. Both the sociological and the socio-psychological theories of voting[7] propose that support for political parties is mainly a result of stable and consistent factors, such as social group attachments, chiefly family, and party ties. It is possible, then, that Albertans remain loyal to the Tories because their friends and neighbours prompt them to do so, or because most Albertans, by and large, are what political scientists call conservative identifiers.[8] That is, Albertans support the Klein government because long-term loyalties of one kind or another bind them to the Conservative party.

A second explanation begins with the premise that citizens today are *less* reliant on either social group or party cues.[9] Downs, for example, contends that voters are "rational utility maximizers,"[10] meaning that they organize their political preferences according to their calculated evaluations of which parties are the most likely to provide the greatest personal gain. Downs' theory assumes that voters distinguish clearly between policy initiatives and that they base their overall political judgements on the effects of government actions. If Downs is right, another reason why Albertans might continue to support the Klein government is because they value the general principles of deficit elimination, spending cuts, and user fees more than they oppose the consequences of large and rapid budget cuts. By this account, Albertans continue to support the Tories because they distinguish between the government's broader policy initiatives, of which they approve, and their hard-hitting approach, about which they may have reservations.

In most democratic societies the governing party competes with other opposition parties for the right to rule. Therefore, a third prospective explanation may be related to a weak or neutralized opposition. We saw in the previous chapter that, half-way through their first term, the Tories began to see they would face no significant threat from the left. It is possible, then, that Albertans continue to support the Klein government because they see no other viable alternative. At least one preliminary study proposes that, despite their best efforts, the opposition Liberals have simply failed to win support away from the governing Tories.[11]

A fourth possible explanation is that the success of the Klein government depends upon the popularity of the leader of the party rather than the policies the government enacts. Thus the Tories really are the "Ralph Party," and support for the Government can be attributed directly to the preference Albertans feel for Ralph Klein over all other opposition leaders, whoever they may be. We have reviewed a good deal of the anecdotal evidence regarding Klein's popularity.[12] The understandable desire of journalists to dramatize electoral contests has made this last explanation the most plausible in the public mind. We will indicate more precisely the effect the premier's popularity has in attracting party support and, conversely, the effect that evaluations of the new Liberal leader, Nancy MacBeth (the former Nancy Betkowski) work against that support. We will provide quantitative evidence to supplement the popular accounts of Ralph Klein's appeal.

We suspect that all four explanations are at least partly responsible for explaining why Albertans continue to support the Klein government. But is any one explanation more compelling than the others? And conversely, which particular arguments are the least relevant overall? Using statistical analysis of data we gathered from three consecutive public opinion surveys—the 1995, 1996, and 1999 Alberta Advantage Surveys (AAS)—we provide an analysis of the Klein government's unprecedented success.

The first two public opinion polls were conducted during the aftermath of the Klein government's initial budget cuts (in 1995 and 1996, respectively). The third and most recent survey was taken in January, 1999, midway through the second electoral mandate and after the government had successfully eliminated the deficit, reduced the debt, and begun to reinvest. Each survey was administered via telephone to a random sample of slightly more than 1000 Albertans. The margin of error for each respective study is approximately +3%. Although these surveys are not panel studies, that is, although we did not interview the *same people* in all three studies (a very expensive procedure) each questionnaire did contain several of the *same questions*. Thus, by comparing the answers to these questions, it is possible to track aggregate public opinion over time. We incorporated a number of different measures—from background factors to attitudes towards Nancy MacBeth that allow us to test the validity of the four possible explanations noted above. The timing of these studies is particularly fortuitous in that they allow us to examine public opinion in Alberta during both the best and worst of economic times.

Approval for the Klein Government's Performance
Each round of the AAS begins by asking Albertans how they would rate the performance of the current provincial government: *"Would you say you strongly approve, approve, disapprove or strongly disapprove of the Klein government's performance?"* Figure 1 illustrates how the Tories approval ratings have varied over time.

Figure 1: Approval for the Klein Government's Performance

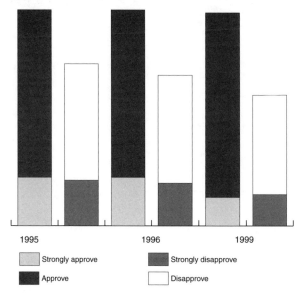

| 1995 | 1996 | 1999 |

| | Strongly approve | | Strongly disapprove |
| | Approve | | Disapprove |

As we alluded to above, one prominent argument has been to suggest that, as time wears on and the impact of the government's budget restructuring becomes more widely felt, support is for the Klein Tories bound to decline. Our data, however, provide no such indication: approval for the government continues to rise, while disapproval continues to fall. Nearly six years have passed since the Tories were first elected, and our evidence shows they are more popular now than ever before. The most recent findings show that almost two in every three Albertans (65%) say that they approve of the government's performance.

We do find, however, a noticeable shift in the *intensity* of support; over the last three years or so, the number of Albertans who strongly approve of the government's performance has decreased by seven percent. Thus, even though more and more Albertans continue to jump on the Tory bandwagon, and there are fewer voters who strongly disapprove of the Klein government's performance, today's Conservative party supporters on the whole are not as likely to be as adamant in their support as they were a few years earlier. Adamant or not, the more general finding remains: most Albertans, support the incumbent government. But, why? What accounts for the Klein government's remarkable success?

The next part of our analysis turns to consider the four conventional explanations discussed earlier. The approach that we employ is designed to indicate the proper weight of each explanations. By pitting alternative explanations against their antecedents, we can evaluate how each con-

Table 1: Approval for the Klein Government's Performance by Socio-Demographics and Stable Party Ties
(Regression analysis)

Predictors	Approval for the Klein Government's performance	
Psychological attachments:		
Stable party ties (conservative)		.27 (.02)**
Socio-demographics:		
Sex (male)	.05 (.02)**	.05 (.02)**
Age (senior)	-.08 (.03)**	-.08 (.02)**
Education (university)	-.07 (.02)**	-.05 (.02)**
Employment/income (employed with high income)	.06 (.02)**	.04 (.02)*
Calgarians (vs Edmontonians)	.05 (.02)*	.03 (.02)
Rural Albertans (vs Edmontonians)	.05 (.02)*	.02 (.02)
Constant	.63 (.02)**	.59 (.02)**
R-squared (adjusted)	.05	.15

Note:
The above figures are unstandardized regression coefficients and (standard errors).
* significant at p<.05; ** significant at p<.01
Coding:
(1) Approval for the Klein Government's performance: strongly approve=1; approve=.75; disapprove=.5; strongly disapprove=0.
(2) Sex: male=1; female=0.
(3) Age: 65+yrs=1; 35-64yrs=.5; 18-34yrs=0.
(4) Education: university=1; technical college=.5; primary and secondary=0.
(5) Employment/income: employed with high income=1; employed with moderate income=.75; employed with low income=.25; unemployed with low income=0.
(6) Calgarians: Calgary residents=1; Edmontonians=0.
(7) Rural Albertans: rural residents=1; Edmontonians=0.
(8) Stable party ties: voted for the Tories both provincially and federally in 1997=1; voted for the Tories provincially, but Reform federally in 1997=.5; voted for the Tories provincially, but the Liberals or NDP federally in 1997=0.
Source: The 1999 Alberta Advantage Survey

secutive explanation affects voters' overall approval ratings, and which particular arguments stand out as being the most powerful overall.

1. The impact of long-term loyalties:
The first explanation proposes that support for the Klein government is a result of long-term social group loyalties and/or partisan ties. Table 1 tests this proposition statistically using two separate regression analyses. The first looks specifically at the effects of various socio-demographic variables (including sex, age, education, employment/income and place of residence) on approval for the Klein government's performance, and the second examines the combined effects of both social and psychological influences all at once.

The point of conducting two separate regression analyses is to determine the extent to which group differences are significant, once psychological explanations are taken into account. When we examine the impact of various socio-demographic variables, independent of other forces, it appears as though the political landscape in Alberta is divided into several polarized camps. Males, for example, turn out to be more approving of the Klein government's performance than females. Similarly, we find other important group differences when it comes to factors such as age, education, employment/income and place of residence. Overall, however, social group differences (as measured by the r-squared statistic) explain only 5% of the variance in popular approval of the government's performance. Moreover, the significance of group differences begins to shrink the moment that other competing explanations are introduced.

The second regression analysis in Table 1, for instance, shows that stable partisan affiliations have more than three times (.27) the effect of the strongest socio-demographic determinant, which in this case is age (-.08). Albertans who are loyal to the Conservatives both federally and provincially are more likely to approve of the Klein government's actions than those who split their votes between the provincial Tories and another federal party. In addition, party loyalty detracts from the effects of both education and employment/income, and it causes the overall impact of place of residence to become entirely insignificant. Although the combined effects of both sociological and psychological loyalties account for more of the variance in approval for the Klein government's performance than do social forces alone, the bottom line is that partisan ties tell us more about approval ratings than do any sociological affiliations.

2. Opposition toward the pace and magnitude of the Klein government's budget cuts vs. support for the general principles of deficit elimination, spending cuts, taxes and user fees.

A second explanation considers the possibility that although Albertans may oppose to the pace and magnitude of the budget cuts, they approve in principle of the goals of deficit elimination, less spending, lower taxes, and increased user fees. Therefore, Albertans may continue to back the Klein government because their support for a balanced budget and less government intervention outweighs their concerns over deteriorating government-delivered or government-supported programs.

Figure 2: Opposition Toward the Pace and Magnitude of the Klein Government's Budget Cuts in Education, Health Care and Social Services

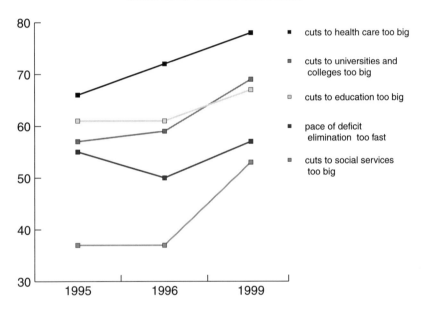

Figure 2 reports Albertan's orientations toward the pace of the Klein government's deficit elimination plan and their concerns over the magnitude of the budget cuts in the areas of education, Health care, and social services. Given the Klein government's hard hitting approach to budget cutting, the data contain no surprises: most Albertans think the pace of deficit elimination in Alberta was too fast. Moreover, as the cuts to government programs began to take greater effect between 1995 and 1999, the strength of public opposition toward the magnitude of the budget cuts continued to grow. Over the last three or four years alone, Albertans have become 12% more opposed to the magnitude of the cuts to Health care, 12% more opposed to the magnitude of the cuts to primary and secondary

Table 2: Approval for the Klein Government's Performance by Orientations Toward the Pace and Magnitude of the Government's Budget Cuts
(Regression analysis)

Predictors	Approval for the Klein Government's performance
Orientations toward the pace and magnitude of the Klein Government's budget cuts:	
Pace of the cuts too fast	-.10 (.03)**
Cuts to education (primary and secondary) too big	-.13 (.04)**
Cuts to universities and colleges too big	-.08 (.04)*
Cuts to health care too big	-.08 (.04)*
Cuts to social services and welfare too big	-.08 (.03)**
Psychological attachments:	
Stable party ties (conservative)	.22 (.03)**
Socio-demographics:	
Sex (male)	.02 (.02)
Age (senior)	-.09 (.02)**
Education (university)	-.04 (.02)*
Employment/income	
(employed with high income)	.03 (.02)
Calgarians (vs Edmontonians)	—
Rural Albertans (vs Edmontonians)	.02 (.02)
Constant	1.00 (.04)**
R-squared (adjusted)	.26

Note:
The above figures are unstandardized regression coefficients and (standard errors).
*significant at p<.05; ** significant at p<.01

New coding:
(1) Pace of the cuts: too fast=1; just about right=5; too slow=0.
(2) Cuts to education (primary and secondary) too big: too big=1; just about right=.5; too small=0.
(3) Cuts to universities and colleges too big: too big=1; just about right=.5; too small=0.
(4) Cuts to health care too big: too big=1; just about right=.5; too small=0.
(5) Cuts to social services and welfare too big: too big=1; just about right=.5; too small=0.

Source: The 1999 Alberta Advantage Survey

education, 6% more opposed to the magnitude of the cuts to universities, and 16% more opposed to the magnitude of the cuts to social welfare.

It is, however, one thing to dislike expenditure cuts but something else to dislike the government because of them. An analogy from personal life may be instructive: very few people enjoy going to the dentist, but they don't for that reason dislike their dentist or stop having their teeth checked. The crucial question, therefore, remains: to what extent does the public's discontent detract from approval for the Klein government's performance? As with the earlier question, regression analysis of the data can sort out the answer.

The findings reported in Table 2 show that concerns over the pace and magnitude of the budget cuts do indeed have a significant negative impact on the Klein government's approval ratings, even after the effects of various long-term partisan allegiances have been taken into account. Albertans who feel that the pace of deficit elimination was too fast, and that the magnitude of the budget cuts was too big, are not as likely to approve of the government's performance.

The major sore spots appear to be both the size of cuts to primary and secondary education and the pace of the government's deficit elimination strategy. Even though the deficit is gone, concerns over the pace of deficit elimination still have a relatively powerful effect. Moreover, given the media-enhanced horror stories about long waiting times in emergency facilities, inadequate hospital staffing, and the general deterioration of health care in Alberta, it comes as something of a surprise that the effect of opposition to health care cuts is only about the same as opposition toward cuts to universities and colleges, and to social welfare.

There is no doubt that approval or disapproval of the pace and magnitude of government cuts are a major influence on Albertans' perceptions of the government's overall performance. Statistically, the addition of these variables increase the explanation of the overall variance by 11%, a sizeable amount. At the same time, these factors take away from the effect of long-term party support, and the impact of differences in sex becomes entirely insignificant.

Granted that opposition toward the pace and magnitude of the budget cuts does detract from approval for the Klein government's performance, why do the government's approval ratings continue to improve? The answer, we suggest, may be tied to the question of priorities. That is, Albertans may continue to support the government because they value the broader policy objectives more than they oppose its hard-hitting approach. They go to the dentist even though it hurts because they think it is good for them. Indeed, they take pride in their achievement of a balanced budget or sound teeth.

Figure 3: Orientations Toward the General Principles of Deficit Elimination, Spending Cuts, Taxes and User Fees

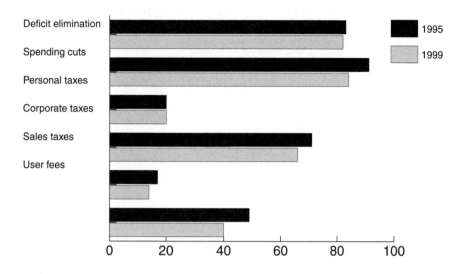

Figure 3 shows Albertans' more general views towards the core principles of deficit elimination, spending cuts, lower taxes and user fees. The data, in this case, appear quite stable, with only a few minor fluctuations. On the whole, more than four in every five Albertans support the principles of deficit reduction and spending cuts. Not surprisingly, however, Albertans are much less supportive when they are asked whether they would rather pay more taxes: no more than one in every five Albertans supports the idea of increasing either personal taxes or introducing a sales tax. Corporate taxes, on the other hand, are another story: two in every three Albertans indicate that the deep pockets of corporations should be picked so that they contribute more to government revenue. Lastly, and perhaps the most difficult to gauge, is the public's view towards user fees. Although relatively popular in 1995, support for this particular proposition appears to be in decline. The most recent results show that only two in every five Albertans agree with the idea of having to pay user fees.

Bearing in mind that the Klein government's overall policy objectives were to eliminate the province's fiscal deficit by implementing a mixture of spending cuts, along with no new taxes and some user fees, it is important to examine how the public's orientations toward these general principles contributes to their appraisals of the government's performance. The results of the regression analysis reported in Table 3 suggest that while support for general policy objectives is indeed important, certain

Table 3: Approval for the Klein Government's Performance by Orientations Toward the General Principles of Deficit Elimination, Spending Cuts, Taxes and User fees
(Regression analysis)

Predictors	Approval for the Klein Government's performance
Orientations toward the general principles of deficit elimination, spending cuts, taxes and user fees:	
Deficit elimination (strongly support)	.30 (.04)**
Spending cuts (support)	—
Personal taxes (oppose)	-.01 (.02)
Corporate taxes (oppose)	.05 (.02)**
Sales taxes (oppose)	.06 (.02)*
User fees (oppose)	—
Orientations toward the pace and magnitude of the Klein Government's budget cuts:	
Pace of the cuts too fast	-.08 (.03)**
Cuts to education (primary and secondary) too big	-.08 (.04)*
Cuts to universities and colleges too big	-.08 (.04)*
Cuts to health care too big	-.06 (.03)
Cuts to social services and welfare too big	-.04(.03)
Psychological attachments:	
Stable party ties (conservative)	.16 (.02)**
Socio-demographics:	
Sex (male)	.03 (.02)
Age (senior)	-.09 (.02)*
Education (university)	-.04 (.02)*
Employment/income (employed with high income)	.02 (.02)
Calgarians (vs Edmontonians)	.01 (.02)
Rural Albertans (vs Edmontonians)	.01 (.02)
Constant	.61 (.06)**
R-squared (adjusted)	34

Note:
The above figures are unstandardized regression coefficients and (standard errors).
*significant at p<.05; ** significant at p<.01
New coding:
(1) Deficit elimination: strongly support=1; support=.75; oppose=.5; strongly oppose=0.
(2) Spending cuts: should do=1; should not do=0.
(3) Personal taxes: should not do=1; should do=0.
(4) Corporate taxes: should not do=1; should do=0.
(5) Sales taxes: should not do=1; should do=0.
(6) User fees: should not do=1; should do=0.
Source:The 1999 Alberta Advantage Survey

principles carry more weight than others. The most important factor, by far, is support for the general principle of deficit elimination: supporters of deficit reduction are the most inclined to approve of the Klein government's performance. Likewise, two other broader policy objectives are also important, but to a lesser degree: Albertans who oppose increases in corporate and sales taxes are more likely than those who support these principles to approve of the government's actions.

The fact that orientations toward other broader policy incentives such as less government spending, lower personal taxes, and user fees turn out to be statistically insignificant may be a consequence of the problem of multi-colinearity as opposed to the fact that these variables are truly unimportant. Our decision to include these indicators despite the fact that they may be correlated with other variables already included within the analysis is based on the reasoning that each variable seems to us to be conceptually distinct. support for general spending cuts is not the same as support for expenditure cuts in specific areas such as education, health care, and social welfare.[13] Moreover, the fact that there are statistical differences between support for corporate and sales taxes lends further support for the need to distinguish between support for different taxes and user fees.

Figure 4: Approval for the Oppostion Liberal's Performance

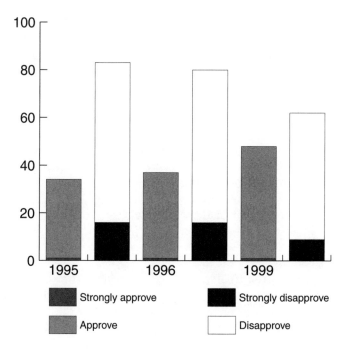

The addition of variables measuring orientations toward general policy objectives, though not always significant, contributes to an 8% increase in the total variance explained. More importantly, the inclusion of these indicators weakens the negative impact associated with orientations toward the pace and magnitude of the budget cuts. That is, once the public's perceptions toward the general principles of deficit elimination, spending cuts, taxes, and user fees are taken into account, the evidence suggests that the impact of opposition toward Health care cuts and cuts to social welfare becomes entirely insignificant. Furthermore, the effects of long-term party loyalties are also considerably reduced; the impact of stable party affiliations, for example, drops by more than 25%. At this point, then, it would appear that the key reason why Albertans continue to support the government is because they unequivocally support the general principle of deficit elimination and they oppose, also in principle, the proposition of having to pay more taxes.

3. The lack of an effective opposition:
A third potential explanation of why the Klein government continues to prosper may be connected to the absence of an ineffective opposition. The data presented in Figure 4 help to illustrate how Albertans feel about the opposition Liberals. The evidence in this case is overwhelming: more than a majority of Albertans consistently indicate they disapprove of the opposition Liberals' performance. This does not mean, however, that the Liberals' position is forever hopeless since they also appear more recently to be making some significant improvements. Over the last three years or so, the number of Albertans who strongly disapprove of the Liberals' performance has declined by nearly half, and approval ratings, in general, appear to be on the rise.

As with the earlier questions we examined, however, to say you think the Liberals are doing a good job is not the same as saying you ever would vote for them. Higher approval ratings for the Liberals do not necessarily translate into an ability to "detract" voter support from the Klein Tories. Once again regression analysis proves instructive. The results presented in Table 4 indicate that the performance of the Liberals in Alberta has no discernable impact on approval for the Klein government's performance, nor does the addition of this particular variable help to improve our overall understanding of why some Albertans continue to support the Tories, while others do not.

The incorporation of this variable does, however, produces some interesting side effects that are nonetheless worth mentioning. For instance after accounting for the performance of the opposition Liberals, we find that the positive impact of support for the general principle of deficit elimination

Table 4: Approval for the Klein Government's Performance by Orientations Toward the Official Opposition
(Regression analysis)

Predictors	Approval for the Klein Government's performance
Orientations toward the Official Opposition:	
Approval for the opposition Liberal's Performance (approve)	—
Orientations toward the general principles of deficit elimination, spending cuts, taxes and user fees:	
Deficit elimination (strongly support)	.28 (.04)**
Spending cuts (support)	.01 (.02)
Personal taxes (oppose)	-.02 (.02)
Corporate taxes (oppose)	.06 (.02)**
Sales taxes (oppose)	.06 (.03)*
User fees (oppose)	-.01 (.02)
Orientations toward the pace and magnitude of the Klein Government's budget cuts:	
Pace of the cuts too fast	-.06 (.03)*
Cuts to education (primary and secondary) too big	-.08 (.04)*
Cuts to universities and colleges too big	-.08 (.04)
Cuts to health care too big	-.05 (.04)
Cuts to social services and welfare too big	-.04 (.03)
Psychological attachments:	
Stable party ties (conservative)	18 (.03)**
Socio-demographics:	
Sex (male)	.02 (.02)
Age (senior)	-.06 (.03)*
Education (university)	-.04 (.02)*
Employment/income (employed with high income)	.02 (.02)
Calgarians (vs Edmontonians)	-
Rural Albertans (vs Edmontonians)	.01 (.02)
Constant	.59 (.07)**
R-squared (adjusted)	.33

Note:
The above figures are unstandardized regression coefficients and (standard errors).
*significant at p<.05; ** significant at p<.01
New coding:
(1) Approval for the opposition Liberal's performance: strongly approve=1; approve=.75; disapprove=.5; strongly disapprove=0.
Source:
The 1999 Alberta Advantage Survey

declines, but only slightly. Conversely, the negative impact of disapproval toward the pace and magnitude of the budget cuts becomes even less pronounced, and the effect of opposition toward cuts to universities and colleges becomes altogether insignificant. In fact, when Albertans think at all about the performance of the opposition Liberals, they are less concerned about the pace and magnitude of the Klein government's budget cuts and more motivated to act in accordance with their long-term party ties. In short, whether people think the Liberals are doing a good job or not makes no difference to whether they approve of the Klein achievement.

4. The impact of leadership

The fourth and final explanation for the Klein government's continued success is that it results from the positive impact of Ralph Klein's leadership. Evidence from a long line of electoral studies indicates that preferences are often based on whether voters support a candidate or a leader, as distinct from a party or a specific policy or policy mix. In the present study, this would mean that support for the Klein government may be contingent upon the strong popular appeal of Premier Klein, and conversely, the lack of voter support for current opposition Liberal leader, Nancy MacBeth, even though many Albertans think she is doing a good job.

Figure 5: Leadership Ratings

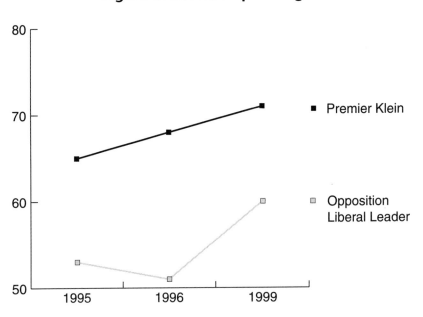

GOVERNING IN POST-DEFICIT TIMES

Table 5: Approval for the Klein Government's Performance by Leadership Ratings
(Regression analysis)

Predictors	Approval for the Klein Government's performance
Leadership ratings:	
Premier Ralph Klein (positive)	.28 (.02)**
Opposition leader, Nancy MacBeth (positive)	-.04 (.02)*
Orientations toward the Official Opposition:	
Approval for the opposition Liberal's Performance (approve)	.04 (.04)
Orientations toward the general principles of deficit elimination, spending cuts, taxes and user fees:	
Deficit elimination (strongly support)	.17 (.04)**
Spending cuts (support)	-.01 (.02)
Personal taxes (oppose)	-.02 (.02)
Corporate taxes (oppose)	.03 (.02)
Sales taxes (oppose)	.03 (.02)
User fees (oppose)	-.02 (.02)
Orientations toward the pace and magnitude of the Klein Government's budget cuts:	
Pace of the cuts too fast	-.01 (.03)
Cuts to education (primary and secondary) too big	-.07 (.04)
Cuts to universities and colleges too big	-.05 (.04)
Cuts to health care too big	-.04 (.04)
Cuts to social services and welfare too big	-.02 (.03)
Psychological attachments:	
Stable party ties (conservative)	.10 (.02)**
Socio-demographics:	
Sex (male)	.01 (.02)
Age (senior)	-.02 (.02)
Education (university)	-.03 (.02)
Employment/income (employed with high income)	—
Calgarians (vs Edmontonians)	.01 (.02)
Rural Albertans (vs Edmontonians)	.01 (.02)
Constant	.47 (.06)**
R-squared (adjusted)	.50

Note:
The above figures are unstandardized regression coefficients and (standard errors).
*significant at $p<.05$; ** significant at $p<.01$

New coding:
(1) Premier Ralph Klein: positive ratings (51 - 100)=1; neutral rating (50)=.5; negative ratings (0-49)=0.
(2) Leader of the opposition Liberals (Nancy MacBeth): positive ratings (51 - 100)=1; neutral rating (50)=.5; Negative ratings (0-49)=0.

Source:
The 1999 Alberta Advantage Survey

Figure 5 compares Albertans' overall assessments of Premier Klein to those of the leaders of the opposition Liberals. As time goes on, the evidence indicates Albertans have grown considerably more fond of Premier Klein. The public's ratings of the Premier are consistently more positive than ratings for various opposition leaders. It is interesting to note, however, that the newly appointed Liberal leader, Nancy MacBeth, rates more positively among Albertans than did the former Liberal leader, Grant Mitchell. More to the point, regression analysis reported in Table 5 shows that leadership is a major factor in maintaining the high approval for the Klein government's performance. If you approve of Klein's leadership, you are very much inclined to approve of his government's performance. Unfortunately for the Liberals, orientations toward the opposition leader also matter, but to a much lesser extent. Nonetheless, the data show that Nancy MacBeth's supporters are not as likely to approve of the Klein government's performance.

The introduction of these "leadership" variables improves our overall understanding of the variance in the government's approval ratings by a whopping 17%. Moreover, the effects of leadership all but wash out the impact of all other factors except for two. And even then, both the effects of orientations toward the general principle of deficit elimination and stable party ties are noticeably reduced. The major conclusion to be drawn from the preceding analysis is that the most important explanation of Albertan's approval of the government's achievements is the leadership of Ralph Klein. This is followed by support for the general principle of deficit elimination and stable partisan ties, although the relative weakening of the latter lends support to the more recent findings by political scientists elsewhere suggesting that long-term party affiliations are less important today than once they were. Conversely, social group affiliations and the performance of the opposition Liberals do not factor as being directly relevant overall.[14] In fact, the only factor that appears to leave any dent in the government's strong popularity is Nancy MacBeth: she gave the Premier a run for his money during the Conservative party's leadership and she continues to be an obstacle even now.

What Explains the Premier's Popular Appeal?
The data clearly suggest that the Premier's personal appeal, more than anything else, is responsible for the Tories overall success. The next logical question is: what explains that popularity? We have seen in earlier chapters that he has plenty of detractors.[15] Data from the AAS permit us to look more closely at this particular question.

The evidence represented in Figure 6 considers three general characteristics of good leadership—effectiveness, trustworthiness, and how "in touch" leaders are with their constituents. As part of the AAS, Albertans

Figure 6: Why is Premier Klein Popular – General Reasons

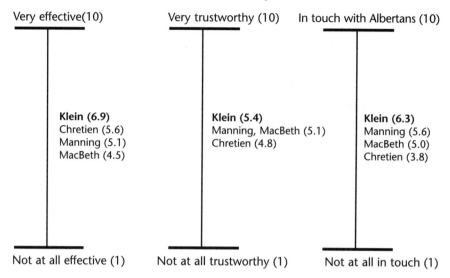

Very effective(10)　　Very trustworthy (10)　In touch with Albertans (10)

Klein (6.9)　　　　**Klein (5.4)**　　　　　**Klein (6.3)**
Chretien (5.6)　　　　Manning, MacBeth (5.1)　Manning (5.6)
Manning (5.1)　　　　Chretien (4.8)　　　　　MacBeth (5.0)
MacBeth (4.5)　　　　　　　　　　　　　　　　Chretien (3.8)

Not at all effective (1)　Not at all trustworthy (1)　Not at all in touch (1)

were asked to rate several political leaders according to each of these qualities. A score of "1," for example, indicates that the leader in question is not very effective, whereas a score of "10" indicates that the leader is very effective. The results in this case correspond to citizens' average ratings of each respective leader, on each particular characteristic. In all three cases the Premier of Alberta stands above all other leaders examined. In the eyes of Albertans, then, Premier Klein is clearly perceived as being the most effective, the most trustworthy, and the most in touch with Albertans. On average, Albertans give the Premier a 6.9 out of 10 on effectiveness, 5.4 on trustworthiness and 6.3 when it comes to being in touch with Albertans.

Turning from the more general findings to more specific considerations, Figure 7 shows how Albertans responded when asked to comment more directly on why they think the Premier is so well liked. At least five potential reasons were brought to mind, some more frequently than others. Slightly more than a third of Albertans (37%), for instance, indicate that the Premier is popular because "he eliminated the deficit and put our fiscal house in order." Another third claim that the Premier is well liked because he exhibits the integrity of a people's politician. Eleven percent of Albertans, for example, contend that the Premier is "a politician who keeps his word;" 8% say that "he listens to voters and does what they want;" and 10% agree that "when he makes a mistake, he isn't afraid to admit it." Lastly, a final third of Albertans (32%) feel that the primary reason why Premier Klein remains at the top is because "he has no real competition or challenger."

Figure 7: Why is Premier Klein Popular – Specific Reasons

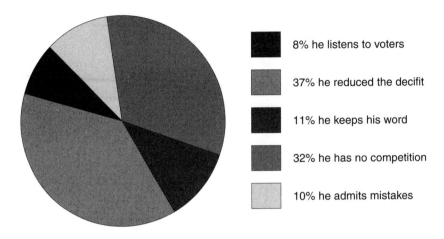

- 8% he listens to voters
- 37% he reduced the decifit
- 11% he keeps his word
- 32% he has no competition
- 10% he admits mistakes

In the final regression analysis, reported in Table 6, we examine the combined impact of each of these factors, both general and specific, in an attempt to determine which particular leadership attributes Albertans perceive as being the most important overall. The evidence produced by this analysis shows that general considerations clearly outweigh the more specific policy achievements. In particular, the Premier's most powerful asset is that he is trusted. The more Albertans trust the Premier, the more they like him. This is not to say, of course, that effectiveness and being in touch are not important; they too are significant, but to a slightly lesser degree.

Likewise, when it comes to more specific attributes, the Premier's perceived integrity and his general appeal are more important than anything else: the fact that he listens to voters and that he keeps his word, is even more important than the fact that he eliminated the deficit. Based on this analysis, it appears as though Albertans continue to approve of their current Premier because at a time when people's general disenchantment with politics is on the rise and trust in politicians is in decline,[16] Ralph Klein stands out as being different from the rest. He's a people's politician: he's trustworthy, he listens and he keeps his word. The fact that he is an effective politician who eliminated the province's deficit doesn't hurt, but it is clearly secondary.

Table 6: Why is Premier Klein Popular?
(Regression analysis)

Predictors	Rating for Premier Klein (positive)
General reasons:	
He's very effective as a political leader	.22 (.04)**
He's very trustworthy	.37 (.03)**
He's very much in touch with Albertans	.20 (.03)**
Specific reasons:	
He's a politician who keeps his word (vs. no competition)	.13 (.04)**
He listens to voters (vs. no competition)	.15 (.04)**
He admits mistakes (vs. no competition)	.06 (.04)
He eliminated the deficit (vs. no competition)	.11 (.03)**
Constant	.04 (.03)
R-squared (adjusted)	.45

Note:
The above figures are unstandardized regression coefficients and (standard errors).
*significant at p<.05; ** significant at p<.01

New coding:
(1) He's a politician who keeps his word: he's a politician who keeps his word=1; he has no real competition or challenger=0.
(2) He eliminated the deficit: he eliminated the deficit=1; he has no real competition or challenger=0.
(3) He listens to voters: he listens to voters=1; he has no real competition or challenger=0.
(4) He admits mistakes: he admits mistakes=1; he has no real competition or challenger=0.
(5) He's very effective as a political leader: very effective (6-10)=1; moderately effective (5)=.5; not at all effective (0-4)=0.
(6) He's very trustworthy: very trustworthy (6-10)=1; moderately trustworthy (5)=.5; not at all trustworthy (0-4)=0.
(7) He's very much in touch with Albertans: very much in touch (6-10)=1; moderately in touch (5)=.5; not at all in touch (0-4)=0.

Source: The 1999 Alberta Advantage Survey

CHAPTER SIX
GOVERNING IN THE POST-DEFICIT ERA

On 11 February, 1997 the Lieutenant Governor delivered a short, bland speech from the throne; the next day Jim Dinning delivered his last budget. Two minutes after Dinning resumed his seat the Speaker dissolved Alberta's twenty-third Legislative Assembly and the Tory caucus repaired to the Pioneer's Cabin in Edmonton for a major party. They had every reason to celebrate. For the previous year their approval rating had floated between 60% and 70%. In a little over three years a $3.4 billion deficit had become a $2.2 billion surplus. Public expenditures were down 20% and oil and gas prices were firm. Alberta had the lowest minimum wage—and Albertans had grasped that legislating high minimums was a sure-fire job-killer. The province also had the lowest per capita costs in health care, which the government said meant that others were wasteful, not that Alberta was stingy. Alberta had the lowest per capita costs in education, which clearly did not mean that high school students were ill educated: the provinces' 13- and 16-year olds rated tops in the country on nation-wide tests in February, 1997. Many people attributed the fine showing to competition introduced by Charter Schools to the traditional provincial monopolies. In nation-wide surveys asking Canadians if they were satisfied with their quality of life, Albertans again came first, five points above respondents living in Ontario, and nine above the national average. Not surprisingly, the premier was happy to point out, this was the "Alberta advantage" in operation.

The 1997 Election

In March of 1996, a year before election day, Ralph Klein predicted the next election campaign would be boring.[1] He repeated the prediction several times for the rest of the year and during the month-long campaign was a promise he kept. In September, 1996, Treasurer Dinning had announced he would not run for re-election, as did the Justice Minister, Brian Evans, Ken Rostad who ran Federal and Intergovernmental Affairs, and Jack Ady in Advanced Education. The departure of these senior cabinet ministers consolidated Klein's control and hardly diminished his front-bench strength.

As in 1993, the opposition was weak, poorly financed, and in the case of the Liberals, badly led. The New Democrats had a new leader in Pam Barrett; she was invariably described as "feisty" and did, in fact, run a tenacious campaign. But the New Democrats were too far off the Alberta political map to have any effect, except to siphon votes away from the inept Liberals. Balancing the distant left wing was an equally distant right wing group in the revived Social Credit Party, led by Randy Thorsteinson. The Socreds were given some editorial support by *Alberta Report*, chiefly because of Thorsteinson's strong position on socially conservative issues, but most of his support was restricted to the Bible-belt east and west of Red Deer.

Spectators looking for a horse race were most disappointed by the Liberals. Leader Grant Mitchell wisely never tried to match Klein in a personality contest, but he was unskilled at packaging his policies as well. A couple of years earlier he had criticized Klein when the premier was on a trade mission in Texas and was branded a saboteur, a traitor, and worse.[2] When the last Dinning budget was passed Mitchell observed: "it was thin, limited. It talked only about budgets. It's a boardroom announcement." This was not incendiary rhetoric, and it turned out that his low-key campaign was deliberate. The strategic mind behind the Liberals' gray-on-gray approach was Harvey Locke, a Calgary environmental lawyer. Mitchell's performance on the televised leaders' debate, for example, was judged by nearly every observer to have been dismal, and yet according to Locke, "that debate went exactly the way we wanted it to go."[3] The Liberals costed their campaign promises at $663 million, but when the Tories said the bill was really closer to $5 billion, the Liberals were at a loss: all they could do was complain that bureaucrats should not have scrutinized the Liberal numbers. The Liberals' campaign strategy cost them dearly: they lost 14 seats, two of them to New Democrats.

There were a couple of minor blips in the Tory campaign as well, but they were contained within the party. Wayne Cao, a PC candidate in Calgary Fort, was accused by members of the Vietnamese community of having ties to the Communists in Viet Nam. He answered by stating that he had praised the Vietnamese government and sent them $200 to get his family out of the country and into Canada, which put the issue to rest.

A second incident had more potential. In Calgary West, Mike Nasser, a friend of the premier, and also his barber (and Colleen Klein's hairdresser), was forced to withdraw because of strong indications of irregular and questionable business practices. The Lebanese-Canadian Cultural Society, of which he was president, owed $57,000 in back taxes and the province was reviewing a grant for nearly $20,000 given to renovate the Society's headquarters. The department of labour was pursuing a complaint by a former apprentice hair-cutter, and others had taken Nasser to court to collect their vacation pay or to get him to return damage deposits on apartments they had rented from him. Despite his closeness to the premier, it was clear to everyone that he was not an attractive candidate. After he withdrew, ten days into the campaign, the Tories looked to Karen Kryczka, who had been the runner-up in the nomination race. She was vacationing in Mexico. By the time she returned, a couple of days after being contacted, her signs, campaign buttons and literature were on order, and when she met Ralph Klein she was greeted by posters indicating that she, too, was a member of Ralph's Team. Two weeks later she won by nearly a two-to-one margin over a former educational psychology professor at the University of Calgary, Paul Adams.

The Klein team coasted to victory with 63 out of 83 seats, up from 51 in 1993. The Tories claimed that a grateful electorate had rewarded them for a tough job well done. Others claimed that the "Alberta political culture" accounted for the PC win, along with "group think" regarding overspending.[4]

As we have seen from the data examined in Chapter Five, invoking such recondite causes, is not very helpful. Nevertheless, it was clear that, by the 1997 election, the Conservatives were no longer as interested in creative fiscal reform as they were in administering their new fiscal regime. They had managed the campaign well. They kept control of the agenda, often by flying Klein to remote daily events, which made it more difficult for the same reporters to cover his announcements. Grant Mitchell relied chiefly on a campaign bus—symbolically, it was still on a hoist when the election was called. Pam Barrett used a car. Things were much more comfortable for the Tories the second time around. On election night, however, the premier looked satisfied with his victory, not elated.

Taking their Bearings
In the throne speech prior to the 1997 election, the Lieutenant Governor noted that his government had "completed the main component of [its] election mandate a year ahead of schedule." This undoubted achievement led many observers to wonder what the premier would do for an encore. One thing seemed certain: since health, education, and welfare were the chief policy areas that had felt the impact of the government's spending reductions, the problems created by the Klein initiative as well as on-going questions of issue management would not simply disappear. Overall, the changes in welfare policy were probably the most successful. The record on education was mixed, and, even in the spring of 2000, health policy remains in flux and may be so for years to come.

Social Welfare:
Traditionally, Alberta's welfare programs, called Social Allowances, consisted of passive grants, which provided relatively low benefits to large

numbers of people. Through the early 1990s, Alberta and B.C., alone among the "have" provinces, provided more direct assistance than the national average. Moreover they were relatively successful in managing their welfare populations. Only 30% of Albertans, for example, thought that welfare was a major concern.[5]

In 1993, the new Family and Social Services minister, Mike Cardinal, changed the traditional passive program of doling out money. It was, he said, nothing but a system of perverse incentives intended to keep people with low education levels, little training, or parental obligations dependents of the state.[6] In its place he introduced an active educational and counselling policy, called Supports for Independence. It aimed at assisting people deemed capable of functioning in a competitive economy to do so. Children and the disabled were obviously excluded, and their level of support was left virtually unchanged under the new policy. The conduit for education and training was the Department of Advanced Education and Career Development, to which immediately were transferred about 20% of the welfare cases and some $60 million. At the same time eligibility criteria for people considered employable was tightened: if you were employable, to receive welfare you had to enroll in one or another Supports for Independence program. At the same time funds for transitional support for single parents were reduced. As a result, between December, 1992 and December, 1995, the provincial welfare caseload declined by over 50% from 98,642 to 49,001.[7]

Cuts to the welfare budget, however, were not across-the-board. Mike Cardinal was Cree. He had experienced welfare dependency first hand, and he had been a social worker. Here was a minister with enough experience and information not to have to cut the stupid way. Under his direction, welfare reform did not just tinker with better ways to serve the interests of "clients" or to advance more efficient ways of serving their interests: it also addressed the question of pride. This was a tricky as well as a difficult issue, because pride and interest are often antithetical. A welfare system that addressed only the interests of its clients ends up increasing dependency. The only ones whose pride is even engaged by such a system are social workers and liberal intellectuals who take pride in working on behalf of, or in support of, the "least advantaged." By so doing, they do not promote their own interests, which is precisely why they take pride in "helping" the least advantaged. Moreover, the government also believed that higher taxes would lead to taxpayer resentment that money was squandered on those whom Mayor Klein once stigmatized as "bums and creeps."[8]

The government addressed the question of pride by recovering an old and forgotten distinction between the deserving poor and mere sturdy beggars. The deserving were those who through age or infirmity could not work along with those who, for the time being, were inadequately educated or trained. The latter group were temporarily deserving because they had sufficient initiative to improve themselves. As long as only the genuinely deserving receive social assistance, there will be no stigma attached to it. This is why, in the past, it was perfectly acceptable to stigmatize sturdy beggars: an able-bodied, intellectually capable young man who accepts welfare and refuses to look for work or to prepare himself to look for work is, by definition as well as commonsensi-cally, undeserving of public support.

Most Albertans found the logic of welfare reform obvious and acceptable, and yet, there was resistance and criticism. Without providing any evidence, Margaret Philip, "Social Policy Reporter" for the *Globe and Mail*, stated: "There is evidence that some of these people [who disappeared from the Alberta welfare rolls] have turned up collecting welfare in other provinces." The sources for this unsubstantiated opinion were unnamed "poverty advocates" and "welfare advocates," which is to say, the very people whose client base was eroded by the new programs.

Jonathan Murphy, executive director of the Edmonton Social Planning Council and one of these "advocates," evoked the imagery of *The Grapes of Wrath*: "The spectre of the poor travelling across the country riding the rails and looking for work."[9] Murphy's "spectre" came more from his own imagination than Steinbeck's but it soon attained the status of another urban legend. Even couple of years later, when there was plenty of hard evidence of the success of the program, Karen Thibault, spokesperson for social workers who were members of the Alberta Union of Provincial Employees, remarked that the cuts in the welfare rolls have simply induced hardship: "It seems you have to go through torture before you can get some help," she said.[10]

Toronto pundit Jeffrey Simpson, took it upon himself to wonder whether all the missing Alberta welfare cases had been off-loaded onto the backs of British Columbians. Some B.C. politicians (including the premier) had complained about indigent Albertans, and B.C. did, after all, institute a three-month residency requirement for welfare recipients, which was later declared illegal.[11] A couple of weeks after Simpson's public musings, *Alberta Report* made an obvious comment: even if all 12,000 new welfare claimants in B.C. trekked across the Great Divide to become lotus-eaters, "that still leaves 40,000 former welfare cases unaccounted for."[12]

In June, 1997 the Canada West Foundation delivered to the Minister of Family and Social Services a report, *Where are they Now? Assessing the Impact of Welfare Reform on Former Recipients, 1993-1996*.[13] It was based on a random sample, stratified by region and family type, of former Supports for Independence recipients. Respondents tended to be young, single, low-wage earners born in Canada. The most significant finding of the study was that two-thirds of the respondents had jobs and the vast majority of them said their lives had improved both materially and spiritually since going off welfare. No policy can ever be perfect, not least of all because of the need to reconcile pride and interest. Even so, the Supports for Independence program was undoubtedly a success, and one of the reasons was that it took pride into account. It is something of a reflection on contemporary journalists, not to mention social workers, that the importance of pride is so ill understood.

Education:
As noted above, education, unlike welfare and health care, received relatively small reductions in funding. Moreover, the structural changes were ambivalent in their effects. Probably the most high profile and experimental change involved Charter Schools. These schools are autonomous but are funded by local Catholic or public school boards and are required to offer innovative programs not available from the major provincial boards. Moreover, they are allowed to hire only teachers approved by the Alberta Teachers Association.

Even within those restraints, a number of interesting innovations were undertaken by parents eager to escape the regular programs of instruction. In January, 1995 the Calgary Public Board gave approval for the first "workplace school." It was to occupy space in the Alberta Government Telephones (AGT) building and would serve primarily the children of AGT employees.[14] This was essentially a regular school in a commercial downtown location. It would help parents working at AGT and would reduce the number of children being bussed. Even so, members of the Calgary Public Board had grave misgivings about taking parents' requests into consideration at all, especially in a commercial context. Jennifer Pollock, Vice-Chairman of the Calgary Public Board, expressed her concern about the "values" of AGT influencing the minds of young scholars, but went on to say: "I can't say I would feel the same way about a large American-based oil company," by which she meant that the "values" of AGT were barely acceptable but that those of such an oil company would not be.

A few months later the Edmonton Public School Board approved the creation of Nellie McClung School, named after one of Alberta's pioneer feminists which offered a slightly modified curriculum with an emphasis on independent studies.[15] This was not quite a charter school either; rather it was experimental insofar as it accepted only girls and required them to wear uniforms. Edmonton Public Board also funded a Christian school, called Logos. Their action was controversial, and was opposed by the Alberta

Teachers Association. One unnamed Board member acknowledged that the decision was made in order to keep students in the public system rather than encourage more private, religiously grounded schools.[16]

Many of the charter schools went quietly about their business, offering programs with special emphasis on art, music, dance, and the like. The Charter School of Commerce in Calgary again raised the issue of "values." Students were required to wear suits, ties, and dress shoes (no jeans and boots for these cowtown scholars); the curriculum was centred on business transactions, report writing, and so on. Educational psychology professors pronounced on the malign effects that were bound to follow from having students tote briefcases to class, and concerned members of the Calgary Public Board wondered whether the whole experiment was "morally right."[17]

It is certainly true that per pupil expenditures were reduced with the spending cuts, and that teachers' salaries came down, both relatively and absolutely, but there is no evidence that the education of young Albertans suffered as a result.[18] It is also true that provincial per pupil expenditures on private schools increased from 50% to 60% of the public per pupil rate, but neither the number of private schools nor of charter schools ever became sufficiently large to mount a serious competitive challenge to the large boards.[19] The centralization of 141 boards into 57 gave the education bureaucracy greater, not less control over finance, curriculum, and staffing. There was, it seems, never any intention to cut costs sufficiently to enable parents to play a more important role in their children's education. More radical measures, such as vouchers, were not even considered. As one observer said, "established bureaucrats, political interests, and unions appear to have defeated" the impetus for reform.[20] Even so, by the end of 1999 ten charter schools were operating and five more were scheduled to open over the following eighteen months, thus reaching the total permitted under the act.[21]

Health care:
The most contentious of the changes introduced by the Klein government dealt with health care. Three obstacles have proved to be particularly challenging. The first centred on inevitable difficulties associated with reorganizing such a complex structure so heavily freighted with human anxieties. Second was the related problem of staffing the reorganized hospitals and health authorities, and the third was the issue of the Canada Health Act (CHA) and the conflict between Ottawa and Edmonton over its proper interpretation.

Saskatchewan, New Zealand and the U.K. had all established regional health care systems to coordinate hospitals, public-health units, home-care facilities and the like before Alberta collapsed 200 hospital boards into 17 Regional Health Authorities (RHAs). Such large-scale, administrative consolidation was bound to involve transaction costs. They became semi-permanent however because the boundaries to the RHAs were drawn on the basis of politics rather than health care considerations. Had the borders of the RHAs been better designed, there might have been fewer patients moving among them and so no need to establish a complex accounting system to keep track of patients treated outside their "home" RHA. However, the strong rural support given to the Klein government has made it politically difficult to close rural and small-town hospitals. Yet at the same time, the fact that only the Capital RHA and the Calgary RHA are capable of providing the full-range of services has led to a number of problems.

For example, if you are an expectant mother living just beyond the boundary of the Calgary RHA, you may prefer to have your child delivered in a big modern urban hospital. As a result, the local small-town hospital will be under-utilized and the city facility will be over-utilized. Moreover, per capita funding, if nominally equal, will result in over-funding of the small facility and under-funding of the larger one, which will then require additional funds to be allocated to the urban RHAs. At the same time, they will have to make a case for supplementary funding, which in turn transforms the RHAs into lobby groups. Between 1993 and 1999, this hypothetical scenario was repeated time and again, which had the effect of both introducing uncertainty and increasing costs.[22]

Then, in November, 1995, 120 laundry workers at the Calgary General Hospital went on strike. They had lost a competition with K-Bro Linen Systems of Edmonton when laundry service was put out to competitive tender despite the fact that laundry workers had already taken a 28% cut in their wages. It was bad enough that laundry workers were poorly paid; trucking Calgary's dirty linen to Edmonton to wash it made the laundry workers a focus both of public sympathy and of public anxiety over changes to the health care system in general. For the first time, the Premier intervened directly: the laundry workers' jobs were saved, Calgary's laundry was washed at home, and critics, both in the unions and among those who questioned the government's long-term commitment to fiscal probity, declared that the Premier had done what he had promised he never would do. Ralph "blinked" in the face of pressure from a particular group.[23]

Within a year, *Alberta Report* observed, "the Klein government is restoring health care spending so fast that it has developed a full-fledged case of political Tourette's disease."[24] The next blink was in the face of the doctors who had never been happy with the consolidation of hospital administration into fewer, larger, and more remote RHAs. The elimination of many senior and middle management positions brought about immediate efficiencies and cost savings, but at the same time it changed the place of physicians in the medical hierarchy. Many of the most vocal complaints, who also occupied leadership positions in the Alberta Medical Association, said they had not been sufficiently consulted in the reorganization.

One particular demand from RHA management was especially irksome: doctors had to account for the use they made of RHA resources, not the resources of individual hospitals. Many expressed nostalgia for the good old pre-RHA days of individual hospital boards. In the old days, duplication and redundancy meant that specialized facilities were available in many of the large hospitals; under the RHAs, specialized facilities were rationalized and concentrated in particular hospitals scattered across the RHA. After reorganization, for example, there might be only one hospital in Edmonton where neo-natal brain surgery could be performed. Likewise other specialized procedures could be undertaken only at one or two facilities across the province. Looked at from the perspective of provincial or even of RHA administrators, such specialization was simply a sensible and efficient allocation of limited resources.

The doctors saw it differently. They were given admitting privileges to all the RHA facilities, but their patients could be in several locations, each of whom may have required specialized treatment available only at one specific hospital. From the point of view of the attending physician, it was a great inconvenience to have patients scattered around the RHA using the specialized facilities. Thus the appeal to physicians of the old-style redundancy where a single hospital could provide many specialized treatments. In addition, of course, the RHA-wide rationalization of redundancies in specialized facilities greatly increased physicians' non-billable travel time.

Hospitals take 75% of the health care budget, employ 20,000 people and are governed and paid by the RHAs. Doctors take the rest; there are around 4,300 of them and they are paid directly by the province. Between 1993 and 1995, the RHAs succeeded in reducing expenditures by 10% but doctors bills were up by four percent. Doctors had agreed to a fee-schedule roll back of 5%, as had other public sector employees, but then they simply saw more patients, which more than made up the difference. They refused to agree to a $100 million cut to their total fees and launched a lavish media operation against the government. Using a toll-free phone number, the AMA invited Albertans to "tell us where it hurts." They then publicized the complaints of the ill and blamed the government for deteriorating service. The result: cuts were restored and assurances given that the AMA would be consulted in the future.[25]

Concessions to the doctors were followed by additional "reinvesting" in RHAs.[26] The dam had been burst, and the highly effective anxiety-inducing media blitz by the province's MDs did the trick. The nurses were next. Even though they were paid by the RHAs, since those bodies were appointed by the government, the government was quite properly held responsible for over a year of fruitless negotiations and then for an impending strike scheduled to take place just before the 1997 election.[27] Wages were one element in the conflict between the United Nurses of Alberta and the RHAs, but, as with the physicians, there were governance issues as well. Just as the doctors were keen to defend their turf against RHA administrators, the nurses were particularly concerned to obtain flexible nurse-to-patient ratios. This too directly challenged the authority of RHA administrators.

The original strategy of the government included the use of private clinics to relieve the inevitable bottlenecks that accompanied the transition to the RHA-based system. To this end they hired Jane Fulton as Deputy Minister in July, 1995. She was said to be an advocate of private medical care, the notorious, Americanized, "two-tiered" system, but she called herself a "competitive socialist" and claimed as well to be a member of the NDP.[28]

She made a number of other claims as well, and these were her undoing. In a series of prominent stories in the *Globe and Mail*, Jane Coutts, the health holicy reporter, indicated that Dr. Fulton had exaggerated some of her achievements. She said she was a "visiting professor" at several important U.S. universities when it would have been more accurate to say she was a professor visiting the university to give a lecture or attend a conference.[29] The *Globe* reporter did not indicate where she had learned about Fulton's inflated resumé beyond noting it was brought to light by "an investigation by the *Globe and Mail*," and the Alberta Health Minister, Shirley McClellan, said she sensed "a bit of a witch hunt." An investigation by the provincial Public Service Commissioner confirmed that Fulton had "overstated" some of the biographical details in her resumé but did not mislead the province regarding her qualifications.[30] In any event, Fulton's credibility was impaired, the government lost a strong bureaucratic voice, and within a year she was gone from the deputy minister's job.

Fulton was hired originally because she strongly believed in freedom of choice for health care. Even if she had been scruptuously accurate in her resumé details, she, McClellan, and Klein still would have run afoul of the federal government. As early as November, 1994, federal health minister Diane Marleau told the provinces they were not to permit private clinics to charge facility fees. These fees are charged to cover rent, supplies, heat and light, and the services of the physician are billed to the province. In January, 1995, Ms. Marleau gave the province nine months to comply or their grants would be reduced by the dollar amounts charged for facility fees.[31]

To the federal government, facility fees were subsidies, and so evidence of a two-tier system. In April, at a provincial health ministers' meeting, Shirley McClelland tried to defend the Klein government's position but met with no success. The Prime Minister then weighed in to signal that Ottawa would not allow any move toward free market health care.[32] Alberta argued that permitting *clinics* to charge facility fees in fact shortened the waiting time for *hospitals*; semi-private clinics, for example, would draw patients out of the public line-up for specialized procedures such as cataract surgery or magnetic resonance imaging. This was the first attempt by any provincial government to find an innovative alternative to the rigid and increasingly unworkable formulas of the Canada Health Act (CHA).

It was clear to Alberta that they were the target of the federal decree. Ottawa's position, if consistently applied, would mean that private abortion clinics in every province would also be illegal, and so would clinics that charge "tray fees," to cover the cost of supplies for procedures done in a physician's office. It was not consistently applied: some facilities that charged tray fees, for example, were not on Marleau's list of prohibited medical centres.[33] When October, 1995 rolled around, Marleau's edict came into force and Ottawa began deducting over $400,000 a month from Alberta's transfer account. Alberta, however, did not go to court as it had said it would, and by 1 July, 1996 that particular experiment was over.

In May, 1997 another controversy between Alberta and the federal Liberals arose, this time over the plan of the Health Resources Group, Inc. (HRG) to open a private facility on two floors of the idle Grace Hospital in Calgary. The new federal health minister, David Dingwall, said that the proposal violates the "spirit" of the CHA and would not be allowed to proceed. If necessary, Dingwall said, he would see the CHA amended to prohibit such a scheme.[34]

The HRG proposal would serve third-party insurance plans, uninsured foreign visitors, and people seeking non-medically necessary treatment, none of which was prohibited by the CHA. Klein wrote to the Prime Minister in protest of Dingwall's remarks. "This arbitrary and ill-informed declaration of public health policy is unacceptable," Klein said. He pointed out that HRG would break no law, as Dingwall himself allowed, and that the Calgary group would do only what the King's Health Centre in Toronto was already doing. The significance of

Dingwall's declaration and Klein's response was that *no* experiments, even if they did not contravene the CHA, would be tolerated.[35]

By the start of 1999, it seemed that the Klein government had abandoned health care reform.[36] At the Conservative Party's annual convention in November in Jasper, the Premier responded to fears that the Party had grown complacent and was no longer interested in innovation. Klein reminded his audience of all the pioneering policies that his governments had introduced and assured them that further changes were coming. "We've got to find new ways of delivering [health care] service," he said. "We're saying: 'Does it violate the Canada Health Act? If it doesn't violate the Canada Health Act, why not?'"[37] He went on to explain that, for example, private companies already provided long-term care, and other changes would follow. Later in November, for example, Klein announced that the government planned to allow RHAs to contract out some procedures, such as hip replacements and laser eye surgery, to "private health facilities," provided the non-taxpayer supported outfits provided a net benefit to the health care system as a whole. His remarks were greeted with considerable skepticism from the advocates of a state monopoly in health care delivery of services.[38]

Most recently the Klein government has tabled Bill 11—The Health Care Protection Act— which proposes to give RHAs the option to contract out (i.e., to out-source) minor surgical services (some of which may require overnight care) to private health facilities, provided it improves access, increases cost-efficiency, reduces waiting lists, and passes the scrutiny of the College of Physicians and surgeons and the Health Minister. Within a short time, critics of Bill 11, most of which, such as the public-sector unions, have a vested interest in maintaining the status quo, have begun to mount a significant attack against the government's proposed plan. The opposition Liberals, union workers, and lobby groups such as the Friends of Medicare have held a number of town hall meetings and taken up a massive media effort in an attempt to convince Albertans that Bill 11 is part of a master plan by the government to dismantle publicly funded health care. The government appears to have taken the criticism to heart and retaliated with its own public relations campaign.

Bill 11 has also aroused the attention of federal health minister Allan Rock, who declared that out-sourcing of services would not reduce costs and improve access—even though the most comprehensive studies contradict the federal minister's claim.[39] When Rock was backed by the prime minister and then flew into Calgary and blasted Bill 11 before a picked audience of Liberal supporters, the premier said in a one-sentence letter to the prime minister that Rock's conduct was a "disgrace."[40] Klein then elaborated his view of the federal government at a fund-raiser by indicating the Liberals were biased against Alberta for the worst kind of political reasons. Klein said he considers health care reform, within the restrictions of the CHA, to be a leadership initiative, akin to the fiscal reforms of 1993.[41] In view of persistent polling information that indicates Canadians and Albertans are very concerned about health care reform and are *not* averse to imposing user fees, which are still prohibited by the CHA, it seems obvious that the debate over health care and the CHA will intensify in the months and years ahead.[42]

Handling the Surplus

Jim Dinning's last budget, delivered on 11 February, 1997, was mostly self-congratulation. *Budget '97* "keeps us on track," he said. It "sticks with what works," to "build the right climate for growth in Alberta's economy so business and industry will prosper and so Albertans will see more jobs—good paying, high quality jobs." As noted above, economic prosperity was the prime objective all along and expenditure reduction was the means. Some ten weeks later, Stockwell Day, the new Treasurer presented a "Post-Election Update." Day is usually billed as a social conservative and, because of his duties as an assistant pastor, a theo-con. The *Toronto Star*, with its customary sympathy for Alberta political leaders, called him a "gay-bashing abortion-hater." Leaving the name-calling aside, Treasurer Day changed very few of Dinning's numbers and, despite alterations in Dinning's narrative style, the "Update" was essentially the same document as *Budget '97*. There was, however, one issue that might be ignored, postponed, and obscured with self-congratulatory rhetoric in the lead-up to the election, but eventually would have to be faced: what to do with the surplus?

In FY 1996-97 Alberta would have a budgetary surplus of nearly $3 billion, despite a cut in transfers from Ottawa of $390 million. On the revenue side, the surplus resulted from higher than expected oil and gas prices ($1.4 billion in royalties), from high tax revenues ($463 million), and from Heritage Fund earnings ($932 million). On the expenditure side, a decline of $595 million was posted, but $572 million of that was a result of low debt-servicing costs and a drop in pension obligations, not deep cuts to program spending. Indeed, considerable improvization or "emergency funding" had been dispensed to the RHAs in order to keep the health care system intact.

In addition, the *1995 Balanced Budget and Debt Retirement Act* had been made more flexible through amendments. "Surplus" revenue on the books at the end of the fiscal year could not be carried over but, as in the original act, had to be applied to the debt. During the year, however, the government could increase spending provided it could still meet the end-of-year target of $450 million dedicated to debt reduction. In other words, the legal impediment against increased spending during the year was lifted.

Editorial writes and other commentators elsewhere in Canada made light of the surplus problem. "How could spending extra money be a problem?" they asked. "What a great problem to have! Wouldn't it be great if Paul Martin had the same problem?" In fact, such derisory comments are misplaced. There may not be much of a financial problem, but there certainly is a leadership problem. In 1932, Winston Churchill asked "is the march of events ordered and guided by eminent men [and women], or do our leaders merely fall into their places at the heads of the moving columns?" In December, 1992, when Klein was elected Tory leader, he answered that question unequivocally. In 1997 he had to answer it again: how would he guide events under the new fiscal circumstances?

Some time prior to the March 1997 election the Tories decided on a course of action that indicated (after the fact) that they would no longer lead by ordering events, but would fall into place at the head of a moving and unstable column of public opinion. They would justify their abdication of genuine leadership by rhetorical gestures in the direction of populism. Their problem was simple: they knew they would win the election, but they had no idea what to do next. The solution: an administrative process similar to the 1993 Red Deer Budget Roundtable. There would be extensive consultation over the summer leading up to a "Growth Summit" held in September, 1997 in Edmonton.[43]

The issue to be discussed over the following five months was *how* to "reinvest," an obvious euphemism for spending, and not *whether* to do so. An Environics West poll taken in midsummer indicated genuine concern among Albertans over where the government was headed, especially after they announced there would be no fall sitting of the Legislature.[44] It looked as if the extra-parliamentary activity leading to the Growth Summit would be a substitute for parliamentary government. Moreover, by focussing on how to increase expenditures, the government could appeal to those who voted against them in the spring without having to answer opposition questions in the house. In short, the initiative was undertaken by an executive that appeared to be abandoning its previous course of fiscal restraint and was afraid to justify its new course of action before the Legislative Assembly of the province.

When parliamentary government is subverted in this way the executive receives neither support nor advice from the assembly. Populist rhetoric may conjure up the subtle support of "the people," the "folks" to whom the premier often directed his words, but unless it is inspired by its own vision, the executive still must receive advice from somewhere. It was clear, after the 1997 victory, that vision was the one thing needed by the government, which meant it was particularly important to attend to the voices the executive chose to hear. The Premier indicated that the recommendations of the Growth Summit would be refined into the next Throne Speech, scheduled for early 1998. In effect, the Growth Summit would replace both the legislature and the Tory caucus.

The non-partisan and non-parliamentary nature of the exercise was indicated by the selection of Michael Percy, a former Liberal MLA and at the time dean of business at the University of Alberta, as co-chairman along with Premier Klein. Moreover, by choosing the Shaw Centre in Edmonton to be the venue, the government was holding out an olive branch to the city that most resented the expenditure reduction. There was some expectation that there would be a dramatic conflict between tax-cutters and tax-spenders, but the astute exercise of agenda-control placed the tax-cutters and their dry, bean-counting arguments first. Heads nodded in agreement or nodded off to sleep but then awoke to a rising chorus of compassionate pleas for increased spending. Indeed, if you look at who was *not* invited you have a clear indication of what the government wanted to achieve. There were no representatives of the Alberta Taxpayers' Federation. The National Citizens Coalition was absent along with the voluntary sector and what *Alberta Report* called "non-state charities" such as the United Way, the Boy Scouts, and the Red Cross. The Centre for Prairie Agriculture, a free-market organization, was not there and neither were any representatives of private or charter schools and certainly not anyone who advocated a voucher program for education.

A total of 243 measures were adopted, but most of them were sufficiently vague that the government could pick and choose and do what it wanted. All, however, pointed to an obvious result: *health, education, and infrastructure "needed" more government spending.* Big government, directed by a benevolent executive without scrutiny from the legislature, was good; expenditure reduction was out of the question.[45] It was unclear, however, whether it was through inadvertence that the executive heard only advice that advocated a return to the default position endemic to Canadian politics or whether they deliberately chose participants who would demand the government do something, and get bigger in order to do it. It was probably a little of both. The government used the Growth Summit to convince those who were in favour of staying the course, the emphatic fiscal conservatives, that politically they had no choice. They were doing what Albertans wanted, but they were not going to submit themselves to the taunts of the official opposition.

The response of interested parties and less interested observers of the Growth Summit exercise in executive action was also significant. Initially for example, the Alberta Federation of Labour refused to have anything to do with the process. Carol Anne Deane, president of the 37,000-member Alberta Union of Public Employees, said, "we are suspicious that part of this exercise is to keep down our wages."[46] At the end of the day, however, at least some of the leadership of the big labour unions were pleased with the results.[47]

Alberta Report, on the other hand, was not. Brian Mulawka's report, called "The Gimmie Summit," began:

> It was a scene worthy of the court of Louis XIV. In the cavernous hall of Edmonton's Shaw conference center, delegates to the Alberta Growth Summit brought the proceedings to a close with a kind of supplication ceremony before Premier Ralph Klein. As 100 participants sat in a semi-circle surrounding the premier, each of the eight "sector leaders" came forward to present him with their group's request for alms from the public purse. None of them actually got down on bended knee, but they nonetheless looked the part of fawning courtiers competing for the beneficence of the emperor.[48]

Similarly, in the pages of the *Globe and Mail*, Calgary journalist George Koch speculated that the Growth Summit was a sign that Klein's commitment to fiscal conservatism was exhausted and that he was now eager to spend the surplus. He viewed the new mood as a bad sign. "Leading from the rear is fine, as long as there is an obvious popular consensus. But now Albertans themselves appear unsure." In the absence of consensus, creative leadership, not executive manipulation, was needed. By squandering his moral leadership with a return to the easy ways of his predecessors, Premier Klein, said Koch, was doing the entire nation a disservice. Instead of pushing ahead with substantial education and health care reform

> after his one big achievement, balancing the budget, Mr. Klein has stalled. Privatizing campground operations hardly qualifies as major reform. That he refuses to follow up with the next logical step—comprehensive reform, and reduction of taxes—is a tragedy for overtaxed working families, and not just in Alberta.[49]

A week later the premier replied to the *Globe and Mail* that reinvestment was not big spending: "we have to reinvest in these systems [i.e., education, health care, and infrastructure] to accommodate the pressures of growth. That's the government's job. It's that simple." Logically, of course, if the government's goal remained prosperity, "reinvestment," particularly in education, and infrastructure might well be necessary. Klein did not single out these areas, however, but went on to reaffirmed that there would be no deficit financing and no tax *increases*.[50] The Premier of Alberta does not usually answer his critics by writing a letter to the editor. It would appear that Koch had touched a sensitive issue.

The annual Tory convention endorsed the Growth Summit proposals, and Treasurer Day hinted in November, 1997 that the surplus was near to $2 billion.[51] On 8 January, 1998 the premier again addressed the province on TV. He stressed that the government was following consistently the principles he had first articulated in his 1994 speech to the province and that they were consistent with the need to reinvest.[52] At the end of January, 225 days after the Legislative Assembly dispersed for the summer, the Lieutenant Governor read a predictable (because widely leaked) speech from the throne. Treasurer Day delivered his budget, entitled *Agenda for Opportunity*, on 12 February, 1998. About the only new item was a modification in the rules for debt reduction. The first $1 billion of a budgetary surplus would be applied directly to the debt; the next $250 million could be directed at "one-time relief" for "pressure points," and the balance to additional debt reduction.[53]

Slightly over a year later Treasurer Day delivered his third budget. It captured many headlines because it proposed for 2002 to decouple Alberta's provincial income tax from the federal tax. Instead of paying a percentage of the federal tax, the new regime would be a flat tax on income. This would effectively end "bracket creep," at least for the province. Day also ended the income surtax and provided additional tax relief for lower income and single-earner families.[54] By and large the budget was well received since it managed to combine increased spending, the promise of lower taxes, and some immediate tax relief.[55] In some respects, however, it was a compromise budget: per capita expenditures were down from the high point of 1986, but up from Dinning's 1996 budget.[56] Moreover, with revenue projections up 1.6% but expenditures up 4.4%, serious tax reductions were not on the agenda.

Budget 2000 was entitled *New Century, Bold Plans*. It too reaffirmed the government's commitment to maintaining balanced budgets and debt repayment, with the expectation of reducing the accumulated debt by another $1.2 billion over the next three years. There was again more money for health and education, although it was selective in the sense of being targeted at those areas that required it the most—such as the need for more front-line staff. There was a new six point plan for health care and $60 million reduction in user fees, which was a step toward making it easier to do business and therefore boost economic development. But the key focus of *Budget 2000*, like its predecessor, was on tax cuts and ending bracket creep, measures that now would go into affect starting January 2001. Treasurer Day moved the delivery of this budget ahead of schedule in order to pressure his federal counterpart to follow his lead. To everyone's surprise, a few days later, Finance Minister Martin unveiled his budget and announced that his government would also be re-indexing tax exemptions to inflation. The provincial treasurer praised his federal counterpart for following where Alberta had led and urged him to further boldness.

VLTs and ATB
Two additional financial issues arose to trouble the second Klein government. On the revenue side was the question of video lottery terminals (VLTs) and the increasing contribution they made to the province's bottom line. On the expenditure side were Alberta Treasury Branches (ATB) and the contribution ATB made to the operational solvency of West Edmonton Mall (WEM).

ATB came into being in 1938 with $200,000 in government capital and the expectation that it would disappear within five years. It was funded in order to extend refinancing to depression-wracked farmers at the time when the large chartered banks, with headquarters in remote cities, were foreclosing at an alarming rate. The ATB offices were, literally, branches of the Treasury Department. Not until 1995 was a board of directors created, and by then it had long been acting all but in name as a bank.

In 1997, at a time when chartered banks were earning record profits, ATB lost $27 million. One of the reasons for its dismal performance was a series of very bad loans. Between 1978 and 1993 ATB lost about $2.3 billion, mostly through unsecured or under-secured loans to well connected Tories such as: Nader Ghermezian of West Edmonton Mall ($487 million), Peter Pocklington ($120 million), real estate developer Norm Green ($120 million), and financial wizard Larry Ryckman, who also owned the CFL Calgary Stampeders for a time ($9 million).

The WEM loan was the big one, and it caught the attention of most Albertans, as well as people interested in the bank business elsewhere. West Edmonton Mall is a huge postmodern collection of discontinuities. It is built on the premise that shopping is entertainment and boasts 15,000 employees along with 150,000 light fixtures, a water slide, more submarines than the Canadian Navy, and an NHL size ice sheet. But big boxes can get too big, and by 1993 it had defaulted on $400 million in loans. Alberta Treasury Branches bailed out the WEM owners, the Triple

Five Corporation, which is owned by the Gheremezian family; $240 million later, WEM still had a high vacancy rate—but it remained very popular with people from Fort McMurray and High Prairie, even if local Edmontonians preferred a vibrant downtown as a place to shop, and Calgarians laughed at the unseemliness of their northern cousins allowing such monsters to be erected at all.

The terms and the circumstances surrounding the WEM loan were the subject of increasing public scrutiny from the spring of 1997 until the winter of 1999.[57] By late 1998, ATB was suing its former acting superintendent for $450 million, charging among other things that he had taken bribes from WEM in exchange for approving their loan package. The former ATB employee involved, Elmer Leahy, then countersued, claiming he was acting under instructions of Ralph Klein, Jim Dinning and Ken Kowalski—at the time still Deputy Premier. The politicians all denied Leahy's allegations.

Reports in the *Calgary Herald* by the legislative reporter, Don Martin, argued that Dinning and Kowalski had diametrically opposed views regarding WEM. Dinning was prepared to see it sold off to a receiver, even one headquartered in Toronto; Kowalski was equally committed to a "made-in-Alberta" solution to WEM's woes, and that meant an ATB solution.[58] When the auditor general issued his report in mid-February, 1999, he found no evidence that any politician interfered directly in the operations of ATB or had ordered the WEM loan package approved. He did, however, say as well that there was "no commercial justification" for the loans, that both Klein and Kowalski exerted "influence" on ATB, and that neither Leahy nor the Ghermezians were willing to cooperate with him so that many facts remain unknown.[59] The government seemed to have dodged a bullet, not acted in a statesmanlike manner.

In December, 1997, the Canada West Foundation began to call into question the increased reliance of the Klein government on revenues generated from gambling on VLTs. A 16-page report by Garry Smith of the University of Alberta indicated that the government would be well advised to reexamine the entire VLT question. At the time the Smith Report appeared, there were nearly 6,000 of these fast, colourful and noisy machines in the province. There had been no public debate during the five years since they first appeared, notwithstanding the fact that, by 1996, the government was netting more than half a billion dollars from VLT operations.

According to Smith, the great appeal of VLTs comes not just from the thrill of someday hitting the jackpot, but from the ability of the machines to provide a kind of electronic companionship that appeals primarily to the lonely, the unhappy, and the vulnerable. They appeal to politicians because they are a dependable cash cow that can be justified by arguing that the proceeds go to the "disadvantaged." In fact, things are a bit more complex than that.

As an illustration, consider the VLT operations in Fort McMurray. In 1997 there were 97 VLTs distributed among 17 bars. The machines had swallowed $43 million the year before, paying out $30 million, for a 70% payback. The government take was $11 million or 26% and the hotel and bar owners raked in $2 million or 4%. Prior to the advent of VLTs there were only small stakes bingo and charity casinos staffed by volunteers and held as local fund-raisers for community projects. After the introduction of VLTs, the local school band or the bantam hockey team had lost a means to raise funds locally—and, incidentally, increase social capital by undertaking genuine "community-building." Instead, in the example of Fort McMurray, they had to settle for their share of the $1.22 million that the government decided to return directly to the community for sports and culture. That was less than 10% of the government take, but more important, the money was doled out by bureaucrats from control central in Edmonton. That takes away a lot of initiative from volunteers in the community to help themselves and increases dependency on government.

A common misconception, encouraged by the government, is that the bulk of gambling revenues go to support worthy causes in the arts, research, amateur sports, and community projects. In fact there are no segregated accounts. Nearly all the VLT take, along with the pot from other forms of gambling, ends up in general revenues, indistinguishable from the proceeds of taxes, royalties and fees. Likewise, all government expenditures, whether for roads or the arts, are taken from general revenues. This means that money returned to Fort McMurray to support the bantam hockey team and earmarked as VLT money is, in fact, just another centrally administered government grant, no different than a capital allocation to build a bridge or pave a road.

Opposition to VLTs is not based on a dislike of having previously local sources of community activity centralized in the provincial capital. For opponents, gambling is simply wrong. Gambling, these critics say, is based on the pernicious and malign doctrine that rewards come from luck, not hard work. Initially the opposition was found among social conservatives whose only temptation was to vote for a party to the right of the Tories, if there was one. Later the Ukrainian and Roman Catholic churches joined their mostly Protestant brethren. They found allies in community groups who were opposed not to gambling but to VLTs having replaced bingos and casinos.

In Calgary opposition was led by a long-time Tory supporter, Jim Gray. In addition to being one of the most successful oilmen in the city, Gray was a prominent community activist and member of numerous non-profit boards, including that of the Canada West Foundation, which has done the most extensive studies of the VLT question.[60] One of the results of this articulate and well supported discussion of the effects of VLTs on Albertans was that the premier called a "gambling summit" for April 1998. As with the other summits, this one was carefully organized: the 125 delegates who gathered in Medicine Hat were told they would have to reach a consensus. Since both pro- and anti-gambling advocates were present, it was almost guaranteed that the recommendations would be vague.[61] Moreover, they were asked to discuss the pros and cons of gambling, not whether it was appropriate for the government to receive such large amounts of money from such a source.

In July, 1998, The Summit Conference Report appeared and recommended that the province:

(1) dedicate more resources to research on issues such as the social impact of gambling and emerging gambling activities; (2) restrict gambling to those at least 18 years old; (3) continue the charitable model of bingos and casinos; (4) not direct gambling profits to the province's General Revenue Fund; (5) direct all gambling profits to non-profit community initiatives; (6) increase visibility of gambling treatment programs; (7) improve disclosure of gambling activity to better inform citizens; and (8) update and adhere to a set of guiding principles for gambling in Alberta.[62]

The biggest change would have been to segregate gambling revenues from general revenues and use them solely for community purposes. If that were done, the CWF report observed it would mean "a fundamental change in the way the provinces use lottery funds."

In August, 1999 the province came up with a policy that did not satisfy critics of gambling and may or may not conform to the recommendation that the funds be used in response to community initiatives. Murray Smith, the minister responsible for gambling, said that school boards, health authorities and chambers of commerce from around the province had approached his office with proposals for infrastructure development. He suggested that up to a third of lottery revenue could be used for bridges, highways and schools.[63] Whether this is laundering gambling money, as critics say, or responding to community initiatives, when lottery revenue exceeds oil revenue by $300 million, as it did in FY 1998-99, there was simply no way that the entire proceeds from gambling could be spent on the likes of junior hockey and museums.

Without question, the financial achievements of the Klein government have been successful. By 1996 or so, they were well on the way to achieving the objectives they had set out in 1993. At the same time, it would appear that the success of the government brought additional problems. In the following chapter we consider them in more detail.

CHAPTER SEVEN

LESSONS LEARNED
OPPORTUNITIES MISSED

After two election victories and seven years in office, the results achieved by the Klein governments are impressive. They have rebalanced the provincial budget, established an economic climate that his enabled large numbers of Albertans and Canadians from other provinces to find work, and have restructured a great deal of the government apparatus. Other governments would doubtless benefit from policies modelled on those of Alberta. And yet, as we have seen in the previous chapter, evidence beginning to appear in 1996 and 1997 indicates that the Government of Alberta was deviating from its own game plan and its own program. There are lessons useful to other governments there as well.

The first question to consider, therefore, is whether the policy initiatives undertaken by the Government of Alberta have attained (or will attain) the long- and short-term goals that the government set for themselves. This is a difficult issue about which to draw firm conclusions. According to Aristotle, politics is a matter of *praxis*, of acting and doing, not of *poesis*, of making. There are no finished political products; not even constitutions, which are supposed to endure, are ever really finished products. They must be interpreted by judges, for example, and can always be amended. Politics generally speaking is the original never-ending story. This means that firm and absolute judgements can hardly ever be made with confidence.

Therefore, in order to understand what the Klein government has actually achieved, it is first necessary to recall the problems they faced. If Osborne and Gaebler were right in *Reinventing Government* and *the* problem is centred upon the structure of governance, on the inability of industrial-model bureaucracies to do their job, then there are plenty of lessons available for other governments to learn—or rather to put into practice according to local circumstances. Privatization or deregulation, for example, are not new and can be introduced more or less along the lines that have been followed in Alberta or, indeed, in other places.[1]

The difficulty is that one cannot simply say with certainty that there is a clear causal relationship between changes to the structure of the Alberta government and changes to the economy, though the government may take every opportunity to claim there is a direct connection between theory and practice, strategy and execution. In his 1995 talk to the Fraser Institute, for example, Klein said:

Since the Alberta government began to get out of people's lives 23 months ago, and keep taxes low, oil and gas activity is up, farm income is up, livestock earnings are up, manufacturing shipments and exports are up, our labour participation rate is the highest in the country, and 50,000 new jobs in the last 18 months have given Alberta an unemployment rate of 7.2%, which is a dramatic drop. Government spending is down, and reorganized and refocused health, education, and social service programs still remain of the highest quality.[2]

Even so, because politics is the story of human action and initiative it is full of surprises, which is to say it is never as predictable, mechanical, or clear as perhaps one would like. It is often easier to see how bad government programs can bring ruin to their citizens than how good ones can induce prosperity.

Lessons from Alberta

Bearing in mind the preceding qualifications, there are a number of useful lessons to be learned from the Alberta experience. Consolidating school and hospital boards, which Alberta did not pioneer, is an easy way for governments to save money with no real reduction in services; some parts of universities or hospitals in Alberta as well as other provinces could easily be turned into profit centres serving, for instance, foreign markets. Ministers and Deputy Ministers in other governments might easily ensure that their ministries submit detailed business plans, and not just policy initiatives and fiscal estimates, for legislative approval. The establishment of accurate and realistic accounting practices is an obvious, simple, but also a necessary place to start. If for no reason other than sheer effectiveness, politicians and senior administrators would be well advised to keep their eye on how these changes in Alberta have taken shape.

When making spending cuts, the need to make rapid and decisive reductions is also an important lesson: gradualism cannot work because the required adjustments never get made. As Sir Roger Douglas said, once you start a program, don't stop until it is completed. Once potential dissenting groups are exposed to market forces, they will not seek to recover past privileges but ensure that others lose their privileges too. Moreover, it helps if the politicians are the first to be hit. Once Klein and his colleagues cut their own pensions and they too had to rely on RRSPs, like ordinary Albertans and ordinary Canadians, they gained credibility. Credibility enabled the government to act, and consistency ensured their credibility would not be damaged. One may not like what the Klein government had done or the manner in which they set about doing it, but the fact that they did what they said ensured they would be respected. This was a lesson that Mike Harris learned, as did his union opponents, who were both more numerous than in Alberta and forewarned.

A similar lesson exists for quiet times. Governments typically set policy first by determining what is popular and then finding the money, either by taxing or by borrowing. In contrast, the Alberta program requires that governments first set tax and borrowing levels and then set budget expenditures within those limits. Thus when the Alberta government decided upon a 20% target for reductions in all departments, it was because that level of cuts would eliminate the deficit with no increase in taxation rates.[3] This, most observers of public policy formation would agree, is a novel approach.

There is, however, one innovation that external observers may easily overlook. The Alberta Economic Development Authority (AEDA) was an initiative instigated by the Premier in the summer of 1993 when he asked Art Smith whether an organization like the Calgary Economic Development Authority (CEDA) could be made to work at a provincial level. CEDA was a classic "steering organization" (to use the Osborne and Gaebler terminology), that Klein established when he was mayor of Calgary; its members were drawn from both public and private sectors. In response to Klein's request, Smith drafted a proposal and circulated it to several business people around the province. Nearly all said they would support a CEDA-style authority at the provincial level; nearly all said they thought it would work. In March, 1993 Smith presented a draft plan to the Premier, and on 8 April, 1993 it was announced.

The March, 1995 Business Plan describes the AEDA mission as follows:

> The Alberta Economic Development Authority (AEDA) will plan and implement economic strategies in Alberta through a partnership engaging government departments and the private sector, drawn from all regions and industrial and commercial components in the Province.

After the departure of Ken Kowalski from Cabinet to the back benches, the Premier for several months thereafter served as Minister of Economic Development. That department serves as the human resource base for AEDA. The Authority's mandate was to develop strategies to encourage investment, to improve the tax regime, to develop trade and export sales, and to deregulate the provincial economy. In short, AEDA was given the task of developing the details of what the Premier called the "Alberta Advantage." In practice, this meant AEDA would examine departmental business plans and if necessary recommend changes to the minister, review future business plans prior to their being submitted to the appropriate Standing Policy Committee, and review departmental budgets. AEDA would also submit its own initiatives to Premier Klein, through a process to be described below; in addition, it was given responsibility for reviewing promotional programs, picking foreign trade office locations, planning future trade missions, and analyzing post-mission results.

To implement its mandate, AEDA established two boards, a 15-member Board of Management, which acts essentially as an executive and operates the Authority on a day-to-day basis, and an Economic Council of up to 80 members, appointed by Cabinet for staggered terms of two and three years. As mentioned above, members are drawn from labour, commercial, industrial, and educational institutions in the province. Whether it accepts Board of Management proposals or initiates its own, the Council conducts its actual work by means of 18 task committees made up of private sector experts.

A typical AEDC meeting is chaired by the premier and includes senior officials as well. They discuss reports from three or four task committees. The premier then has the option of dealing with the report as discussed either by accepting it as is, returning it to the task committee, or taking it to cabinet for further study. Both the private sector executives and the senior civil servants are placed in a forum where they are required to discuss and justify their proposals.

The role of AEDA in bringing together two kinds of experts, namely private and public sector senior management, each with its own distinct operating cultures, has been described as "catalytic." AEDA is an innovative way of creating an informed as well as an energetic executive. It would be no surprise to Osborne and Gaebler because they repeatedly found "that the fiscal imperative provided the impetus to unleash creative and innovative energy that had been constrained by the status quo."[4]

Another major lesson stemming from the Klein initiatives concerns what political scientists call "priming." To use the Premier's own analogy, the government has been successful in persuading Albertans to accept the disruptions that have accompanied the "renovations."[5] Albertans did not mysteriously wake up one fine morning and decide that today would be the day they turned their collective attention to provincial finances. Nor were they infected with a perverse political virus that made them unaware of, or insensitive to, the costs of reducing services without reducing taxes.

On the contrary, the Klein government persuaded Albertans of the importance of deficit elimination, by continuously pointing out its significance for debt reduction and for overall economic prosperity. Granted, the Alberta Tories did have some help; both the Decore Liberals and the federal Reform Party had been vocal at expressing the need for governments to be more fiscally prudent, more effective and less intrusive. Even so, the government was successful in capitalizing on the efforts of others and in exercising their own leadership on the issue.

Among the means used, pride of place must go to the effective but simple rhetorical structure they employed: here is a problem, the deficit and accumulated debt; here is the solution, cut expenditures. The implications were clear to all: none but the wilfully ignorant, the unredeemably stupid, or the incorrigibly selfish were unaware that debt was Alberta's, and indeed is Canada's greatest problem and that the only way to deal with it is by reducing annual deficits to zero followed by several years of budgetary surpluses. Once having captured the political and rhetorical high ground, commonsense alone indicated the next step: the only way to run a surplus and get rid of the debt is to cut expenditures.

Many observers and critics have argued that, in fact, debt reduction is a very complex problem requiring close attention over many years. There are even a few dinosaurs left who dispute the importance of deficit elimination and debt reduction, but Klein and Dinning were not among their number. "We don't have a revenue problem in Alberta," the Premier said in his 1994 TV address to the province. "Your government should be able to live on $11.5 billion a year."[6] A sales tax was not the answer either, even if there was tax room for one. "If sales taxes are so good at eliminating deficits," said the premier, "why don't the nine provinces that have one have balanced budgets?"[7] Likewise Treasurer Dinning helped drive home the point by observing that "if deficits created jobs, everyone in Canada ought to have two or three of them." Moreover, "tax increases," he said, "damage incentives to work, save, and invest by reducing the after-tax rate of return of those activities," and they hurt "the future prosperity of Albertans."[8]

The second phase of the Klein government's persuasive "priming" effort was to convince the public that the financial crisis was also a symptom of a deeper problem: the traditional policies and the traditional model of government no longer worked as they once had done, so that the long-term answer was to change the modes of governance and adopt a new approach. "This plan," said the Treasurer, "is not just about reducing spending. It is about restructuring government so Albertans can receive essential services at an affordable price."[9]

The value of a confident leader is another lesson to bear in mind. Unlike Peter Lougheed, Ralph Klein is not a hands-on premier. During the 1992 Tory leadership campaign he went so far as to criticize one opponent, Rick Orman, for promising he would be a hands-on premier. Klein charged that "Orman would never have any time for politics. He would never have any time for people, if that's his style of government."[10] Shortly after his election as leader, Klein said of his next task, "I'll get out there and do some hard-nosed selling."[11] The first Speech from the Throne made essentially the same point, but more elegantly: "Our Premier will make it part of his job to sell Alberta as one of the best places in the world to visit and do business."[12] Klein's personality and media savvy made his proposed salesmanship credible. It was also sound strategic leadership, and increased both his trustworthiness and popular perceptions or his integrity.

Even Mark Lisac, who has been highly critical of many of the Klein government's policies, allowed that the Premier was outstanding at "selling" Alberta: "When he talked [in Seoul], you could close your eyes and swear you were in Ponoka or Lethbridge. Alberta voters, Korean business leaders, they were all the same to Ralph Klein. They were all just plain folks. And here was the most surprising thing of all—they responded to him much like a crowd in Lethbridge or Ponoka."[13]

The Premier has grown particularly adept at handling his opponents. While he has always been capable of direct and vigorous responses to his critics, he often resisted what must have been a great temptation and presented himself as being open, flexible, inclusive, and not confrontational by choice. Perhaps most refreshing among the habits of successful politicians, Klein was willing to admit his mistakes and, like a master of political judo, turn errors to his own advantage.

This is not to say that Klein made concessions to his opponents. The difficulty with the "special interest groups," for example, was not that they would succeed. That would never happen. As with the opposition parties, the problem was getting them to help and not simply opposing every government initiative on the basis of an unthinking reflex.[14] "We don't want to bring anyone into this process kicking and screaming," Klein said, "we just want to have a buy-in. If everyone just gives a little bit, five percent, we can get this thing back on course."[15] To Decore's charge that he was "dismantling Alberta," Klein gently replied, "if Laurence has any ideas of how to make the system better, I would ask him to pass them on to me because he won't be able to use them for at least the next four years."[16] And at the 1994 Tory convention in Banff, the Premier reiterated, this time to his own party, that he would be happy to consider alternatives: "If they come up with an easier way to reach our destination, then fine, we will detour. Instead of going around the mountain, if it's easier to go through, we'll do that. But there's no going back."[17]

In addition to being rhetorically adept, and able to deal successfully with their opponents, the Klein government also appealed to Albertans' sense of pride. Thus when it came to dealing with such emotionally charged issues as the indignity of welfare dependence, the government simply recast the issue, giving it a more positive spin: the issue was one of self-respect. Likewise, the first Speech from the Throne began and ended with an appeal to Albertans not to neglect or forget the achievements of their past when dealing with the undoubted difficulties that lay ahead.

> The government understand fully that following these plans will be strong medicine for all of us, but it will stand by them, and all that my government asks is that Albertans stand by these commitments alongside the men and women in this House. Let us not abandon our course, for any feeble attempts to avoid the challenge will be labour lost.[18]

With each budget address the government referred to this same theme, calling upon Albertans to "stay the course." There was no question, Klein said, of "going back to the old ways of spending," only of "doing it right this time."[19]

By asking Albertans to stay the course, the Klein government was appealing to their patience, and so to their virtue. High approval ratings can be seen as an indication that Albertans were willing to wait for better times to come. There may, however, be an element of unexportable particularism involved: Albertans have always been optimistic inhabitants of next-year country.[20] Moreover, as Machiavelli pointed out, an appeal to virtue is particularly effective when it is combined with dislike of one's enemies rather than with gratitude to one's friends; Albertans have never lacked enemies to dislike and have been roundly disliked in turn. Many non-Albertans consider Albertans too proud, which is why they call us rednecks. But if it is true, as Harvey Mansfield astutely observed in a different context, that "pride takes pride in rising above interests,"[21] then this insight that applies not merely to virtuous Albertans, but to citizens everywhere. Consequently, although Canadians elsewhere may lack what Treasurer Dinning called the pioneer spirit, that does not mean they lack pride, self-respect or virtue. Governments elsewhere need only be creative and find their own particular expressions of common human qualities. Albertans cannot help them with this effort, though they can encourage them by saying "look at what we have done. You can do it, too."

Straying from the Course
Federal Politics
A key element in the advice given by Sir Roger Douglas is that you don't stop until you complete the program. Treasurer Dinning was fond of quoting another of Sir Roger's aphorisms: you can't leap a canyon in two

jumps. Now governments need support to be effective, and supporters need arguments as well as the pungent rhetoric of exhortation. Arguments provide an internal gyroscope to policies; without them, a government can easily lose its sense of direction as well as its momentum, as supporters drift away. Some dangers can be prudently foreseen,[22] but others are more insidious. Sometime around 1995-96, after it had eliminated the deficit and had begun to accumulate a surplus, the Klein government appeared to lose sight of its original purpose. The 1993 Red Deer Roundtable on the acceptability of business plans, fiscal restraint, mission statements regarding the "core business" of ministries, and so on seemed to be genuinely consultative as well as an attempt to gather support.[23] But by the time of the gambling summit, the growth summit and the health summit a few years later, there was widespread belief that the consultative aspect had been greatly reduced and the public relations aspect greatly enhanced.

After the 1997 election, the government had decided to opt for a new policy of making strategic cash injections at various "pressure points" (health care, education, and so on) rather than "stay the course" and complete the program as Sir Roger Douglas had counselled. The objective remained a prosperous Alberta and the means, government restructuring, had proven effective. Tax reform or the introduction of education vouchers would be a logical sequel. When those easily anticipated steps were not taken, there was a great deal of speculation on the possibility that Premier Klein was about to leap into federal politics, either through the federal PC party or via the United Alternative (later the Canadian Alliance).[24] The speculation proved misplaced. On the federal scene, Klein was a distant but lukewarm supporter of his federal party. Then, after they became a confined rump of Red Tories in Atlantic Canada, he remained a supporter of the Liberals at least as much as he has supported Reform and the United Alternative. This was a complex and ambiguous strategy with a very uncertain payoff.

Ever since Preston Manning delivered his talk to the Calgary Chamber of Commerce in February, 1997, asking Klein to declare his views on the question of Quebec's distinctiveness, relations between the two men had been guarded.[25] Klein saw Manning's remarks during his election campaign as a crude attempt to serve the interests of the Reform Party by driving a wedge between Klein and Jean Charest, who at the time was still leader of the federal Tories.

Manning had concluded that Klein was not going to help him in the next federal election and so he wished to neutralize whatever support for Charest that might still exist. From the Reform point of view, a strategy of "wedge politics" made perfect sense. From as far back as October, 1996, the federal Liberals had been trying to get Klein "on board the national unity train." He was, said one anonymous federal official, "potentially a swing vote on distinct society."[26] This meant he would also be the focus of considerable federal Liberal attention. Klein responded to the rumour by strongly denying he had any interest in going to Ottawa: "Pie in the sky, a red herring, absolutely ludicrous, not on my agenda. I haven't given it a thought."[27] Moreover, during the early days of the UA, Klein's endorsement of the first official convention was highly qualified. It is true that he did give a major speech and that Rod Love and Stockwell Day were major players in the organization of the initiative; but it is also true that, just prior to his talk, Klein praised Paul Martin for his budget and Joe Clark as well! Preston Manning, the chief architect of the UA, was not amused.

Social Union
Then came the "social union" negotiations in January, 1999, which provided further evidence to support the view that the Klein government had drifted off course. The social union discussions grew from the 1997 Calgary Declaration, a post-Charlottetown initiative directed at Quebec and pregnant with the possibility of "rebalancing" the federation in such a way that "federal, provincial and territorial governments [would] work in partnership while respecting each other's jurisdictions."

Premier Bouchard responded positively and put his own interpretation on the social union: he saw it primarily as a means to limit the federal spending power. Since the days of Premier Maurice Duplessis, limiting the ability of Ottawa to spend taxpayers' money on any public policy, including those assigned by the Constitution Act to the provinces, with or without conditions and with or without provincial cooperation, has been high on every Quebec premier's political agenda. Bouchard repeated his comments at the August, 1998 premiers' meeting in Saskatoon and added that the other premiers had agreed: there would be no separate deals.

Limiting the federal spending power is also in the interest of Albertans. Power follows money in any federation. So long as Ottawa is without self-restraint, the only way the bright ideas of ambitious centralizing bureaucrats and politicians can be thwarted is through the opposition of the provinces. Given the ability of Ottawa to create fiefdoms in Atlantic Canada through the expedient use of transfer payments and shared cost initiatives, the only provinces with a realistic ability to resist are Ontario, Quebec, B.C., and Alberta.

Early in December, 1998 Premier Klein received a pointed reminder as to why it was important to limit what Ottawa could do. At 2 p.m., on

7 December, a smiling Jean Chrétien, flanked by his dapper Human Resources Minister, Pierre Pettigrew, announced to a group of beaming youngsters at an Edmonton YMCA, that "his government" would spend $465 million on a three-year youth employment scheme. Three hours later, the premier stood beside Chrétien at a press conference and said all that he knew about the program he had just read in a news release. Klein added that he was not even sure that the provincial minister responsible, and Minister Pettigrew's counterpart, knew about it. The two federal politicians, in Edmonton to consult on the social union, had somehow failed to inform their hosts. Then, to make matters worse, Chrétien said, "but Ralph, it's not a new program." Perhaps not, but a 50% increase in an existing program undertaken by Ottawa without consulting anybody was not a prudent way to promote federal-provincial cooperation. The message was apparently lost on Premier Klein. In spite of the insult he had just received, he supported the Liberals' position: that the social union was a keystone in the great arch of national unity.[28]

In early January, the ministers from each province met in Halifax under the chairmanship of the federal Justice Minister, Anne McClellan. "I don't anticipate failure," she said, "we're making very, very good progress." At the end of the month, they met again, this time in Victoria. It seems the federal position had changed: what looked like an agreement that would allow provinces to opt out had changed. "Some of the things that were said by Ms. McLellan in Halifax," said Alberta Family and Social Services Minister, Lyle Oberg, "were not written down. I'm certainly not happy with the federal position now." Indeed, by the time the ink had dried the provinces were saying they had been double-crossed by Ottawa.[29]

Double-crossed or not, on 4 February, 1999, nine provinces and two territories signed the social union agreement, "A Framework to Improve the Social Union for Canadians." The ones who signed agreed to three broad principles. First, they supported nation-wide access to "essential social programs and services of comparable quality." This meant that B.C.'s residency requirement for welfare was illegal; it might mean that lowering welfare payments or changing the conditions of eligibility, as Alberta had done, would also be illegal. Nor would it be legal for universities to charge out-of-province students higher tuition fees. Second, the signatories committed themselves to "ensure adequate, affordable, stable and sustainable funding for social programs." Third, they reaffirmed the sanctity of universal, accessible and state financed and state-administered medicare, which seemed to bring an end to the possibility of private hospitals.

From the Alberta perspective, the second principle is by far the worst of a bad lot. It is the key to the whole social spending account but it contains no indication of what might be meant by adequate, affordable, stable and sustainable. There is no provision for a binding settlement mechanism if one province should decide that a certain level of spending is adequate and affordable but federal bureaucrats disagreed. This might be particularly difficult if the provincial sums were lower than what the federal government considered adequate and affordable. As with the earlier dispute over the proper interpretation of the Canada Health Act, if Ottawa and Alberta disagreed, the federal government alone would decide if Alberta complied with the correct understanding of adequacy and affordability.

Moreover every province (except Quebec) acknowledged the legitimacy of the federal use of the spending power by agreeing with the provision that states "the use of the federal spending power has been essential to the development of Canada's social union," and explicitly mentions conditional social transfers. Perhaps even more astonishing, all provinces, including Alberta, agreed to issue compliance reports on the performance of social programs. In return, the federal government rescinded a provision announced in the 1996 Speech from the Throne that committed Ottawa to an opting-out provision that would have allowed provinces to refuse to participate in a federal initiative and still receive federal funding provided they established a similar program. Under the new agreement there can be no opting out: you either were in the program and received federal cash or not and received none. To the extent that federal-provincial relations are a zero-sum game, Ottawa gained two points. First, the provinces (except Quebec) gave up on the whole spending power package and second, Ottawa took back its previous concession.

The most obvious question is: why did the provinces do it? The most common answer is: because the federal government promised more money for health care. The problem with this explanation is that federal funds are not provided on a per capita basis. For every new dollar Newfoundland receives from Ottawa for health care expenditures, the taxpayers of that province remit only fifty cents to Revenue Canada. Alberta, in contrast pays $1.37 for every loonie it gets back. In other words, Ottawa simply recycles dollars after the style of Robin Hood—by taking from the rich provinces and giving to the poor. Thus, while self-interest might explain the motivation of Brian Tobin, premier of Newfoundland, it cannot explain the motivation of Ralph Klein. The $188 million in new federal health dollars received by Alberta cost provincial taxpayers $257 million in federal taxes.[30] To make matters even worse, when the federal budget was delivered a few weeks later, the new federal money scarcely kept up with the pace of inflation and of an ageing population.

A more focussed question, therefore is: why did the premiers of the "have" provinces, B.C., Alberta, and Ontario, agree? The NDP government of B.C. has been ideologically committed to a national plan for time out of mind, and B.C. receives about as much as it puts in. Ontario lost on the deal, but Mike Harris was facing the uncertainty of a spring election, and the last thing he needed was to hand the opposition such a potent symbolic weapon as having refused "more money for medicare." But Ralph Klein faced no election. Moreover, his refusal to accept the "new" federal money would have benefitted Albertans nearly $70 million.

If there is a coherent answer to the question it may lie in the fact noted above that the federal government had long hoped that Klein would endorse their national unity strategy. The reason seems obvious enough. Along with their cousins across the mountains, Albertans have long and loudly held that Quebec is the spoiled child of confederation, that the separatists are no better than blackmailers, and that a long train of prime ministers from Quebec have made matters worse by devoting an inordinate amount of attention to the province and by attempting to appease its insatiable demands for more. From this perspective, the obvious criticism—pointed out, for example, by Lorne Gunther in the *Edmonton Journal*—is as follows: "by hanging Bouchard out to dry, the English [-speaking] premiers have reinforced Quebecers' feelings of isolation in confederation."[31] There is, however, another way of looking at the issue.

Shortly after the social union agreement was signed, Rod Love remarked somewhat facetiously that Canada now enjoyed a 9-1-1 federalism. Roger Gibbins, current president of the Canada West Foundation, explained:

> The nine English Canadian provinces will work more closely together as a group, and in consultation with the federal government. The nine will then negotiate as a group with Ottawa, which will in turn conduct one-on-one bilateral (or binational) negotiations with Quebec. The federal government has assured Quebec that it will not incur any financial penalty for being outside the Social Union framework, and thus Quebec is free to join any intergovernmental agreements as it sees fit.
>
> Because Quebec will only be at the table as an informal observer, it will be possible for other governments to discuss national programs and national standards without treading on Quebec sensitivities. For its part, Quebec will have no incentive or need to block policy initiatives from the rest of Canada; Quebec can simply remain apart (and at no financial risk) if it disapproves, or opt in if it approves.[32]

On social policy questions, then, Quebec might enjoy *de facto* sovereignty-association, packaged to English-speaking Canada as flexibility.

At the same time, none of the premiers outside Quebec need concede anything from the position that the provinces all retained their formal equality. Given the enormous anxiety that the national unity question has induced in prime ministers since the days of Pierre Trudeau, and given as well the evident impossibility of reaching a formal, constitutional definition of the place of Quebec in Canada (or out of Canada, for that matter), 9-1-1 federalism may well be the most creative approach to the Quebec question that has arisen in the past generation. The defect, however, is obvious as well: it is sufficiently mendacious that no politician in Ottawa, in Quebec City, or in any of the nine provincial capitals can ever admit to it.[33]

Judicial Activism and Social Policy
At about the same time as the Government of Alberta was conciliating and abetting federal government ambitions in the area of social policy and creativity on the constitutional file, they stumbled yet again when the opportunity to limit the influence of the judiciary emerged. On 23 February, 1996 the Alberta Court of Appeal overturned a Court of Queen's Bench decision that would have compelled the government to change the Individual Rights Protection Act, the precursor to the Alberta Human Rights Citizenship and Multiculturalism Act. The original case involved a man, Delwin Vriend, who had been fired from King's University College in Edmonton because he was sexually active outside of marriage, which behaviour contravened the terms of his employment. In addition, Vriend was homosexual and, more important, had engaged in homosexual activities, which was also against the religious teaching of the Christian Reformed Church, which operated King's College. Vriend had been brought up within the Christian Reformed Church and was well aware that he was violating an important moral teaching of the religious community to which he belonged, or once belonged. Moreover, Vriend proclaimed his defiance of the moral teachings of the Christian Reformed Church to *urbi et orbi* and especially students with whom he was in contact during the course of his work in one of the university labs. In the terminology he favoured, Delwin Vriend was "openly gay."

In his Statement of Claim, Vriend alleged that he was fired not for his practices but for his sexual orientation, the difference being that, while one may be responsible for one's actions (or practices) one is not responsible for one's orientation. Thus, he said, he was the victim of discrimination against which he was protected by the "equality clause" of the Canadian Charter of Rights and Freedoms.

It is true, of course, that section 15 of the Charter protects individuals from discrimination on the basis of "race, national or ethnic origin, colour, religion, sex, age or mental or physical disability," all of which are personal characteristics for which individuals are not responsible. However, "sexual orientation" was deliberately and explicitly excluded from s.15 of the Charter because as Justice Minister Jean Chrétien, as he then was, observed: "It is because of the problem of the definition of those words that we do not think that they should be in the constitution...that is why we do not want them there...we have a Parliament to decide that."[34] It was, however, "read in" to the Charter as an "analogous ground" to the explicit and enumerated grounds of race, age, mental disability, and so on. But nowhere in the Charter or in any other Constitutional document can one find a basis for establishing an analogous ground. Indeed, the doctrine was invented entirely by the Supreme Court in the 1985 *Egan* decision. Thus, in *Egan* the court established the grounds to expand its own jurisdiction, which it proceeded to do to an even greater extent in *Vriend*. This may not be the most egregious engrossment of its own authority by the Supreme Court, but it is surely one of the most notable instances of judicial creativity.

Let us, however, return to Delwin Vriend. After having been dismissed by the College, Vriend then approached the Alberta Human Rights Commission but was denied a hearing because sexual orientation had been thrice rejected by the legislature as being a valid consideration for human rights legislation. It was as if the Legislative Assembly of Alberta had taken heed of Justice Minister Chrétien's reflections and, in their wisdom, decided one way and not another.

Vriend then appealed his rejection to the Court of Queen's Bench on the grounds that sexual orientation *ought to have been included* in order to make the Individual Rights Protection Act compatible with the Charter. Madame Justice Anne Russell agreed and, anticipating the Supreme Court's ruling in *Egan* by a month, "read in" the equality provisions of the Charter to the Alberta statute even though, to repeat, it had been three times considered by the Legislature and three times excluded. Justice Russell, in other words, declared: notwithstanding the deliberations of the chief law-making body of the province, and notwithstanding their considered exclusion of sexual orientation, I, Justice Anne Russell of the Court of Queen's Bench of the Province of Alberta, have the unquestionable ability to "find" sexual orientation to have been included. Voilà! I so find. Thus the Alberta law was deemed to contain a sexual orientation provision and the Alberta Human Rights Commission was judicially empowered to hear Vriend's complaint.

Neither the procedure of a judge "reading in" provisions to a duly passed act of the legislature that had deliberately excluded those provisions nor the substantive effect of that procedure was universally acclaimed by Albertans. Not surprisingly, the *Vriend* case became polarized around the question of "gay rights."[35] The government, as expected, appealed on the grounds that the Legislative Assembly, not the courts, had responsibility for drafting the provisions of human rights legislation.

The case then went to the Alberta Court of Appeal. Writing on behalf of the majority in the split decision Mr. Justice J.A. McClung said that "Alberta's legislative calendar must be set by the elected representatives of voting Albertans, not outside agencies," which specifically included judges. "The Order Paper of the Alberta Legislature," he went on, "is not to be dictated, even incidentally, by federally appointed judges brandishing the Charter." The fact is, the ability of legislatures to set their own agenda is a fundamental aspect of parliamentary privilege and one of the most basic principles of responsible or parliamentary government.

More specifically, Mr. Justice McClung determined that, while it was certainly true that the Charter could be used to determine the constitutionality of government action, it could not be used to judge government inaction. Justice McClung therefore found that the Alberta government did not violate the Charter when it refused to act in such a way that a specific provision, thought highly desirable by some citizens, was not included in the legislation. Failure to exercise its undoubted authority to legislate in a way that some citizens thought just or at least desirable was not, he said, a valid basis to turn back the government's appeal just because a lower court directed the Legislature to do so.

Two important principles lie behind the ruling of the Alberta Court of Appeal. First, in a parliamentary regime, responsibility for drafting statutes to include or exclude specific provision in laws of general application is the chief purpose of legislatures. It is not the purpose of courts to second-guess legislatures when it comes to giving form to what we often call "core values." Rather, the courts have the purpose of adjudicating the peripheral question of the limits of rights based on those values.[36]

Second, legislatures are not obliged to enter what McClung called every "morally eruptive controversy" to try to rectify it, for the simple and obvious reason that if morally eruptive controversies are ever to be resolved by political institutions—and it is by no means obvious that they are—the only institution that is even remotely appropriate is through a general election or perhaps a referendum. One of the fundamental doctrines of Anglo-American jurisprudence is that there are limits to the applicability of adjudication as a means of arriving at authoritative political decisions.[37]

Although Justice McClung did not mention this point, it is a fundamental purpose of the Charter to protect citizens and non-citizens alike from government action. Charters and similar constitutional documents protect individuals by limiting what governments may do. Their purpose, however, is not to protect individuals from what governments do not do. The very premise of liberal constitutionalism is citizen responsibility, not the dependence of subjects on the grace of the sovereign. In his own way, therefore, Justice McClung was simply recalling the principles of limited and parliamentary government to litigants who may never have known them and to an inferior court that apparently had forgotten them. McClung in no way propounded a novel judicial doctrine.

The case was then appealed to the Supreme Court of Canada. During the months prior to the decision on *Vriend*, handed down on 2 April, 1998, the government indicated that, should the Supreme Court find the Alberta Human Rights Citizenship and Multiculturalism Act, as it had become, to be unconstitutional, they would use the constitutional provision contained in section 33 of the Charter, the "notwithstanding clause," to set aside the Court's ruling. The weekend before, Premier Klein broadly criticized judicial activism in an address to the annual Tory convention, held that year in Red Deer.[38] The expectation was that, under the circumstances, the government was prepared to respond to the Supreme Court when as expected they overturned the Alberta ruling.

The circumstances, however, looked unpropitious. On 10 March, 1998 the government had introduced Bill 26, an act to limit compensation to persons who had been involuntarily sterilized between 1928 and 1972 when such procedures were legally administered by the provincial Eugenics Board. Bill 26 was based on workers' compensation legislation and was designed to ensure that awards would be made on the basis of an administrative process rather than litigation. To ensure compliance with this intent, a Charter-based challenge to it was prevented by including section 33 as one of the bill's provisions. The Conservative caucus was not strongly committed to the use of section 33 and, when the proposal was loudly criticized by lawyers for plaintiffs who had undergone involuntary sterilization, by the opposition, and by the media, the government withdrew the bill. The premier said, by way of explanation "my political sense probably didn't click into gear...yes, I was out of tune here."[39]

Klein also went on at some length about the importance of the Charter and that using "the notwithstanding clause to undermine it is something you do only very, very rarely." Klein's choice of words was revealing. Once the issue of using section 33 was framed in terms of *undermining* the Charter, it would probably never be used. The fact is, however, that section 33 does not undermine anything; it is a means for legislatures to resolve matters about which reasonable people may disagree. For example, does the religious freedom provision of section 2(a) prohibit secular day-of-rest legislation? What is the balance between freedom of expression and regulation of obscenity? The questions do not answer themselves, and judges disagree on specific cases. Moreover in the *Vriend* decision, the Supreme Court of Canada acknowledged that the use of section 33, under the circumstances, was part of a healthy dialogue between two branches of government. In light of Premier Klein's later remarks in Red Deer, one might have expected at least a gesture in the direction of dialogue.

In the sterilization bill, however, the government had no interest in dialogue. The pre-emptive use of section 33 meant there would be no dialogue because there would be no litigation. Nothing would come before the courts, because one partner to the dialogue was legally silenced. There can be no question that Bill 26 was legal, but it gave the political impression that the government was unsure about the justice of its action and took steps to ensure no one questioned it. If that is what Klein meant when he admitted to being politically inastute, no one is likely to disagree. The pre-emptive use of section 33 under the circumstances was also ill advised because it prevented "dialogue" between the courts and the legislature. But those circumstances did not obtain in the *Vriend* case at all.[40]

The real issue in *Vriend* was precisely the existence of a "dialogue" between the courts and the legislature. Delwin Vriend had been fired by a religious-based educational institution, not Wal-Mart. He was well acquainted with their moral teachings; indeed he was flamboyant in his flouting of them. Most Albertans, as most Canadians, would object to Wal-Mart firing an employee because of their sexual practices—though even here there may be limits, and so occasion for further dialogue. The court nevertheless accepted the contention of Vriend that his was a case of general employment discrimination, overlooking the particularities of his actual employer. If the Alberta government wished to engage in judicial dialogue, the way to do so would have been to amend the Human Rights Act to protect homosexuals against workplace discrimination, excepting religious institutions such as King's College. Then, if Vriend again went to court, the rhetorical and so the political ground would have been prepared for the use of section 33.

On 2 April, 1998, as expected, The Supreme Court overturned the Alberta Court of Appeal's decision and, in effect, upheld the decision of Madame Justice Russell. The reaction of Delwin Vriend was clear, if not grave: "Ha, ha. I win." The reaction of Ralph Klein was grave if not clear: "It's pretty hard to go against that kind of judgement."[41] The Tory caucus debated the *Vriend* decision and the wisdom of engaging in dialogue by means of section 33, but voted by a two-to-one ratio against the idea. Instead, they appointed a ministerial task force to consider ways of limiting or "fencing in," to use the term of Stockwell Day, the impact of *Vriend*.[42] The government also took out half-page advertisements in the major newspapers of the province to explain the *Vriend* decision. It stressed that "in some circumstances" such as "religious belief" there may be exceptions granted by the courts and, in a fine display of irony, cited *Egan* as a case in point because while it expanded the court's self-proclaimed jurisdiction, it denied pension benefits to a homosexual couple. It also indicated that *Vriend* did not mean that gay sex education was required or that homosexual marriages would be allowed.

Like President Bush in Operation Desert Storm, Premier Klein claimed he drew a line in the sand. He would, he said, "respect" the Supreme Court's decision. But as George Koch pointed out, his was "a supreme act of followership." During his press conference after the *Vriend* decision, Koch said, "at times he was literally incoherent, like an anglophone Jean Chrétien. Legislative reporters who routinely massage the Premier's quotes nearly gave up, or grew so annoyed that they printed his words verbatim."[43] The premier was well aware that the political consequences of *Vriend* went far beyond the individual litigant and his association with King's College. Klein was probably most concerned about the split in his caucus. And the caucus was split because about a third of the members saw in *Vriend* not so much an unwarranted exercise of judicial activism as the thin edge of a gay-rights movement agenda that had extensive policy implications of which they did not approve.[44]

On 25 February, 1999, the government introduced Bill 12, the Domestic Relations Amendment Act. Among its provisions was the exclusion of homosexual couples from spousal support for dependent partners—which looked like a "fence" against homosexual marriage.[45]

On the other hand, the government also indicated it would consider favourably a "domestic registered partnership" act that looked very similar to a legal definition of the notion of homosexual spouse.[46] Homosexual adoption would likewise be permitted if it was "in the best interest of the child," which at least *pro forma* has a bearing on every adoption.[47]

The position of the government in all this social policy ferment was not easy to determine. Both caucus and the electorate appeared divided, and no obvious bridge appeared.[48] Early in March, 1999, Longwoods International delivered a polling report to the government. The whole gay rights agenda, and the issues associated with it, the report said, are bound to be controversial. The focus of the poll was on the circumstances under which section 33 would be used to nullify judicial decisions that the government considered unwise—or to use the language of the Supreme Court in *Vriend*, the focus was on those circumstances when it would be appropriate to engage in dialogue. The use of section 33, the report warned, "is an issue where government will have a difficult time taking a leadership position when there is no consensus and the views of Albertans on a moral, religious and personal issue are divided."[49]

A solution, however, was found a couple of weeks later. "The power of deciding when to use the notwithstanding clause," said a government press release, "is in the hands of Albertans. The Alberta Government decided today, that in future, a province-wide referendum plus a vote in the Legislative Assembly will be required before a decision is made to use the clause." The only exception would be a Supreme Court decision upholding homosexual marriage, in which case it would unquestionably be used.[50]

Both the *Calgary Herald* and the *National Post* asked the obvious question: why bother with a referendum?[51] "Mr. Klein's argument," said the *National Post*, "is ridiculous and perhaps disingenuous. While proclaiming his devotion to democracy, he wants to subject the Charter's only democratic element to a popular veto." That is, plebicitarian democracy was introduced as a check on parliamentary democracy, though no constitutional provision required it, and parliamentary democracy was already inhibited in its ability to constrain judges, though its constitutional soundness has never been in doubt.

That the government has veered from its original plan by "strategic" reinvesting, that it has opted to sign on to the social union agreement despite the fact that the deal makes further government restructuring more difficult, and that it shied away from taking a leadership position on controversial issues such as arose *Vriend* are all indications of the changes that took place between the first and second Klein administrations. It is so much easier to lead a consensus than to steer a course between competing and antithetical claims. In the following chapter we will consider what the changes from the first to the second Klein government may mean for the future of government restructuring and continuing prosperity in Alberta. Can the Klein government still achieve its medium- and long-term objectives? Can it get back on track?

CHAPTER EIGHT
GETTING BACK ON TRACK

Flaccid Federalism

Quebec alone has pretensions to a ministry of foreign affairs. The other provinces make do with federalism. The conflict between Ottawa and Alberta during the period of the National Energy Program was easily described using military metaphors and imagery. The conflict between the survivalist myths of the St. Lawrence valley, in both Quebec French and Loyalist English, provide a great contrast to the myths of cooperative pioneer individualism that permeate the consciousness of Albertans. Besides, ambitious politicians never lack for reasons to quarrel. After 1997 the most arresting thing about the relations between Alberta and Ottawa is the absence of serious conflict. There were, however, several opportunities for conflict. As Sherlock Holmes explained in his *Memoirs*, the absence of a dog's bark during the night is also a "curious incident." Consider for example, the prominence of environmental concerns among the public at large. With shared jurisdiction between Ottawa and the provinces regarding environmental policy, disputes in this area might easily have resulted in a great deal of barking.

Greenhouse Gasses

Starting in the 1980s, environmental activists have claimed that elevated levels of carbon dioxide and other "greenhouse gasses" are causing the temperature of the atmosphere to rise at such a rate that humans will soon go the way of the dinosaurs. "Global warming," as it is called, is particularly alarming to the climatologists at Environment Canada. In addition, most people for whom global warming is a fact attribute the cause of increased $CO2$ production to the burning of fossil fuels—coal, oil and natural gas. From these two assumptions they conclude that the trend can and must be reversed. The Kyoto Agreement, negotiated in December, 1997, provides for just such a reversal through mandatory reductions in greenhouse gas emissions. Ottawa pledged at Kyoto to reduce such emissions to 1990 levels by 2010. In order to effect the reductions contemplated in the treaty, however, agreement between Ottawa and the producing provinces is needed. Moreover, it is by no means clear that the agreement is workable. What is clear is that Ottawa signed a treaty in December the terms of which clearly violated the terms of a federal-provincial agreement signed the previous summer in Regina.

The Kyoto agreement followed logically from the 1992 Framework Convention on Climate Change signed in Rio de Janeiro. This event, usually called the Earth Summit, was orchestrated by Maurice Strong, the founding president of Petro-Canada and a highly committed environmentalist. The intentions of Rio were opposed by the administration of President George Bush, and nothing concrete followed. A change in administrations in the US brought the views of Vice-President Al Gore, who was at least as green as Maurice Strong, into prominence. There is some debate over whether Gore and Strong are "reform environmentalists" or "radical ecologists" that is, whether they want to curb environmental pollution and use natural resources more prudently, or whether they favour a fundamental alteration in the relationship between human and natural being. In either case, the facts surrounding global warming were questionable, which meant that to proceed with implementing the Kyoto agreement seemed to many Albertans and many Canadians to be an imprudent and questionable enterprise.

Worse, even if Canada and the US agreed to the Kyoto Agreements provisions, no poor country has agreed to abide by them. In concrete terms, it is proposed that Canada, which generates some 2% of all global greenhouse gasses, through the agency of the federal government, wreck the economy of the oil and gas producing provinces. As Alberta energy minister Steve West put it, "We can't just shut down Canada to demonstrate to the world our individual responsibility while underdeveloped countries stand back and say 'that was nice.'" Steve West was not alone in objecting to the implications of Kyoto while implicitly accepting the global warming notion as if it were fact when in fact it is subject to much controversy. More important, however, is the fact that the premier has been relatively quiet on this issue and that, as a result, opposition to Ottawa bureaucrats and politicians has been mounted chiefly by people in the private sector whose arguments can easily be dismissed as being solely expressions of their self-interest. They are that, of course, but one would have also expected a vigorous defence of provincial responsibilities and jurisdiction, particularly when the expansive activities of the federal government is based on a "science" that may well prove as reliable as the projection of hundred dollar oil proved to be in 1980.

In 1994, the Canadian Association of Petroleum Producers (CAPP) accepted the premise so fervently espoused by Ottawa, even though it possessed numerous studies showing the questionability of man-made global warming. "We think we can get a lot closer to the goal through voluntary measures than if we wait for regulations to be passed forcing the reductions," said Gary Webster, CAPP's manager for environment and health policy. It was clear that the energy industry saw the latest move by

Ottawa as a threat—a National Emissions Program, NEP II, would be the successor to the National Energy Program, NEP I. After Kyoto, federal energy minister Christine Stewart revealed that Ottawa was more interested in the iron fist of legislative or administratively mandated compliance than with the velvet glove of voluntarism. Analysis of the impact of CO_2 reductions, she said "is not intended to determine whether the target is realistic, but to determine the most cost-effective way of reaching it." And if it is not realistic? Well, we'll have compliance anyway. Kyoto is about the exercise of federal power, not greenhouse gasses or the salvific redemption of "the planet." The Klein government seemed not to have noticed.

Some people in the oil business have nevertheless objected to the position taken by CAPP as well as to what they consider to be the hidden agenda of the federal government. Mike Tims, CEO of Peters and Company, a Calgary investment banking firm said, "it's an economic agenda wrapped up as an environmental issue." James W. Buckee, CEO of Talisman Energy, and holder of an Oxford doctorate in astrophysics, is even more blunt. "Global warming," he says, "is 'junk science' and CAPP President, David Manning, doesn't know a damn thing about climate change." Roger Phillips, CEO of the Regina-based steel company, IPSCO, and a physicist, is similarly dismissive: "Kyoto means needless sacrifice for all of us with no payback."[1] Global-warming "science" relies more on megaphones than commonsense or reason to persuade and bamboozle. Megaphones in the hands of federal ministers of the crown who can actually do something are an obvious challenge to provincial governments.

It is probably fair to say that Sheila Copps, former federal environment minister, knows even less about the question of global warming than does CAPP president David Manning. Her voice, however, has been raised in alarm: "the lower mainland of British Columbia, which has a fairly low sea level, will experience flooding. The prairies will see an increase in forest fires. The province of Prince Edward Island will become a series of islands." Her remarks about the lower mainland are scarcely intelligible, and one is more likely to encounter prairie fires on the prairies than forest fires, but her excited tone is unmistakable. The cause of it all, according to her unnamed scientists is, naturally, global warming. As if the prospect of an archipelago of PEI were not enough, Ms. Copps has more horrors to evoke: a record number of turkeys and chickens died from heat prostration in 1997; a record number of icebergs were sighted off Newfoundland; every piece of property in Oxbow, Saskatchewan sustained wind damage; more Canadians than ever have suffered migraine headaches. The list goes on. Something must be done!

When governments behave with such obvious irrationality, there is likely to be a hidden agenda to give order and direction to their efforts. So far as Ottawa is concerned, "global warming" is but remotely related to scientific climatology. Its real focus is taxes collected at the point of production. Just as in the days of Premier Lougheed, a full exchequer quickly attracts the predatory attention of the big spenders in Ottawa. Premier Klein, however, has raised few alarms. The dog has not yet barked.

Rewilding Banff

A second vaguely "environmental" issue concerns Banff National Park, which in her new job as heritage minister came within Sheila Copps' sphere of power. In 1883 Banff was called Siding 29 but was renamed by Donald Smith, later Lord Strathcona and Mount Royal, after his hometown in Scotland. From the start, this part of the Bow River Valley 100 km or so west of Calgary has been a source of contention among the federal government, the CPR, and tourists. In 1885, the 10-acre sulphur-water Hot Springs Reserve was set aside by the Dominion government for public use; in 1887, the Rocky Mountains Park Act was passed, establishing what is now Banff National Park. A year later the first Banff Springs Hotel opened for business. Over the next few years the government and the CPR worked together to establish the other great mountain parks: Yoho, Kootenay, Glacier, Revelstoke, Waterton and in 1907, Jasper. William van Horne, President of the CPR expressed the enduring attraction of the place. "Since we can't export the scenery," he said, "we'll import the tourists."

From the beginning, then, the history and purpose of Banff have been bound up with tourism. It has never been a mere nature preserve. The hot springs was made accessible by both provincial and federal governments, which encouraged or built railways and highways through the mountains, though today the Cave and Basin is closed to public swimming in order to protect snails that find the warm water as congenial as humans do. Hotels, restaurants, transportation services and recreation facilities were then built to accommodate visitors. An infrastructure was constructed for people who owned or worked in the tourist facilities. The CPR, the hotel owners, and especially the federal government have promoted tourism in Banff Park for over a century with great enthusiasm. They built, and the people came, as Van Horne foresaw.

There has always been tension between commerce and tourism and the natural beauty of the place upon which it depends. In recent years, however, with the increased visibility and activity of romantic environmental preservationists, the federal government has been listening almost exclusively to one very loud, but not very reasonable voice. The

Heritage Minister has become convinced, like the preservationists, that the park is threatened beyond measure.[2] More importantly, she is also of the opinion that only bureaucrats in her ministry, living thousands of kilometres away in Ottawa or taking orders from them, can save the park by reversing what she sees as beauty-destroying commercial activity. Banff residents, some 6,100 of them, do not all agree. They point to the 75% reduction in commercial development potential undertaken in the first ten years that the town of Banff has existed as an Alberta munici-pality. As the *Community Plan*, published in June, 1997 observed, "the Town of Banff has demonstrated more responsibility towards the National Park in the eight years since Incorporation than the Federal Government did in the 110 years it controlled the community."

The Minister and her minions in Parks Canada did not take kindly to such comparisons. In September, 1997, Minister Copps swooped down on Banff to veto a decision taken by the Banff Town Council the previ-ous June. The Council had voted to permit commercial expansion amounting to some 850,000 square feet, about the size of a small shop-ping mall, onto land that was already developed in the townsite. Cheered on by pristine environmentalists, Ms. Copps determined this develop-ment "would create a town without a soul," and she sent the councillors back to the drawing boards to come up with something more soulful. In fact, however, the Town Council had met every one of the conditions established by Parks Canada: residential capacity, zoning restrictions, annual growth rates, and stringent architectural guidelines.[3]

Other issues were also involved. First of all, Banff is a town incorpo-rated under the laws of Alberta and unlike the Minister, reached a deci-sion only after conforming to a lengthy and mandatory process of public hearings, committee discussions, debate in town council, and a referen-dum. A lot of time, energy and toil went into creating a plan that pro-vided for orderly commercial development of space that was about a third of what had already been approved by Ottawa. Indeed, as the June, 1998, plan explains in detail, "The Banff Community Plan is not an expansion plan. It is a reduction plan."

The Incorporation Agreement between Ottawa and Alberta gives final say to the Heritage Minister. This is what she said: "given the directions that we gave to council to come up with a plan that was environmental-ly benign, I'm disappointed they haven't the foresight to create an eco-community for the next century." The town mayor, Ted Hart, was more than a little irritated at having his efforts and those of the town sum-marily dismissed in favour of something so vague and wistful as "an eco-community for the next century." He was not buying the green babble for a moment. There was, he said, "a bigger issue involved: the federal political system is just not working when a minister can make a statement basically saying the people of Banff are pond scum so you don't have to consult with them." Not until December, 1998, did Minister Copps lift her ukase and permit the town plan to come into effect—again without consultation.

For many Albertans and British Columbians the mountain parks are local recreational facilities. As with the residents of the town, local park users have no interest in despoiling the beauty of the place. During the winter, for example, half those who visit Banff are Albertans, and another fifteen to twenty percent are from B.C. and Saskatchewan. This aspect of the park seems to be of no concern to Ms. Copps or to her deep green allies. According to the Minister, Banff is connected to the "identities of all Canadians. We all feel that Banff is a part of us, and it goes far beyond a local planning issue." Harvey Locke, President of the Canadian Parks and Wilderness Society, a loyal Liberal whom we have met in these pages above as the campaign manager for Lawrence Decore in the 1993 provincial election, agrees: "It's not a question for the people of Banff alone. It's a national park." The views of residents regarding development, he said, "are not a national majority." Mayor Hart agreed that the park is a national institution, but that is also what makes it vulnerable to the coarse manipulation by politicians such as Ms. Copps. "Everybody knows Banff," he said. "It's easy to twist information, to give people a distorted vision. The federal government obviously wants to look good on the international environmental stage." The "pond scum" in the townsite are presumed to have antithetical views, but no one has explained why they are so keen on despoiling the world they live in every day.[4]

The views of environmentalists have resulted in some very strange proposals that nevertheless have received serious consideration from the Heritage Ministry. They include such things as elevating lengthy sections of the Trans-Canada Highway and even of the CPR mainline in order to create large wildlife underpasses. Environmentalists have also proposed shutting down the ski hills at Sunshine, Lake Louise, and Norquay because they are "historical anomalies" and "mechanical."[5] Parks Canada has sought to evict residents of the Banff townsite and have succeeded in shutting down the summer gondola at Lake Louise.[6] But it was not until they proposed a cap on the number of skiers that Jon Havelock, the Alberta Intergovernmental Affairs Minister, wrote a letter of protest.[7] Premier Klein, however, said little by way of response to the increasingly intrusive administrative rule by Ottawa.

As with private sector opposition to Kyoto, the actual business people whose livelihoods were threatened by Parks Canada and their ideological allies in the environmental movement led the resistance to Ottawa. For example, there is Charlie Locke (no relation to Harvey Locke, the environmentalist connected to the Liberals) who owns the Lake Louise Ski Area. He is a qualified mountain guide, a climber, and outdoor enthusiast who once skied, unsupported, the glacier route between Jasper and Lake Louise through what was, in 1967, partly unmapped territory. He considers himself a responsible conservationist but he is public enemy number one for the preservationists of the Alberta Wilderness Association. What the environmentalists want to do, says Locke, "is first push tourism operators out of the park, thereby denying the park to the average user who isn't a hard-core back-country enthusiast, a bear researcher or his girlfriend, and finally 'rewild' the park. The millions of people who come to see and enjoy the park now aren't part of the equation."[8] Operators like Locke and Ralph Scurfield, who owns Sunshine, say they have addressed every demand by Parks Canada and the environmentalists—except to surrender their right to exist. That is just not good enough: "I'm not interested in seeing compromise," said Mike McIvor, an environmentalist with the Bow Valley Naturalists.[9] A similar attitude and the deep American pockets of the Sierra Club's Legal Defence Fund has shut down the development of the $250 million Cheviot Mine near Hinton, Alberta, east of Jasper, even though it too met every environmental standard established by Edmonton and Ottawa.[10] Again the response of the Klein government to the ideological litigousness of the environmentalists backed by Ottawa has been minimal.

Explaining the Change

That Alberta adopted a pusillanimous attitude towards the engrossment of federal power did not pass unnoticed. Looking back, in June, 1999, Link Byfield wrote in *Alberta Report* that there was not much to choose between the Getty government of 1992 and the Klein government seven years later.

> The government got ahead of its debt (a genuine achievement), and businesses stopped collecting provincial grants. But apart from that, nothing is different. People still look to the government to teach their children, heal them when they're sick, and support needy relatives and neighbours. In short, we still expect our politicians to solve our problems and carry out our responsibilities. And we have no more say today in how it goes about doing this than we did before.
>
> Well, what's so wrong about that? what's the alternative?
>
> There is plenty wrong with it. It creates a nation of whiners and dullards. People stop taking responsibility for the most important things entrusted to them—their family and their community.

The "Ralph Revolution," Byfield went on, was nothing but "an adjust-ment of fiscal policy." Instead of turning over cash and responsibility to communities and to citizens in the form of devolution and lower taxes, "the Tories still see the government in the role of 'service provider'.... Despite all the talk of 'reinventing government,' nothing fundamental has changed."[11] This was not simply rhetorical exaggeration. Peter Menzies, editor of the *Calgary Herald*, made essentially the same observa-tion as Byfield at about the same time.[12] Before considering whether the government can get back on track, it is important to see why it was derailed in the first place.

One likely answer is that several of Klein's important advisors have left caucus or assumed more peripheral responsibilities, thus leaving the Premier without the same quality of advice he had when he redirected the party during 1992-94. Rod Love, for example, whom many believe to have been the mastermind behind the "Alberta Advantage," left provin-cial politics for more lucrative opportunities in the Calgary private sector at the end of February, 1998.[13]

On occasion, Love's departure was linked to Klein's alleged ambitions in federal politics. In the event, however, it was Love who moved in that direction, becoming a key organizer in the United Alternative/Canadian Alliance efforts. In any event, it has been clear since 1996 at least that Ralph Klein has no intention of heading for Ottawa.

In any event, Love is only a phone call away. In this respect moving from the Premier's Office into his own consulting business is more akin to privatizing a former government service than a major career shift. As with Jim Dinning, whose departure to the private sector was also widely seen as a grievous loss to the Klein government, in due course the premier brought him back to government service, this time as Chairman of the Calgary Regional Health Authority (CRHA).[14]

When Rod Love became a communications consultant, Peter Elzinga replaced him as the Premier's Executive Assistant. Elzinga had been an MP from the Edmonton area and so suitably exposed to "national" influ-ences. At the time of his appointment, he was Executive Director of the Conservative Party of Alberta. His concern with the profile of the provin-cial party would easily enough lead him to focus on areas of weakness to be remedied rather than of strength to be reinforced. For example, it is conventional wisdom that Alberta has three constituencies: Calgary, Edmonton and the rest. If a party wins two of them it will always form the government. Klein had won Calgary and the rest so he did not need to win Edmonton. But Elzinga had every reason to persuade him to try.[15]

If the flaccid intergovernmental policies of the Klein government in its second mandate are akin to the dog that did not bark, the major domestic initiative, the courting of Edmonton, is as Holmes also observed "a long shot, Watson; a very long shot." In 1997 the Tories won two of Edmonton's 21 seats, thereby matching the NDP in the capital city. A year later Gene Zwozdesky walked across the floor and, renouncing his Liberalism, became a Conservative. In May, 1999, he became an "Associate Minister." Now the Tories could boast they had three Edmonton MLAs, two-thirds of whom were in cabinet. In contrast, Calgary, which returned 19 MLAs, had but 5 Ministers to show for their fidelity to Ralph's Team. Moreover, the May, 1999 cabinet changes increased the number of ministers to twenty (twenty-one including the premier) and added two "caucus liaison" members. A larger cabinet and "associate ministers" might have been useful when the major changes of the first administration were underway. In 1999, it looked more like padding the front benches and making a gesture to Edmonton.[16]

But this raises yet another question: what compelled the Klein government to change a strategy that had been so successful? Why risk offending his strongest supporters by trying to gain the votes of those whom he had already offended?

If one were to ask Klein himself, the response would be that he was simply following the instructions of the people of Alberta. He has simply done what he said he would do. "When people get mad, they go to the right and to the left," he said. "When people feel comfortable, there is a moderating effect."[17] There is much truth in that. The Klein government has, indeed increased the comfort of Albertans and "moderation" is consistent with comfortableness. The interests of Albertans have been well served by what the Klein governments have achieved, and the data analyzed in Chapter Five support this observation.

But what of pride? Arguably Albertans were most proud of their government when, during Premier Lougheed's time, the battles with Ottawa were at their most intense. We have seen, however, that for two years after the 1997 election the eastern or the federal front grew quiet, even in the face of great provocation by the Chrétien government.

There remains the pride of Ralph Klein. As Dabbs explained at considerable length and with great insight, Klein has always been something of an outsider and, as the subtitle of his book proclaimed, a "maverick."[18] He is, however, a highly competitive maverick with no competition in the ring. Under the circumstances, it is not uncommon for politicians to look to history. In this instance, Klein would look not to his immediate predecessor but back to Ernest Manning and especially to Peter Lougheed.

Prior to the 1997 election there was considerable speculation that Klein might sweep the province.[19] He won 63 of 83 seats and 51% of the vote, which ought to have given him sufficient reason to rejoice. Instead, as Rich Vivone, author of a weekly political newsletter, *Insight into Government*, observed with great astuteness: "a province-wide television audience [on election night] saw a little rotund man wearing a face more fitting a kid who had just lost his dog. Klein's words, his demeanour, and his body language betrayed that, although he had won, he was not pleased."[20] He was not pleased because he expected to win more: he wanted 80 seats and 60% of the vote because that would put him in the same league as Manning and Lougheed. Three times Lougheed won over 90% of the seats; three times Manning won over 85%. Klein's 76% is by those standards less impressive. In the popular vote, he was behind even Don Getty, and nowhere near Lougheed.

The secret of the success of Manning and Lougheed, according to Vivone, is that they "understood the power of government. Their governments used economic, fiscal, and social policies to build a wealthy province with a material quality of life comparable to any in the world." They did, indeed, build wealthy governments; but their policies also led to indebted governments. Moreover, it is not self-evident that wealthy governments any more than wealthy individuals are always a good thing, nor that, if there is a trade-off between wealthy governments and wealthy individuals, it is always wise to prefer the former.

Even so, Vivone is undoubtedly correct to say that "Klein wants to be well remembered." Moreover, he may well be correct in his opinion that "Klein's overhaul is designed to devastate the Liberals by transforming the Conservatives into a more moderate, more positive, more active government."[21] Equally, however, Klein may be running against the memory of Peter Lougheed. Whether the temptation of "active government," which is to say, big, expensive, and intrusive government, can succeed in 2001 as it did in a quarter-century earlier is highly questionable. Seven years after having set a new course in Canadian politics towards smaller, more efficient, and more fiscally prudent government, perhaps his initiative has run out of momentum.

Getting Back on Track
It would be an amazing achievement, and one that Albertans and other Canadians would no doubt admire and reward, if Ralph Klein and his would recover their flair for producing creative and innovative policies. In order to move in the right direction, Klein must recall and heed the advice of Sir Roger Douglas: don't quit until the program is complete. In Chapter Five, our analysis of the popularity of the Klein government indicated that the premier had defied the logic of Anthony Downs' famous *Economic Theory of Democracy*. "Reinvestment strategies," accommodating

teachers unions, and acquiescing in the predatory ambitions of Liberals at Ottawa and their armies of administrators, indicate that Downs, not Douglas, seems to have triumphed in the end.

The long-term goals of the Klein government indeed, the very meaning of the term, "conservatism in Alberta," combined economic development and prosperity with government restructuring. As Klein and Dinning said many times during the early months of the first government, deficit elimination was a contingency, a means, not a purpose or goal. Time and again the Premier indicated he would not blink. Those notions and sentiments are as important today as they were then. Opening the provincial purse and throwing money at various pressure points, including health care, carries a major downside risk. Not only will government be spending taxpayers' money, they will be undoing all the political education and electoral "priming" that the original agenda had achieved. The policies and the justifications of them offered by the Klein government gave Albertans good reasons to vote for them. The danger with "reinvesting" is that is contradicts many of those reasons. There will always be pressure to spend, but more money is not always the answer. Albertans are committed to deficit-free expenditure increases, not a quick return to the days when governments spent more than they could afford.

As we saw in Chapters Four and Five, one of the reasons why Ralph Klein is such a popular premier is that he is willing to admit his mistakes. It is, accordingly, possible to present this deviation from the course of economic development and government restructuring as a temporary phenomenon—*a mistake*. This means recollecting the agenda that led to such widespread support for the Klein achievement. It means paying attention to the recommendations of the Alberta Economic Development Authority. It means using the ministerial business plans as effective guidelines for expenditures, not viewing them as an inconvenience to tax-eating bureaucrats. It means coming through on tax reform as promised in *Budget 2000*.

The government is bound to spend money on new policy initiatives. This is simply unavoidable. But it does not necessarily mean increased expenditures if old policies are defunded at the same time. Moreover, genuine reinvestment can be done in ways that are consistent with the goals of prosperity and restructuring if it is accompanied by a modest amount of strategic forethought. Reinvestment as a euphemism for increased expenditures is nothing more than a bottomless pit. Genuine reinvestment, in contrast, advances the long-term economic and restructuring objectives with which the entire Klein achievement began. Two issues, in particular, seem obvious public policy areas where the government can act consistent with their earlier successes.

The first is to build a consensus that the best way to deal with the budgetary surplus is through tax reductions. There are plenty of economic arguments to bolster an inherently appealing policy and so give Albertans good reasons to be comfortable with an initiative, for example, to eliminate the provincial income tax. Of course there will be opposition, but as we saw from the Alberta Advantage Surveys, support for general principles outweighs opposition to particular points.

A second area, restructuring health care delivery, is more complex. One of the principal dogmas of the supporters of state-supported and state-delivered medicare is that it is a fundamental, culture-defining institution, and that the Canada Health Act (CHA) is a hallowed document, at least as important as the Canadian Charter of Rights and Freedoms. That is why such a second-rate Minister as Diane Marleau was able in 1995 and 1996 to compel Premier Klein to back down and submit to Ottawa's interpretation of the CHA—notwithstanding his 70% approval rating. Over the past few years, however, a number of polls have also indicated considerable discontent with the CHA and with medicare.[22]

About the only thing that can make an expensive, irrational inefficient and misguided policy acceptable in a democracy is its popularity. And the growing unpopularity of the CHA is an obvious opportunity for the Klein government to act. One of the reasons Ms. Marleau could dictate Alberta's health care policy was because the federal government could withhold a significant amount of funding. In 1995, before Alberta had achieved a budgetary surplus, the opportunity cost of refusing dollars transferred from Ottawa was much higher than it is today. Indeed, federal funding of Alberta's health care system hovers around 10% of its actual cost. With the current surplus, Alberta can easily afford to ignore the CHA, forego the federal government's modest contribution, and implement modest user fees. Indeed, one econometric study has shown that the province, along with Ontario, would be better off.[23]

Besides, should a private delivery of health care prove more efficient than state-delivered medicare, that would be a net gain to the country as well. If federalism is to work, John Stuart Mill's "experiments in living," which the *National Post* called "competitive federalism,"[24] ought to be encouraged. In any event, the CHA requires only that health care be "publicly administered," which is to say, paid out of public funds. It says nothing about the necessity of a public provider.

Bill 11, The Alberta Health Care Protection Act, may provide the opportunity the Premier needs to indicate he means business in just the way he did in 1992-93 when it came to government pensions. the most contentious provision allows RHAs to out-source some surgical procedures provided it means cost savings and shorter waiting times. Bill 11 is certainly consistent with the kind of innovative and cost-effective restructuring initiatives that are likely to lead to greater prosperity. Moreover, evidence suggests that Bill 11 may not be as contentious as opponents of it believe. The Alberta Advantage survey data show, for instance, that Albertans are not as concerned about privatization as they are about accessibility: "What truly matters, in other words, is not who provides the services, but whether they are easily accessible."[25] Thus, for example, the CRHA's decision to contract out MRIs to private facilities is a step in the right direction.[26]

Allan Rock, the current federal health minister is widely despised in the province and elsewhere across the prairies and the north for his ill-considered gun-registration law, Bill C-68. In November, 1999, the Premier criticized Rock for his comments on the proposal that crystalized as Bill 11, the Alberta plan to out-source hip surgery the way Ontario does with hernia surgery. On March 10, 2000, Allan Rock paid a flying visit to Calgary to express his negative opinion of Bill 11, returning to Ottawa the same evening. Klein wrote the prime minister a one-line letter indicating that "the conduct of your health minister, the Honourable Allan Rock, last week in Calgary, was a disgrace to you and your government."[27]

A couple of days later at a party fund-raising dinner, Klein elaborated his criticism of Rock and extended his analysis of the harm the Liberal government of Jean Chrétien had done. There is, he said, "an anti-Alberta agenda at work in Ottawa today." Before dismissing the "old trick" of "Ottawa-bashing," Klein went on, "look at the evidence." Alberta was excluded from federal farm assistance extended to Manitoba and Saskatchewan, even though Alberta's eastern border is invisible from the air. In the 2000 budget, corporate income taxes were reduced from 28% to 21%, except in the energy industry, which will eventually cost Alberta oil and gas producers nearly $600 million. The heritage minister, Sheila Copps was mentioned, along with the federal government's rejection of elected senators. Finally he mentioned Allan Rock:

> I have written a one sentence letter to the prime minister. I would have written a shorter letter but I couldn't think of less to say. One sentence was what I needed to express my disgust at the tactics used by Allan Rock—(the same minister, by the way, who introduced the gun control legislation currently being challenged by seven provinces and territories). He gave the media more notice of his visit than he gave the Alberta minister of health. He made no effort to meet or talk with Alberta health officials to discuss his concerns directly. The audience for his speech was hand-

picked and included our most prominent political opponents to Bill 11. His political staff barred an Alberta minister of the crown entry to his news conference. He used discredited studies to make his case, and he left Alberta without so much as a phone call to provincial health minister, Halvar Jonson. That, my friends is why I say to you tonight, in both sadness and anger, that there is an agenda at work in Ottawa that once again seems unable, or unwilling to grasp the emergence of the new west.[28]

Granted, Ralph Klein was speaking to loyal supporters of the "Ralph party." Nevertheless, his willingness to defend Alberta's own agenda against the federal government and to do so on a matter of principle had not been evident for several years. It seems clear that Premier Klein has rediscovered something that his predecessors, Lougheed and Aberhart, learned in the heat of political strife as well: that Ottawa was almost invariably opposed to the interests of Albertans.

By taking control of the agenda and standing up to Ottawa, the Klein government may, like other Alberta governments, be able to articulate the division between federal and provincial responsibilities in ways that enhanced the pride of Albertans. Premier Klein appears to be increasingly aware that Albertans have few friends, whether elected or merely official, at Ottawa. He knows as well that the political culture of Alberta is clearly at odds with the agenda of successive prime ministers and especially with the bureaucracy. A fully functioning internally gyroscope would, in the past, have steered the Alberta Government away from policies such as the social union, which abandoned control to Ottawa in exchange for nothing; it would have used section 33 in cases such as *Vriend*.

The conflicts over Bill 11 suggest a new opportunity. We may, for example, expect Klein to play the "linkage" card, and to do so aggressively: in return for support on devolution of power and rebalancing the federation, Alberta might exact concessions on health care, gun registration, the Kyoto agreement and Banff. Likewise with domestic Alberta politics, the logic of the restructuring agenda would include increased privatization—through greater endorsement of charter schools or a voucher program, for example—and greater experimentation in the delivery of health care—by exploring "alternative" or "complementary" medicine, for instance. In fiscal reform, Stockwell Day's partial decoupling from the federal income tax regime was a start, but it could be extended to areas such as pension reform. These agenda items, if followed by the kind of consensus building of which Premier Klein has shown himself the master, could be followed by further action and greater achievement.

In politics it is never too late to recover from earlier mistakes because the story never ends. In the present context, creative and conservative politics in post-deficit times requires a recovery of the clear-sightedness that characterized the government in 1993, along with prudence, and courage. These virtues are far from absent, even if they are never fully present, and they are needed to ensure the government stays back on track.

ENDNOTES

INTRODUCTION

1   The political philosophy behind this understanding of political activity is borrowed mostly from Hannah Arendt, *The Human Condition*, (Chicago, University of Chicago Press, 1958), Michael Oakeshott, *On Human Conduct*, (Oxford, Oxford University Press, 1975), Bernard Crich, *In Defence of Politics*, (Harmondsworth, Penguin, 1993), and Kenneth Minogue, *Politics: A Very Short Introduction*, (Oxford, Oxford University Press, 1995).

2   2 February, 1995.

3   *Calgary Herald*, 28 August, 1994.

4   The longest version of this theme is Edmonton journalist Mark Lisac's, *The Klein Revolution*, (Edmonton, NeWest, 1995).

5   Klein, *Talking with Albertans: Reinvesting in Albertans*, (17 January, 1995). See also Alberta Report (3 April, 1995) cover story "'Don't Call Me Radical': As long as Klein has a winning fiscal agenda, he wants no part of a real right-wing revolution."

6   *Alberta Report*, 3 april, 1995.

7   See, for example, the self-indulgent and flaccid exploration of what the author calls a "faux-cowboy" motif, Gordon Laird, *Slumming It At the Rodeo: The Cultural Roots of Canada's Right-Wing Revolution*, (Vancouver, Douglas and McIntyre, 1998).

8   One of the most amazing (and amusing) examples of this approach to the Klein Government is by Brooke Jeffrey, who teaches political science in Montreal, *Hard Right Turn: The New Face of Neo-Conservatism*, (Toronto, Harper Collins, 1999). According to Professor Jeffrey, Klein is a "folksy fascist" (p. 137ff), among other things. See also Cooper's review, *The National Post*, 26 May, 1999, B5.

9   *Calgary Herald*, 30 September, 1994.

10 Osborne and Gaebler, *Reinventing Government: How the Entrepreneurial Spirit is Transforming the Public Sector*, (Don Mills, Addison-Wesley Publishing, 1992).

11 Compared to the ten states nearest Alberta there is still an Alberta disadvantage, though much less than any other province. See *Alberta Report*, 21 February, 1994.

12 *The Wall Street Journal*, 12 January, 1995.

13 *The Wall Street Journal*, 2 February, 1995; 23 February, 1995.

14 23 February, *The New York Times*, 1 January, 1995. The *Times* story was closely based on a report by Calgary writer, George Koch, in *Barron's* (12 December, 1994).

15 See *Globe and Mail*, 27 June, 1995, 21 July, 1995. Later in the year it was clear that the Klein achievements were a model for B.C. Liberal leader Gordon Campbell as well. Unfortunately for Mr. Campbell (and arguably for the fiscal health of B.C.), he lost the election to Glen Clark. See *Globe and Mail*, 8 December, 1995. *Alberta Report*, 18 December, 1995.

16 See Edward Greenspan and Anthony Wilson-Smith, *Double Vision: The Inside Story of the Liberals in Power* (Toronto, Doubleday, 1996), 163-70; Donald J. Savoie, *Governing From the Center: The Concentration of Power in Canadian Politics* (Toronto, University of Toronto Press, 1999), 172-87.

17 See *The Globe and Mail*, 22 November, 1994; *Alberta Report*, 12 December, 1994 contains a long excerpt from Klein's acceptance speech at the NCC awards banquet; see also *Fraser Forum* (March, 1995).

18 *The Globe and Mail*, 2 February, 1995.

19 According to Alberta Treasury, from 1981 to 1985, Alberta's resource revenue, the greatest amount of which comes from non-renewable sources, averaged $4.3 billion a year; from 1987 to 1992 it averaged $2.3 billion a year. See *Right on the Money: Alberta's Debt and Deficit*, 1993, 17.

20 *The Globe and Mail*, 3 February, 1995. As we shall see below, the issue of caseload exportation was greatly exaggerated.

21 *The Financial Post*, 17 February, 1994.

22 *Maclean's*, 7 March, 1994. The headline of Ken Whyte's "West" column for the 24 February, 1994 *Globe and Mail* made the same point: "Martin pays lip-service to what Alberta budget actually does."

23 *Macpherson's Democracy In Alberta: Social Credit and the Party System*, (Toronto, University of Toronto Press, 1953) served as the chief interpretative document for two generations of left-wing and eastern Canadian appraisals of Alberta political life. The latest version, to which reference has already been made, is Jeffrey's *Hard Right Turn*.

24 *Maclean's*, 5 December, 1994.

25 Chris Bruce, Ron Kneebone and Ken McKenzie, economists at the University of Calgary, *The Globe and Mail*, 27 June, 1995, offered their summary of seven "lessons" that Premier Harris could learn from Premier Klein. These very specific suggestions were, no doubt, quite sound, and, in his own way, Harris has adopted many of them—which is no surprise if a government claims to act on the basis of commonsense.

CHAPTER ONE

1 See Barry Cooper, "Western Political Consciousness," in Stephen Brooks, ed., *Political Thought in Canada*, (Toronto, Clarke Irwin, 1984), 213-38 and Cooper "The West: A Political Minority" in Neil Nevitte and Allan Kornberg, eds., *Minorities and the Canadian State*, (Toronto, Mosaic, 1985), 203-20. W.L. Morton's "The Bias of Prairie Politics" remains the classic statement of this point. See *Contexts of Canada's Past: Selected Essays of W.L. Morton*, ed. A.B. McKillop, (Toronto, Macmillan, 1980), 149-61.

2 Royal Commission on Dominion-Provincial Relations, *Report* (Ottawa, King's Printer, 1940), I, 239.

3 See the account in J.R. Mallory, *Social Credit and the Federal Power in Canada* (Toronto, University of Toronto Press, 1954), 128-35.

4 H. Blair Neatby, *William Lyon Mackenzie King*, vol. III, *1932-1939, The Prism of Unity* (Toronto, University of Toronto Press, 1976), 159.

5 See his *Essays on the Constitution: Aspects of Canadian Law and Politics*, (Toronto, University of Toronto Press, 1977), 296-7, 398-9.

6 *Edmonton Journal*, 21 August, 1939. The first Social Credit budget also contained a provision to impose Alberta's first and only sales tax. The tax was removed after the war and has since become a point of honour among successive Alberta governments to avoid reinstituting a tax so closely identified with bad economic times.

7 This interpretation follows that of Eugene Forsey, generally considered one of the foremost constitutional experts of his times. See his "Canada and Alberta: The Revival of Dominion Control Over the Provinces" (1939) reprinted in his *Freedom and Order*, (Toronto, McClelland & Stewart, 1974), 177-205. See also J.R. Mallory, *Social Credit and the Federal Power in Canada*, ch. 9.

8 See Frank R. Scott, *Essays on the Constitution: Aspects of Canadian Law and Politics*, (Toronto, University of Toronto Press, 1977), 320-21.

9 See E.J. Hanson, *Dynamic Decade: The Evolution and Effects of the Oil Industry in Alberta*, (Toronto, McClelland & Stewart, 1958).

10 There was another alternative but it was purely notional. Under the system used to open both crown lands and private property to oil and gas exploration, firms bid for the right to drill and the government collected the rents. (Virtually all subsurface mineral rights are vested in the Crown.) Theoretically it was possible to auction production or exploration rights on the basis of royalty returns rather than pre-exploration cash. This would have meant that the province would have shared the risk of finding nothing and would have deferred revenue collection. If Canadian banks were reluctant to expose themselves to such risk, it is perhaps not surprising that the Alberta government was equally risk-averse. The effect was to encourage concentration and to make it relatively difficult for Canadian junior companies to bid on exploration. Most Canadian exploration companies in fact have prospered by means of farm-in agreements with the majors.

11 The most thorough, though decidedly left-wing, account is still John Richards and Larry Pratt, *Prairie Capitalism: Power and Influence in the New West*, (Toronto, McClelland & Stewart, 1979). See also Allan Tupper, Larry Pratt and Ian Urquhart, "The Role of Government," in Allan Tupper and Roger Gibbins, eds., *Government and Politics in Alberta*, (Edmonton, University of Alberta Press, 1992), 31-66, and Mark Dickerson and Stan Drabek, "Provincial Revenue and Expenditure in Alberta: The Boom and Bust Cycle," in Roger Gibbins, Keith Archer, Stan Drabek, eds., *Canadian Political Life: An Alberta Perspective*, (Dubuque, Kendall Hunt, 1990), 135-44.

12 For details see Robert L. Mansell and Michael B. Percy, *Strength in Adversity: A Study of the Alberta Economy*, (Edmonton, University of Alberta Press, 1990), ch. 1.

13 The Alberta Heritage Fund stands in contrast to its counterpart in Alaska. There the state government cuts an annual cheque for each Alaskan, the amount depending upon the size of the fund that year. In Alberta the Government, not the citizens, control the disposition of assets, a reflection of crown rather than popular sovereignty.

14 Mansell, "Fiscal Restructuring in Alberta: An Overview," in Christopher J. Bruce, Ronald D. Kneebone and Kenneth J. McKenzie, eds., *A Government Reinvented: A Study of Alberta's Deficit Elimination Program*, (Toronto, Oxford University Press, 1997), 26-7.

15 Robert L. Mansell and Michael B. Percy, *Strength in Adversity*, 100-1.

16 Economists are not agreed upon the soundness of this strategy. One argument holds that a booming resource sector in a relatively small, open economy will result in even more specialization, not diversification. This often called the Dutch disease. See Ken Norrie, "A Regional Overview of the West since 1945" in A.W. Rasporich, ed.,

The Making of the Modern West, (Calgary, The University of Calgary Press, 1984).

17 See Alain C. Cairns and Edwin R. Black, "A Different Perspective on Canadian Federalism," *Canadian Public Administration*, 9(1966) 27-44.

18 Edward A. Carmichael and James K. Stewart, *Lessons from the National Energy Program*, (Toronto, C.D. Howe Institute, 1983), 1.

19 See Bercuson and Cooper, *Derailed*, ch. 4, for details and an analysis of one of the most malign policies in a questionable Trudeau legacy.

20 Foster, *The Sorcerer's Apprentices: Canada's Super-bureaucrats and the Energy Mess*, (Toronto, Collins, 1982). A more detached and certainly more sympathetic and academic account is in G. Bruce Doern and Glen Toner, *The Politics of Energy: The Development and Implementation of the NEP*, (Toronto, Methuen, 1985). Subsequent quotes are from these sources.

21 See Lusztig, "Canada's Long Road to Nowhere: Why the Circle of Command Liberalism Cannot be Squared," *Canadian Journal of Political Science*, 32(1999), 451-70.

22 See Whalley and Trela, *Regional Aspects of Confederation*, Royal Commission on the Economic Union and Development Prospects for Canada, vol. 68, (Toronto, University of Toronto Press, 1986).

23 See Mansell and Schlenker, "The Provincial Distribution of Federal Fiscal Balances." *Canadian Business Economics*, 3(1994-5), 3-19.

24 Whether federal transfers to the provinces have had the intended effect is highly questionable. They may have contributed to an increase in the size of the regional "have-not" economies, but they have also caused regional dependency and other political pathologies and other factors, such as private investment, have been far more important. For Atlantic Canada, see Fred McMahon, *Looking the Gift Horse in the Mouth*, (Halifax, AIMS, 1996).

25 See also Mansell, "Fiscal Restructuring," 16-20.

CHAPTER TWO

1 Mansell, "Fiscal Restructuring in Alberta: An Overview," in Christopher J. Bruce, Ronald D. Kneebone and Kenneth J. McKenzie, eds., *A Government Reinvented: A Study of Alberta's Deficit Elimination Program*, (Toronto, Oxford University Press, 1997), 32-3.

2 Sheila Pratt, "The Lougheed Party," in Andrew Nikiforuk *et al.*, *Running on Empty: Alberta After the Boom*, (Edmonton, NeWest, 1987), 92.

3 Mansell, "Fiscal Restructuring," 39.

4 Quoted in *Alberta Report*, 20 December, 1993.

5 *Maclean's*, 7 March, 1994.
6 *The Calgary Herald*, 25 October, 1994. This theme is considerably augmented in Kevin Taft, *Shredding the Public Interest: Ralph Klein and 25 years of One-Party Government*, (Edmonton, University of Alberta Press, 1997). We will examine Taft's argument below in chapter six.
7 Lisac, *The Klein Revolution* (Edmonton, NeWest, 1995), 34-5.
8 Quoted in Don Gillmor, "The People's Choice," *Saturday Night* (August, 1989).
9 Dabbs, *Ralph Klein, A Maverick Life*, (Vancouver, Greystone Books, 1995), 62.
10 City of Calgary, 1995 *Budget Summary*.
11 In 1968, for example, a 25-year old Ralph Klein was impressed by and attracted to Pierre Trudeau. He campaigned for Peter Petrasuk, the Liberal candidate in Calgary North, during the general election. Notwithstanding Trudeaumania, Petrasuk was defeated.
12 *Calgary Herald*, 15 November, 1992.
13 These and other data are taken from David K. Stewart, "Electing the Premier: An Examination of the 1992 Alberta Progressive Conservative Leadership Election," a paper presented to the Annual Meeting of the Canadian Political Science Association, Calgary, June 1994. A more edgy version of the CPSA paper is "Klein's Makeover of the Alberta Conservatives," in Gordon Laxer and Trevor Harrison, eds., *The Trojan Horse: Alberta and the Future of Canada*, (Montreal, Black Rose Books, 1995), 34-46.
14 *Alberta Report*, 21 December, 1992.
15 *Edmonton Journal*, 1 December, 1992.
16 *Maclean's*, 14 December, 1992.
17 *Alberta Report*, 21 December, 1992.
18 Dabbs, *Ralph Klein*, 103.
19 *Alberta Report*, 20 April, 1993.
20 *Toronto Star*, 6 December, 1992.
21 *Alberta Report*, 21 December, 1992.
22 *Alberta Report*, 21 December, 1992.
23 *The Financial Post*, 9-1 January, 1993.
24 Jock Osler and Ron Ghitter were close advisors to Clark; Clark, in turn endorsed Nancy Betkowski when Osler and Ghitter were working for her.
25 *Alberta Report*, 28 December, 1992.
26 See Ronald D. Kneebone and Kenneth J. McKenzie, "The Process Behind Institutional Reform in Alberta," in Christopher Bruce, Ronald Kneebone and Kenneth McKenzie, eds., *A Government Reinvented: A Study of Alberta's Deficit Elimination Program*, (Toronto,

Oxford University Press, 1997), 183-4; and Paul Boothe, "The New Approach to Budgeting in Alberta," in *A Government Reinvented*, 226-7. The five SPCs were: Agriculture and Rural Development, Health, Community Services, Financial Planning, and Natural Resources and Sustainable Development. It is perhaps worth noting that there was no SPC devoted to Urban Development.

27 *Calgary Herald*, 6 December, 1992.

28 See Tom Flanagan, *Waiting for the Wave: The Reform Party and Preston Manning*, (Toronto, Stoddart, 1995), esp. ch. 3.

29 Taras and Tupper, "Politics and Deficits: Alberta's Challenge to the Canadian Political Agenda," in Douglas Brown and Janet Hiebert, eds., *Canada: The State of the Federation, 1994*, (Kingston, Queen's University Institute for Intergovernmental Relations, 1994), 66-7. Critics of the new agenda, especially of fiscal restraint, found the connection between Manning, Klein, and later, Mike Harris, to be an outrageous conspiracy.

30 Klein, "The Alberta Advantage," *Fraser Forum*, (March, 1995), 5.

31 Alberta Financial Review Commission, *Report to Albertans*, (31 March 1993), 5-6.

32 *Report*, 17.

33 Moody's Investors' services rated Alberta AA2, and Standard and Poor's Corporation rated it AA with a "negative" outlook during 1993. Peter Plaut of Salomon Brothers, "Province of Alberta—A Credit Review," 8 September, 1994 endorsed the bond rating agencies judgement and concluded that Alberta's economic outlook "remains bright for the medium term" and drew attention to the efforts made during the spring and summer of 1993 to balance the budget.

34 *Dinning, Budget '93: A Financial Plan for Alberta*, (6 May, 1993), 9.

35 The Deficit Elimination Act was replaced *by The Balanced Budget and Debt Retirement Act* shortly after the 1994 budget was introduced. It applied the same principles of deficit elimination to debt reduction and projected paying off the "debt mortgage" by FY 2021, a 25-year "amortization." See *Budget '95: Building a Strong Foundation*, (21 February 1995), 16-23.

36 The contrast with the last major document tabled by the Getty government is striking. *Toward 2,000 Together: A Discussion Paper on Alberta's Economic Options and Choices*, (1991) allowed that a "balanced budget is important," but went on to discuss as the first "option" continuing "to provide loans, equity, grants and loan guarantees." The last option was "providing no special funding...but offering an attractive climate for all business in Alberta." By 1993 the order of priority was reversed.

37 These are collected in *A Better Way II: A Blueprint for Building Alberta's Future*, 1995/96 to 1997/98.

38 In addition to the chapters by Kneebone and McKenzie, and by Boothe, cited above, see also Robert L. Mansell, "Fiscal Restructuring in Alberta: An Overview," in *A Government Reinvented*, 16-73.

39 Whyte, "Klein of the Times," *Saturday Night*, (May, 1994), 50.

40 Whyte, "Klein of the Times," 50.

CHAPTER THREE

1 Shortly after the campaign started, Decore was asked about the Liberal Party's position on abortion—which is directly a matter of federal legislation, not of provincial responsibility except indirectly through health care funding of abortion facilities. Decore said that he and his party favoured the pro-life or anti-abortion position. In fact, that was Decore's personal position, which he maintained on religious grounds. His slip of the tongue caused a week of anti-Liberal headlines detailing his retractions and clarifications. Premier Klein's handling of the question at the 1995 Tory convention is a study in contrast. Social conservatives in the Party proposed a motion to end funding of abortions. The Premier responded by saying that this was a legal matter covered by the federal Canada Health Act and so not a topic that ought to be considered by a provincial party. Morally considered, he said, it was a difficult question between a woman, her doctor, and God.

2 Don Gillmor, "The People's Choice," *Saturday Night*, (August, 1989), 36.

3 *Maclean's*, 28 June, 1993.

4 *Alberta Report*, 20 December, 1993.

5 David Osborne and Ted Gaebler, *Reinventing Government*, (Don Mills, Addison-Wesley, 1992); Douglas, *Unfinished Business*, (Auckland, Random House, 1993).

6 *Unfinished Business*, 53.

7 Lisac, *The Klein Revolution*, 68.

8 Jeffrey, *Hard Right Turn*, 92-3.

9 *Alberta Hansard*, (24 February, 1994), 258.

10 *Calgary Herald*, 1 September, 1993.

11 Mark Lisac's *The Klein Revolution*, is highly critical of what the Klein government has done. At one point in his book he remarked: "These were days when I asked myself if I were watching the creation of a sugar-coated fascism. But I also wondered if I was losing my grip on reality." Perhaps the two options were related. Lisac's hostility was also expressed in his curious literary conceit of addressing his remarks to

Lincoln Steffens, the great American muckraker and advocate of the reinvention of government during the early decades of this century. In Steffens' day bureaucratic control of corruption was an appropriate response. If Steffens could witness the Klein achievement why would he not applaud? If muckraking is to be done today, surely the greatest amount of muck is to be raked from the bureaucracy. What, after all, do they do but regulate adults? Catherine Ford, writing in the *Calgary Herald* (11 June, 1996), also thought Premier Klein was a fascist.

12 *Alberta Hansard*, (31 August, 1993), 10.
13 *Alberta Hansard*, (31 August, 1993), 8.
14 *Alberta Hansard*, (31 August, 1993), 9.
15 *Alberta Report*, 20 December, 1993.
16 Ronald D. Kneebone and Kenneth J. McKenzie, "The Process Behind Institutional Reform in Alberta" in Bruce, *et al.*, *A Government Reinvented*, 177. Likewise Robert Mansell observed: "The typical approach has been to set policy primarily on the votes for expenditures, with determination of how finance the expenditures, through tax increases or borrowing, being mainly the secondary decision. In contrast, the Alberta program would now first involve a determination of the votes for tax and borrowing levels, with expenditures to be decided mainly within this budget constraint." Mansell, "Fiscal Restructuring," in ibid., 55.
17 The Speech from the Throne was delivered on 10 February, 1994 and was short, bland and congratulatory. See *Alberta Hansard*, (10 February, 1994), 1-3.
18 *Alberta Hansard*, (24 February, 1994), 255. *Budget '94: Securing Alberta's Future: The Financial Plan in Action*, and *A Better Way: A Plan for Securing Alberta's Future*. Both were published on 24 February, 1994.
19 The four pillars were: (1) balanced budgets; (2) business plans; (3) measuring performance; (4) debt retirement. *Budget '95* was accompanied by *A Better Way II*, the business plans of each of the ministries.
20 *Budget '95: Building a Strong Foundation*, presented by Jim Dinning, Provincial Treasurer, 21 February, 1995, 7.
21 *Agenda '96: Balance, Responsibility*, Opportunity, presented by Jim Dinning, Provincial Treasurer, 22 February, 1996.
22 Cardinal, "Welfare Reform in Alberta," *Fraser Forum* (June, 1995), 6.

CHAPTER FOUR

1 *Calgary Herald*, 8 May, 1993.
2 *Alberta Report*, 16 August, 1993.
3 *Calgary Herald*, 7 October, 1993.

4   *Calgary Herald*, 22 October, 1993.

5   *Calgary Herald*, 31 October, 1993

6   *Calgary Herald*, 3 November, 1993.

7   Maclean's, 15 November, 1993.

8   The actual fee is $466 p.a. or $450 for 10 months. A fee waiver is available for low income families—which, in turn, has been denounced as "humiliating" for the recipients rather than praised as humane or generous by those who pay.

9   *Calgary Herald*, 25 November, 1993.

10 *Calgary Herald*, 25 November, 1993.

11 *Alberta Report*, 10 October, 1994

12 The Roman Catholic School Boards had constitutional protection under the Alberta Act and the ordinances of the North-West Territories incorporated into it, so their independence was maintained. They are, however, prevented by an administrative ruling from collecting more from their supporters than they would have received directly from the Government.

13 *Calgary Herald*, 19 January, 1994.

14 *Calgary Herald*, 18 January, 1994.

15 *Calgary Herald*, 23 January, 1994.

16 "Road Kill...." On the other hand, as M.S. Shedd pointed out, "Barring an extraordinary degree of administrative inefficiency, it is impossible to cut welfare without disproportionately hurting the poor and, by extension, women, children, and the aged." Family and Social Services, the Alberta Deficit Elimination Program, and Welfare Reform," in *A Government Reinvented*, 260.

17 *Calgary Herald*, 14 February 1994; 18 February, 1994.

18 *Alberta Report*, 14 March, 1994.

19 *Calgary Herald*, 28 April, 1994.

20 *Alberta Hansard*, (1 September, 1993), 14.

21 *Alberta Hansard*, (28 September, 1993), 524.

22 *Alberta Hansard*, (10 March, 1994), 543.

23 *Alberta Hansard*, (1 June 1994), 2384-5.

24 *On Balance*, vol. 8:2 (March, 1995).

25 *Calgary Herald*, 29 November, 1994.

26 *Montreal Gazette*, 26 December, 1992.

27 Lisac, *The Klein Revolution*, 74. A few years later, on the occasion of his induction as an Officer in the Order of Canada, Don Getty remarked that the Klein government had "blundered" on health and education policy: "They broke the system and now they're pouring money in trying to fix it. Well, it's broke. It's busted." Premier Klein replied that Don Getty is a nice man and a private citizen with his own ideas with

which Klein does not agree. *Globe and Mail*, 16 April, 1999. According to William Thorsell, (*Globe and Mail*, 14 September, 1996), Peter Lougheed likewise "doesn't want to be lumped in with his successors, either as an individual or as a maker of policy." See also Lougheed's interview with Peter C. Newman, *Maclean's*, 7 August, 1995. This is also why, at the celebration of 25 years of PCs in office (held, symbolically, at the venerable Palliser Hotel), Ralph Klein was not invited—though Joe Clark was. *Globe and Mail*, 6 September, 1996. Thus Colby Cosh distinguished between the Lougheed-Getty "state capitalists" and the "radical rightists" of the first Klein government. *Alberta Report*, 16 September, 1996.

28 Rod Love confirmed an essentially identical version of Kowalski's fall to Frank Dabbs, and subsequent events have given it a ring of truth. Begin with the fact that Klein owed something to Kowalski for having won the second ballot in December, 1992 and gaining the premiership. Certainly Kowalski was an old-style politician at a time when Klein had a much different agenda. Dabbs also describes the meeting between Kowalski and his own Calgary supporters in a way that reminds one of another famous Machiavellian meeting (*The Prince*, ch. 8). Kowalski met a number of Klein's Calgary supporters at the McDougall Centre, a beautifully renovated sandstone schoolhouse in downtown Calgary that houses the southern Alberta office of the premier and of several political officials. The rooms are large, high ceilinged, well appointed chambers reeking of manly power. There is plenty of brass, leather, and dark wood. On 28 October, 1993, there was plenty of liquid refreshment and a splendid selection of hors d'oeuvres. "The conversation," said Dabbs, "was easygoing, confident, well lubricated." Klein gave a short speech in praise of Kowalski; Kowalski allowed as he had no interest in power, was ever devoted to the interests of Klein and would much rather be golfing than have anything to do with politics. None of Klein's Calgary supporters was impressed except by Kowalski's highly polished mendacity. He was both disliked and considered a liability, though it would be an exaggeration to say that Kowalski was feared. See Dabbs, *Ralph Klein*, 129.

29 Under Kowalski's successor, Murray Smith, the Department took a 40% cut (188 positions). It was estimated that another 90 positions would go when the tourism side was privatized. *Calgary Sun*, 2 May, 1995.

30 *Alberta Hansard*, 21 October, 1993), 988. See also the report in the *Calgary Herald* the next day.

31 *Calgary Herald*, 10 October, 1993.

32 *Alberta Report*, 28 February, 1994.

33 *Alberta Report*, 26 September, 1994.

34 *Calgary Herald*, 26 November, 1993.

35 *Calgary Herald*, 10 March, 1994.

36 *Alberta Report*, 18 October, 1993.

37 *Calgary Herald*, 20 January, 1995.

38 For example, one such story told of a person who died on the way to a Calgary hospital because he had been denied a bed in Edmonton. The government responded by saying that the reporter neglected to point out that he could have had his operation earlier, in Edmonton, but at the hands of a surgeon other than his first choice. *The Globe and Mail*, 17 September, 1994.

39 *Calgary Herald*, 28 April, 1994.

40 See Shedd, "Family and Social Services...," 257ff for examples.

41 *The Globe and Mail*, 18 January, 1994. See also 1995-96 *Government Estimates*, presented by Jim Dinning to the Legislative Assembly 21 February, 1995, 7.

42 *Alberta Hansard*, 1 March, 1994, 324.

43 See the perceptive comments on the production values of the 1995 broadcast in Dabbs, *Ralph Klein*, 152-3.

44 *Globe and Mail*, 3 April, 1995.

45 See Tom Flanagan and Stephen Harper, "Neo-Cons and Theo-Cons," *Calgary Herald*, 3 May, 1997; and a longer version "Conservative Politics in Canada, Past, Present and Future," in William Gairdner, ed., *After Liberalism*, (Toronto, Stoddard, 1998), 168-92.

46 *Financial Post Magazine*, (8 April, 1995), 20.

47 *Globe and Mail*, 20 July, 1995.

48 *Globe and Mail*, 25 September, 1995.

49 *Globe and Mail*, 26 September, 1995. See below, Chapter Six.

50 *Globe and Mail*, 7 March, 1996.

51 *Globe and Mail*, 11 March, 1996. In February, 1996 another controversial social issue, the exclusion of "gay rights" from the Individual Rights Protection Act, was justified in the Alberta Court of Appeal en route to its ultimate reversal in the Supreme Court of Canada. See below, Chapter Six for details.

52 *Globe and Mail*, 9 November, 1995.

53 *Globe and Mail*, 11, 12 November, 1995.

54 *Globe and Mail*, 30 May, 1996; 13 November, 1996; 19 November, 1996; 20 December, 1996.

54 The role of Ken Kowalski in alerting the media to share purchases of Multi-Corp. stock by Hugh Dunne, who managed the Calgary office of the premier, and by Rod Love's wife, increased the animosity between him and Klein. See *Globe and Mail*, 24 April, 1996.

55 *Alberta Report*, 16 January, 1995.
56 *Financial Post Magazine*, 8 April, 1995.
57 *Alberta Report*, 5 June, 1995.
58 *Alberta Report*, 10 July, 1995.
59 *Alberta Report*, 8 January, 1996.
60 *Financial Post*, 3 February, 1996.
61 *Financial Post*, 23 February, 1996. 20% wanted increased spending; 8% lower taxes; 30% favoured a combination of all three.
62 *Alberta Report*, 10 June, 1996.

CHAPTER FIVE

1   Johnson, André Blais, Henry E. Brady, Jean Crête, *Letting the People Decide: Dynamics of a Canadian Election*, (Kingston and Montreal, McGill-Queen's University Press, 1992), 4-5.
2   Downs, *An Economic Theory of Democracy*, (New York, Harper, 1957), 69.
3   In 1993, the Klein government received 44% of popular support. In 1997 support rose to 51%.
4   Of course, not everyone agrees as to the intensity of Alberta's economic crisis. archer and Gibbins, for example, "reject any premise that the actions of the alberta government were driven solely by economic realities," see archer and Gibbins, "What Do Albertans Think? The Kle9in Agenda on the Public Opinion Landscape," in C. Bruce, R. Kneebone and K. McKenzie, eds., *A Government Reinvented: A Survey of Alberta's Deficit Elimination Program*, (Toronto, Oxford University Press, 1997), 462.
5   See, for example, K. Hughes, G. Lowe and A. McKinnon, "Public Attitudes Toward Budget Cuts in Alberta: Biting the Bullet or Feeling the Pain?" *Canadian Public Policy*, XXII: 3 (1996, 268-84)); J. Stokes and k. Archer, "The De-Klein of Government in Alberta," paper presented at the Annual Meetings of the Canadian Political Science Association, (Montreal, Quebec, 1995); see K. Archer and R. Gibbins, "What Do Albertans Think?" The Klein Agenda on the Public Opinion Landscape"; M. Nemeth, "to Tax or Cut," *Maclean's*, (February 13, 1995), 17; and, A. Geddes, "The Klein Revoluiton: Provinces Paying Heed to 'Ralph-Onomics,'" *The Financial Post*, (January 22, 1994), S14-15.
6   *Calgary Herald*, (March 23, 1996); *Calgary Herald*, (December 13, 1996).
7   See P. Lazarsfeld, B. Berelson and H. Gaudet, *The People's Choice: How The Voter Makes Up His Mind in a Presidential Campaign*, (New York, Columbia University Press, 1948); B. Berelson, P. Lazarsfeld and W. McPhee, *Voting: A Study of Opinion Formation in a Presidential Campaign*, (Chicago, University of Chicago Press, 1954); and A.

Campbell, P. Converse, W. Miller and D. Stokes, *The American Voter*, (New York, Wiley, 1960).

8   See Keith Archer, "Voting Behaviour and the Political Dominance In Alberta, 1971-1991," in A. Tupper and R. Gibbins, eds., *Government and Politics in Alberta*, (Edmonton, The University of Alberta Press, 1992).

9   See M. Kanji, "Information, Cognitive Mobilization and Representative Governance in Canada," paper presented at the Value Change and Governance Seminar, (Toronto, Ontario, June 11, 1999); M. Kanji and K. Archer, "When and How Canadian Voters Decide: Searching for Systematic Trends in Canadian Election Campaigns," paper presented at the Annual Canadian Political Science Association Meetings, (Ottawa, Ontario, May/June, 1998); R. Dalton and M. Wattenberg, "The Not So Simple Act of Voting," in Finifter, ed., *Political Science: The State of the Discipline*, (Washington, DC, The American Political Science Association, 1993).

10 Downs, *An Economic Theory of Democracy*, ch. 3.

11 See Archer and Gibbins, "What Do Albertans Think?" 482.

12 See Peter Newman, Maclean's, 6 February, 1995; *Globe and Mail*, 22 November, 1994; *New York Times*, 1 January, 1995.

13 See w. Jacoby, "Public Attitudes Toward Government Spending," *American Journal of Political Science*, 38 (194): 336-61.

14 Of course, it is possible that these factors have important indirect effects by way of "intervening" variables, but that analaysis is beyond the scope of this investigation.

15 See, for example, the revealing portrait by Frank Dabbs in the Epilogue to his generally admiring account, *Ralph Klein*, 173ff.

16 See, for example, Clarke, Jenson, LeDuc and Pammett. *Absent Mandate*, (Toronto, Gage 1989); Mancuso, M., M. Atkinson, A. Blais, I. Greene and N. Nevitte, *A Question of Ethics: Canadians Speak Out*, (Toronto, Oxford University Press, 1998); Nye, J. Jr., P. Zelikow and D. King, *Why People Don't Trust Government* (Cambridge: Harvard University Press, 1997); and Norris, P., *Critical Citizens: Global Support for Democratic Governance* (Oxford: Oxford University Press, 1999). R. Dobell and B. Perry, "Anger in the System: Political Discontent in Canada," *Parliamentary Government*, 39:3 (1990), 3-20.

CHAPTER SIX

1   *Globe and Mail*, 11 March, 1996.

2   *Globe and Mail*, 29 March, 1998; see also 5 April, 1996; 9 September, 1996.

3   *Globe and Mail*, 3 March, 1997; *Calgary Herald*, 28 February, 1997.

4 *Globe and Mail*, 12 March, 1997; *Calgary Herald*, 12 March, 1997.

5 *Alberta Report*, 23 December, 1996. The data were from an Angus Reid survey.

6 See Cardinal's remarks in *Fraser Forum*, (June, 1995), 5-10. See also his earlier assessment in the *Globe and Mail*, 3 October, 1993.

7 See the account by Sheed, "Family and Social Services," in *A Government Reinvented*, 251-60.

8 Actually, he called the young men who flocked to Calgary looking for work when the NEP had begun to devastate the oil industry "eastern bums and creeps," since most of them came from central and Atlantic Canada and, instead of returning whence they came, stayed in town and cost the city money as they drifted into welfare dependency, and crime. Naturally enough, eastern Canadian politicians took umbrage at his remarks. Klein quickly apologized and distinguished between the genuine bums and creeps "who were robbing banks and pimping young girls," and who were not welcome, and those "who were looking for a future and were ready to help build a great city [and who] were welcome even in hard times." Dabbs, *Ralph Klein*, 60.

9 *Globe and Mail*, 9 February, 1995.

10 *Globe and Mail*, 8 November, 1996.

11 *Globe and Mail*, 9 February, 1996.

12 *Alberta Report*, 26 February, 1996.

13 Calgary, Canada West Foundation, 1997.

14 *Globe and Mail*, 6 January, 1995.

15 *Globe and Mail*, 1 May, 1995.

16 *Globe and Mail*, 19 February, 1996.

17 *Globe and Mail*, 23 May, 1998; 28 May, 1998.

18 *Calgary Herald*, 5 September, 1997; *Alberta Report*, 15 September, 1997.

19 See Christopher J. Bruce and Arthur M. Schwartz, "Education: Meeting the Challenge," in *A Government Reinvented*, 387-97.

20 Stephen B. Lawton, "Comments [on Bruce and Schwartz]" in *A Government Reinvented*, 419.

21 *Calgary Herald*, 16, January, 2000.

22 See the account by Richard H.M. Plain, "The Role of Health care Reform in the Reinventing of Government in Alberta," in *Reinventing Government*, 294-9, 316-19. *Calgary Herald*, 22 September, 1999; 19 November, 1999.

23 *Globe and Mail*, 23-24 November, 1995.

24 *Alberta Report*, 30 December, 1996.

25 *Alberta Report*, 4 December, 1995; *Globe and Mail*, 16 December, 1995; 12 February, 1996.

26 *Globe and Mail*, 1 August, 1996; 11 January, 1997; 21 March, 1998.

27 *Globe and Mail*, 7 March, 1997.
28 *Globe and Mail*, 10 July, 1995; *Alberta Report*, 17 July, 1995.
29 *Globe and Mail*, 28-29 February, 1996.
30 *Globe and Mail*, 14 April, 1996.
31 *Globe and Mail*, 7 January, 1995.
32 *Globe and Mail*, 10, 11, 14 April, 1995.
33 Nor were a couple of Ontario facilities, IVF Canada in Toronto, and Shouldice Hospital in Thornhill, both of which engaged in practices prohibited explicitly in Alberta.
34 *Globe and Mail*, 16 May, 1997.
35 In March, 1998, the government introduced Bill 37, which would have established a restricted kind of private hospital. In November it withdrew the proposal because of the strength of the political opposition to it in the Legislature, and the premier announced a "health summit" to look at Bill 37 and other measures to deal with the heath care issue.
36 See *The National Post*, 18 January, 1999.
37 *National Post*, 1 November, 1999.
38 *Globe and Mail*, 19 November, 1999; *Calgary Herald*, 19 November, 1999; *National Post*, 19 November, 1999.
39 See Martin Zelder, "Will Alberta's Health Care Reforms Succeed?" *Fraser Forum* (January, 2000), 7-15.
40 *Calgary Herald*, 14 March, 2000. A news release provided ten reasons why Rock's behaviour was disgraceful.
41 *Calgary Herald*, 71 March, 2000.
42 See, for example, the results of a Pollara poll on paying for medicare. *Calgary Herald*, 12 January, 2000. *National Post*, 12 January, 2000.
43 *Globe and Mail*, 26 April, 1997.
44 *Globe and Mail*, 28 July, 1997.
45 *Alberta Report*, 13 October, 1997; *Globe and Mail*, 1 October, 1997. The exclusion of organizations such as the NCC or the Alberta Taxpayers' Federation ought to give leftwing observers a reason to reassess their views on the gigantic rightwing conspiracy against big government. See, for example, Brooke Jeffrey, *Hard Right Turn*, ch. 10.
46 *Globe and Mail*, 26 April, 1997.
47 *Globe and Mail*, 30 October, 1997.
48 *Alberta Report*, 13 October, 1997.
49 *Globe and Mail*, 30 October, 1997.
50 *Globe and Mail*, 7 November, 1997.
51 *Calgary Herald*, 18 November, 1997.
52 The speech is available on the provincial website and exerpted in the *Calgary Herald*, 10 January, 1998.

53 *Globe and Mail*, 14 January, 1998; *Alberta Report*, 12 January, 1998.
54 *Budget '99: The Right Balance*. Presented by Stockwell Day, Provincial Treasurer, 11 March, 1999.
55 *Globe and Mail*, 12 March, 1999; *Calgary Herald*, 12 March, 1999.
56 *Alberta Report*, 22 March, 1999.
57 *Globe and Mail*, 12 February, 1997; *Financial Post Magazine*, 26 April, 1997. In March 1997, Monier Rahall self-published an exposé of ATB, *Banksters and Prairie Boys*, (Edmonton, Monopoly, 1997).
58 *Calgary Herald*, 9 September, 1998. See also , 9 September, 1998. See also *Alberta Report*, 7 September, 1998; 8 February, 1999; *National Post*, 6 February, 1999.
59 *Alberta Report*, 22 February, 1999.
60 In addition to Smith's *Gambling and the Public Interest*, (November, 1997), CWF published *Rolling the Dice: Alberta's Experience with Direct Democracy and Video Lottery Terminals*, (September, 1998); *The State of Gambling in Canada: An Interprovincial Roadmap of Gambling and Its Impact*, (October, 1998); *Gambling in Canada: Triumph, Tragedy or Tradeoff*, (July, 1999). Additional studies are also underway at CWF.
61 "The first guiding principle is that the guiding principles, whatever form they take, must be respected and followed." *Globe and Mail*, 27 April, 1998.
62 Quoted in CWF, *The State of Gambling in Canada*, 6.
63 *Calgary Herald*, 5 August, 1999.

CHAPTER SEVEN

1 See, in addition to the many examples in *Reinventing Government*, Michael A. Walker, ed., *Privatization: Tactics and Techniques*, (Vancouver, The Fraser Institute, 1988); Walter Block and George Lermer, *Breaking the Shackles: Deregulating Canadian Industry*, (Vancouver, The Fraser Institute, 1991).
2 *Fraser Forum*, (March, 1995), 7.
3 Kneebone and McKenzie, "The Process Behind Institutional Reform," in *A Government Reinvented*, 177.
4 "Introduction" to *A Government Reinvented*, 12.
5 There was another rather more specialized lesson involved in the rapidity and thoroughness with which the incoming Tories distanced themselves from their predecessors and then effectively repudiated them. Had the federal Tories been less parochial in their obsessions with Quebec, the constitution, and loyal to the remarkable legacy of Prime Minister Mulroney, they might have been able to avoid being extinguished in 1993. Such circumstances, however, do not frequently recur.

6   Ralph Klein, *Talking With Albertans: Building the Alberta Advantage, Reaching the Destination Together,* 17 January, 1994.

7   *Alberta Report,* 18 October, 1993.

8   *Maclean's,* 7 March, 1994; *Budget '94: Securing Alberta's Future, The Financial Plan in Action,* (24 February, 1994), 109; *Alberta Hansard,* (24 February, 1994), 256.

9   *Budget '94,* 7.

10   *Calgary Herald,* 15 November, 1992.

11   *Toronto Star,* 6 December, 1992.

12   *Alberta Hansard,* (31 August, 1993), 9.

13   Lisac, *The Klein Revolution,* 164.

14   *Calgary Herald,* 23 September, 1993

15   *Calgary Herald,* 5 October, 1993.

16   *Calgary Herald,* 23 January, 1994.

17   *Calgary Herald,* 8 April, 1994.

18   *Alberta Hansard,* (31 August, 1993), 10.

19   *Klein, Talking With Albertans: Reinvesting in Albertans,* (17 January, 1995). See also *The Globe and Mail,* 14 June, 1994; *Calgary Herald,* 1 March, 1994.

20   See Jean Burnet, *Next-Year Country: A Study of Social Organization in Alberta,* (Toronto, University of Toronto Press, 1951).

21   Mansfield, *America's Constitutional Soul,* (Baltimore, Johns Hopkins University Press, 1991), 74.

22   When the Government introduced Key Performance Indicators (KPI) in 1993, there was always the possibility they would introduce perverse incentives—bureaucrats would aim to meet the criteria, not to provide good service. It is also foreseeable that when government, citizens, and bureaucrats all agree on a course of action there may be no brakes. As Kneebone and McKenzie observed, the civil service in particular may "neglect its traditional role of warning the government against ill-conceived policies." The Process Behind Institutional Reform," 204. Astute political leaders can take precautions against such dangers, however.

23   Mansell, "Fiscal Restructuring," in *A Government Reinvented,* 48-52.

24   *Globe and Mail,* 28-9 January, 1998.

25   Later it was evident in Klein's support for Stockwell Day in his run for the Leadership of the UA/CA.

26   *Globe and Mail,* 27 February, 1997.

27   *Calgary Herald,* 25 February, 1997; *Globe and Mail,* 30 March, 1998.

28   *Globe and Mail,* 8 December, 1998; *Calgary Herald,* 8 December, 1998.

29   *National Post,* 30 January, 1999.

30   *National Post,* 1 February, 1999.

31 *Edmonton Journal*, 5 March, 1999.

32 Roger Gibbins, "The Western Pulse: 9-1-1 Federalism," *Western Landscapes*, I:3 (April, 1999), 4.

33 There may have been some purely domestic factors involved as well. On 20 February, 1999, we published an article in *The Calgary Herald* based on the third Alberta Advantage Survey, discussed in Chapter Five. In it, we showed that health care remains a very sensitive issue. Almost all Albertans support universal health care and think that Ottawa ought to set national standards. To the extent that health care was identified with the social union, it may have limited the government's flexibility in dealing with Ottawa.

34 *Minutes and Proceedings of the Special Joint House-Senate Committee on the Constitution*, (1980-81), No. 48:31-2 (29 January, 1981).

35 *Globe and Mail*, 25 July, 1997; *Alberta Report*, 24 November, 1997; 20 April, 1998.

36 See Peter Russell, "Standing Up for Notwithstanding," *Alberta Law Review*, 29 (1991), 476.

37 See Hon. L. Fuller, "The Forms and Limits of Adjudicaiton," *Harvard Law Review*, 92(1978), 353-409.

38 *Globe and Mail*, 30 March, 1998.

39 *Globe and Mail*, 11-12 March, 1998.

40 The imprudent use of s.33 in Bill 26 with the expectation that *Vriend* would likely be decided against Alberta led, as one might expect, to a great deal of speculation that the "error" in Bill 26 was deliberate so that s.33 would be sufficiently discredited that it could not be used in *Vriend* either. The great problem, as with all such far-sighted Machiavellianism is to find evidence.

41 *Calgary Herald*, 3 April, 1998.

42 *Globe and Mail*, 10 April, 1998.

43 *Globe and Mail*, 16 April, 1998.

44 *Calgary Herald*, 9 April, 1998.

45 *Calgary Herald*, 26 February, 1999.

46 *National Post*, 19 March, 1999.

47 *Calgary Herald*, 22 April, 1999.

48 The data from the Alberta Advantage survey are clear enough. A large majority (82%) agree with the proposition that homosexuals should not be discriminated against for their sexual orientation. Far fewer (42%) would recognize the legitimacy of same-sex marriage, with adoption being permitted to homosexual couples (42%), or with having homosexual materials available in schools (33%). See also the series of op-ed articles by Rainer Knopff and Fred Wall based on this survey in *The Calgary Herald* (30 March to 3 April, 1999).

49 *Calgary Herald*, 3 March, 1999.
50 In March, 2000, Bill 202, the Marriage Amendment Act became law. It defined marriage to be exclusively "between a man and a woman." As the Alberta justice minister observed, however, it may be constitutionally questionable insofar as marriage is, under section 91(26) a matter of federal jurisdiction. See *National Post*, 15 March, 2000.
51 *Calgary Herald*, 14 February, 1999 (in response to Premier Klein's musing on the conditions under which the use of s.33 would be appropriate). *National Post*, 19 March, 1999 (in response to the announced policy).

CHAPTER EIGHT

1   *Calgary Herald*, 27 February, 1999; *National Post*, 6 August, 1999.
2   *Calgary Herald*, 8 June, 1998; *Alberta Report*, 13 April, 1998.
3   *Globe and Mail*, 23 September, 1997.
4   *Globe and Mail*, 28 March, 1998; *Globe and Mail*, 17 June, 1998.
5   *Calgary Herald*, 4 January, 1998; *National Post*, 16 December, 1998.
6   *National Post*, 27 April, 1999; *The Calgary Herald*, 2 September, 1999.
7   *Calgary Herald*, 2 July, 1999.
8   *Calgary Herald*, 27 December, 1998; *Calgary Herald*, 8 September, 1999.
9   *Calgary Herald*, 27 December, 1998; *National Post*, 16 December, 1998.
10 See *Globe and Mail*, 3 October, 1997; *Financial Post*, 14 January, 1998; *Alberta Report*, 313 October, 1997; 18 May, 1998.
11 *Alberta Report*, 7 June, 1999.
12 *National Post*, 26 May, 1999.
13 *Globe and Mail*, 11 December, 1997, 22 February, 1998.
14 See *Calgary Herald*, 23 September, 1999, for an assessment of Dinning's effectiveness.
15 The fact that the Alberta Advantage Surveys indicate that place of residence explains very little voter preference is irrelevant. The fact is, Edmonton elected hardly any Tories, and Klein wanted to change that.
16 *Calgary Herald*, 26 May, 1999.
17 *Globe and Mail*, 20 October, 1997.
18 Dabbs, *Ralph Klein: A Maverick Life*. Particularly eloquent in this respect, is Dabbs' Epilogue.
19 See, for instance, Ted Byfield, *Financial Post Magazine*, 15 February, 1997.
20 Vivone, "The Klein Revolution: Part II," *Alberta Views*, 2:4 (1999), 11.

21 Vivone, "The Klein Revolution: Part II," 11, 15.
22 *Fraser Forum*, February, 1999. See *National Post*, 6 September, 1999; 12 January, 2000; *Calgary Herald*, 3 February, 2000.
23 See Martin Zelder's analysis in *Fraser Forum*, February, 2000.
24 *National Post*, 3 December, 1999.
25 *Calgary Herald*, 19 February, 2000.
26 *Calgary Herald*, 15 March, 2000.
27 Press Release, Government of Alberta, 13 March, 2000. *Calgary Herald*, 14 March, 2000.
28 Speaking notes, Calgary Premier's dinner, 16 March, 2000.